The Age of
Innovation

FINANCIAL TIMES

Prentice Hall

In an increasingly competitive world, it is quality
of thinking that gives an edge. An idea that opens new
doors, a technique that solves a problem, or an insight
that simply helps make sense of it all.

We work with leading authors in the fields of
management and finance to bring cutting-edge thinking and
best learning practice to a global market.

Under a range of leading imprints, including
Financial Times Prentice Hall, we create world-class
print publications and electronic products giving readers
knowledge and understanding which can then be
applied, whether studying or at work.

To find out more about our business and professional
products, you can visit us at www.business-minds.com

For other Pearson Education publications, visit
www.pearsoned-ema.com

Pearson
Education

The Age of
Innovation

Making business
creativity a competence,
not a coincidence

Felix Janszen

An imprint of Pearson Education
London · New York · San Francisco · Toronto · Sydney · Tokyo · Singapore
Hong Kong · Cape Town · Madrid · Amsterdam · Munich · Paris · Milan

PEARSON EDUCATION LIMITED

Head Office
Edinburgh Gate
Harlow CM20 2JE
Tel: +44 (0)1279 623623
Fax: +44 (0)1279 431059

London Office:
128 Long Acre, London WC2E 9AN
Tel: +44 (0)20 7447 2000
Fax: +44 (0)20 7240 5771
Website:www.business-minds.com

First published in Great Britain in 2000

ISBN 0 273 63875 0

British Library Cataloguing in Publication Data
A CIP catalogue record for this book can be obtained from the British Library.

10 9 8 7 6 5 4 3 2

Typeset by Northern Phototypesetting Co. Ltd, Bolton

Transferred to digital print on demand, 2002

Printed and bound by Antony Rowe Ltd, Eastbourne

The Publishers' policy is to use paper manufactured from sustainable forests.

Contents

Preface

The idea of writing this book started about four years ago. It was at the start of my sabbatical leave that my Dean asked me what my plans were. I told him that I planned to write a book about how management could profit from the non-linearities of the innovation process. At that time I had already been working on this topic for five years and had the idea that my approach was well developed.

I started my sabbatical in the Institute Solvay in Brussels, where Ilya Prigogine headed a large group of scientists, ranging from mathematicians, physicists and biologists to economists, studying the principles of self-organization in their various fields. This stay changed my plans. The group on economics I joined was headed by Michelle Sanglier who used computer modelling to study the behaviour of economic systems. It was in this group that I made computer models of the product development process. During my three-month stay I succeeded in modelling this process, and I elaborated this approach during the rest of my sabbatical. A too short stay at the Santa Fe Institute in New Mexico also helped me to formulate my ideas about the importance of non-linear behaviour of the innovation process more precisely.

From that time it still took another three years before I started to write. During this period I adjusted my thinking to be applicable to real management problems. This was the biggest challenge and even more rewarding than the development of the modelling principles during my sabbatical. Due to the vision of a number of managers at companies such as Unilever, Philips, British Steel and Agritech 2007, I was able to apply my approach to a large number of management issues, such as scenario planning, developing new business models in dynamic markets, speeding up the product development process, portfolio management and planning product architectures. However, as important as these projects were, it was my discussions with consultants at various consulting firms who convinced me that I was on the right track and encouraged me to continue.

I realized that after the sabbatical I had a solution and now I had to find the right problem relating to this. I also realized that previously I had fallen into the same trap as many companies, of being too technology driven. Now I can state with more conviction to my students that you have to develop new methodologies and products closely with the users. I can also say to my colleagues with more conviction that developing applications is even more rewarding than just developing new theoretical concepts. I even obtained empirical evidence for one of my earlier statements that developing applications has to go hand in hand with the development of theoretical concepts and to develop those beyond the initial state.

Ultimately eighteen months ago I started writing this book. Again, it was the enthusiasm of many managers of companies I worked with, consultants and last but not least the publishers that encouraged me to continue and gave me the energy to finish the book. In this respect, I want to mention Cees Groenewegen and Marc Vloemans, who not only read the manuscript carefully and gave comments on the text, but also suggested a number of case studies that clarified the points I wanted to make.

When I started my studies ten years ago, to understand better the mechanisms behind the non-linear behaviour of the innovation process, almost nobody understood why I had chosen this topic. I had the impression that most of my colleagues found it too far removed from reality. I can understand that because the main management paradigm at that time was directed at forecasting and precise planning. A number of them also had problems with the idea that I wanted to simulate the innovation process by computer modelling. They found my approach too complicated and too hard to validate and calibrate such models to such an extent that they could be used for exact forecasting and precise planning. During a large part of my study I received greater understanding from the outside world, visionary managers and consultants than from inside academia. The publication of books such as Peter Senge's *The Fifth Discipline* and Arie de Geus's *The Living Company* did not change that. It was only after the publication of the book by Shapiro and Varian, *Information Rules*, that the tide changed. This book has made evident to mainstream economists that studying the non-linear behaviour of economic systems is respectful. Everybody now discusses the new economy and it has become a fashionable topic.

I suppose that, after all, the timing of the book is now perfect. The growth of the Internet has convinced everyone that thinking along the old economic paradigms is no longer tenable. Internet-time makes the non-linear behaviour of the economy a fact of life nobody can deny. It has made the old management paradigm obsolete. To develop new management practices, new approaches to analyze the business situation and to translate this into possible actions are needed. This is exactly what I want to achieve with this book. Not only to make management students, managers and consultants aware of the peculiarities of the non-linear behaviour of the innovation process, but also to support them in analyzing this behaviour, understanding the mechanisms behind it and in this way becoming more successful innovators.

It is evident that the content of this book is my responsibility. Readers have to blame me when they think differently or find all kinds of imperfections in the text. However, writing the book was not possible without the input of many who encouraged and helped me during the long course of developing concepts and the methodologies, and in writing the book. Especially I want to thank the following: Cees van Mourik, Grada Degenaars, Cees Groeneveld, Marc Vloemans and the numerous students who followed my courses on Management of Technology and Innovation and gave comments on the texts of many versions of the manuscript that preceded this book.

Felix Janszen
Rotterdam
January 2000

Part 1

Introduction – the shape of innovation

1 | To understand the present, you have to study the past – the development of innovation management

Introduction

After the age of efficiency in the 1950s and 1960s, quality in the 1970s and 1980s, and flexibility in the 1980s and 1990s, we now live in the age of innovation. Increasingly, industry is applying the new technology to new products and/or services. Even the strongholds of economists, with their elephant-grey suits, the banks, are changing rapidly and new financial products are developed in larger and larger numbers and at a faster and faster pace. In these organizations, technology has become one of the main engines of change and innovation. If banks and insurance companies are not fast enough with their innovations, they might even encounter software houses, such as Microsoft, making inroads into their territory. In those industries where innovation was already commonplace, companies compete on time. Being the fastest with respect to new features, better quality, more attractive styling and so on is the way to beat the competition.

We now live in the age of innovation.

Innovations may come in many different shapes. The term 'innovation' has been defined by the great Austrian economist Joseph Schumpeter as:

the commercialization of all new combinations based upon the application of:

1 new materials and components;

2 the introduction of new processes;

3 the opening of new markets;

4 the introduction of new organizational forms.

In other words, according to this definition, innovations are the composite of two worlds – namely, the **technical world** and the **business world**. When only a change in technology is involved, Schumpeter terms this **invention**. As soon as the business world is involved, it becomes an **innovation**.

Innovation can be seen as an event, the introduction of something new to the business world, as well as a process; one innovation causes another. A change in technology results in a new product that, when used efficiently, requires a change in the organization of business processes. New products, ultimately, may also lead to the development of new markets.

Innovations may also come in many different sizes. We distinguish small, incremental innovations, large innovations, breakthrough and radical innovations, modular and architectural innovations. Often, radical innovations are composed of a number of smaller ones that, once combined, lead to a breakthrough. The first microcomputers were developed in the 1970s in back yards by teenagers in California. They were composed of components that already existed and could be bought in the shops. The innovation started as a new assemblage of existing components. Rebecca Henderson and Kim Clark (1990) have called this an architectural innovation. The new product opened a new market. When the market developed further and the market's needs were better articulated, adaptation of components started to fit better in the new type of product. In a short period of time, a whole new industry evolved from it. This shows how the introduction of a new application of a new combination of technologies led to a new market. This led to the emergence of new industrial organizations and to the development of improved and new technologies.

With possibly a few exceptions, competition will increase dramatically for all companies. From a strategic point of view, there are only limited numbers of options to deal with this situation. Building up sustainable competitive advantage – be it in terms of price, quality or customer contact – can be realized in two ways. Either we buy it from someone who already has it or we create it ourselves. Statistics show that the risk of failure for mergers and acquisitions is very high. Numerous examples exist of situations that did not deliver what they looked to promise. On paper, announced mergers and acquisitions often look very good. In reality, they are a difficult beast to manage. Now, we are not saying that innovation is easy to manage! Not at all. However, we do feel that the risks involved are much lower, the opportunities are much greater and the operational difficulties are reduced if the innovation process is well understood and properly managed. Therefore, we believe that permanent innovation is the one real means of realizing sustainable competitive advantage for most companies, now and in the near future.

To be able to permanently innovate, knowledge is paramount. Knowledge management is one of the key constituents of the innovation management process. Whoever has the greatest insight in innovation and better skills in applying this insight will be more successful than the competition.

Innovation is, by definition, unique and, therefore, also by definition, every innovation process is unique. We will distinguish between:

- the general attributes of innovation processes – that is, what makes innovation processes different from other business processes;
- the company-specific attributes;
- accidental attributes, that are unique to certain innovations.

In this book, we will provide tools for the analysis and modelling of company-specific attributes of the innovation process. As input for this analysis, we will provide process models that encompass the general attributes of innovation processes. Furthermore, we will discuss how this insight can be applied, how knowledge about the dynamics of the innovation process can lead to competitive advantage. In other words, how it will create value for the various stakeholders of the company, such as the shareholders, its customers and its employees.

InCyte's business model

InCyte is a dedicated biotechnology firm that is located in Palo Alto, California. It was founded in 1990 thanks to the joint efforts of a biotechnologist and an IT specialist. The company's core technology is bio-informatics. It helped to develop this technology and apply it to the creation of new medication. InCyte's core asset is a huge and ever-growing database of information about genes. The most important aspect is that diseases can be related to differences in the DNA structure of genes in different tissues. Day and night, batteries of automated DNA sequencing machines are unravelling the DNA codes of hundreds of genes of different tissues from various patients. It is now possible to do this using a minimal amount of tissue. Therefore, a second asset of importance to the company is its network of physicians in hospitals all over the world.

The value of InCyte's databases depends on the extensiveness of its gene libraries. Researchers in the R&D departments of drug companies can hook up their computers to the databases of InCyte. Using these databases, they can search for deviant genes in tissues that play critical roles in the diseases they are developing medication to treat. For example, when they develop medication against atherosclerosis (a degenerative disease of the arteries), they can search for deviant genes in the coronary artery. When a researcher has found such medication, they can start a new programme to investigate the function of the protein that is coded by the gene. When the function of that protein is known, the protein can be cloned and used in a test programme for screening for interesting new chemicals, which may lead to finding a new medicine. Of course, researchers can only hook up their computers to the database when their companies are licensed to do so. They have to pay for it. InCyte can use this money to interest investors and banks as they are willing to invest money in high-tech companies that demonstrate their viability in such a clear way. This relatively cheap money can be invested in more sequencing machines, and in further growth of the networks of collaborating physicians. The physicians are willing to cooperate not only for their financial revenues but also, more importantly, for the fact that now they can play a

case study

bigger role in improving the health of future patients. Of course, it is the patients – last but not least – who will benefit from all this.

We have observed a few very potent reinforcing loops between shareholders, their customers (the big drug companies) and their indirect customers (the physicians – who are at the same time their suppliers to the end customers, the patients). Also, their employees will profit from this success.

Who will not benefit? Those companies that are direct competitors. Also, the established pharmaceutical companies may start to feel uneasy. The information about genes is, very rapidly, becoming crucial in the whole drug development business. A number of other techniques to develop drugs are entering the mature phase of their lifecycles and, in the future, it may be that you will not be able to build competitive advantage on these competences any more. The Chinese and Indian companies, which hire skilled researchers for a tenth of the salaries of western researchers, will have an advantage. What can companies such as Merck do? Of course, in the short term, they must use all available information. In the long run, they must prevent themselves from being in the same position as IBM with respect to Microsoft. They must devalue the possession of such a database. They can do so by giving their information about gene codes for free. In such a way, they prevent other companies from becoming too powerful and, in the meantime, they will strengthen their own core abilities in product development and marketing.

This case reveals the emergence of new ways in which the competitive game can be played. In this chapter, we will discuss these new rules of the game.

In this opening chapter, we will introduce a number of concepts that will help us to study new business development processes in more detail. We will start by defining the arena in which innovations take place and, subsequently, discuss some of its basic attributes. We will explain the non-linear dynamics of innovation processes. Next, we will discuss the consequences of non-linear behaviour for innovation management and, briefly, how management can handle and even profit from this non-linear behaviour.

In the rest of this chapter, we will explain how insight in the relationships between management, structure and process has evolved, consciously and unconsciously. We will discuss the two basic forces that influence the interactions between structure and process – namely, evolutionary, and self-organizing forces. We will apply this especially to innovation management. Next, we will discuss the co-evolution of technologies, products, markets, industries, organization and management practices. We end the chapter with a discussion of a number of theories about the type of organizations at the research and development (R&D) departmental level and at the industry level.

Innovation as the route to growth

Innovation is generally accepted as being the golden route to building a growing and prosperous company. By means of innovation – that is, by introducing new technologies (T), new applications in the form of new products and services (A), the development of new markets (M) and/or the introduction of new organizational forms (O) – we increase net value for customers and, eventually, their loyalty. By developing new businesses, we create extra sources of cash

> *Innovation is the golden route to building a growing and prosperous company.*

flow and increase shareholder value. By creating value for our stakeholders, we may increase our cash flow, enabling us to invest in further development of products, services and processes, closing a reinforcing loop that is depicted in Figure 1.1.

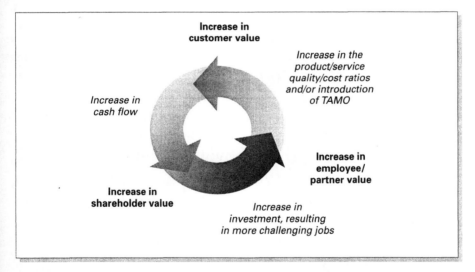

Figure 1.1 Reinforcing loop resulting in a growing and prosperous firm

The logic of this is simple and is nowadays recognized by everyone as the basis for growth. This has resulted in an increasing number of companies investing in new product and new business development. However, this has also led to the 'innovation paradox', which is that when everyone is following the same type of strategy, it becomes ineffective and loses its attractiveness. The increasing innovation efforts have led to a pressure to decrease product development throughput times. These have decreased in some cases to less than half the time needed five years ago (Smith and Reinertsen, 1998). Doing this requires extra resources and so diminishes the return. This has led to what some (see Kauffman, 1995, p 216) have called the 'Red Queen effect', from *Alice in Wonderland*:

'It takes all the running you can, to keep the same place.' A situation emerges that is similar to the arms race between the USA and the USSR in the 1950s and 1960s. However, as in arms races, the one who is smarter, better understands the battlefield, has better technology and better weapons and has more endurance will win in the end.

Companies such as Intel, 3M, Xerox and Microsoft seem to win more battles than others. They outperform their competitors, not solely because they have hired smarter technologists and designers, but for a combination of strategy, tactics in the marketplace, innovative products and so on, and sheer luck. The choice of the DOS operating system by IBM was partly the result of smart negotiation by Bill Gates, but also partly luck. However, it is amazing that certain companies have more luck than others do. To be able to recognize opportunities and react adequately is part of 'good management practice'.

The important lesson we can learn from many examples, such as those mentioned above, is that innovation is still the best way to prosper in business, but that just being innovative is not enough. You also have to be smarter than the competition and understand the battlefield better than they do. Especially important is that you must not only be able to understand better what may happen in the business, but also, more precisely, be able to understand better the innovation process.

Some basic innovation concepts – the dimensions of innovation and the innovation arena

Before starting to discuss some of the most important attributes of innovation, we have to define more precisely what we mean by this word. Referring once again to our mnemonic mentioned earlier, we define innovation as:

the commercialization of something new, which may be:

T a new technology;

A a new application in the form of a new product, service or process;

M a new market or market segment;

O a new organizational form or a new management approach;

or a combination of two or more of these elements.

Innovations can be described as having four aspects:

- Technology
- Applications
- Market segments or customer groups
- Organization.

These four aspects define the innovation arena. Within this arena we can position companies with respect to their technology, applications, market and organization combinations.[1] A change from one position to a unique and new one in this arena is an innovation and the consequence of the company's innovating activities. When we consider the subsequent track of innovations in time of a certain organization, we obtain an innovation trajectory. We can depict the past trajectory and the planned future one. The process of change along this trajectory can be identified as the innovation process. In Figure 1.2 this innovation arena is depicted.

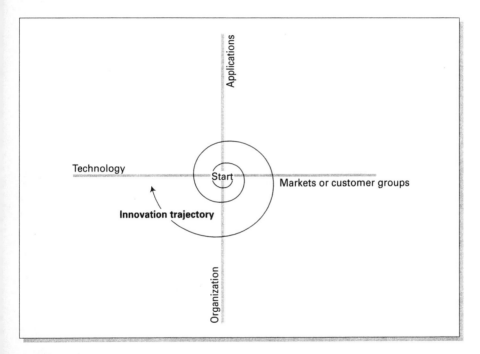

Figure 1.2 The innovation arena

The innovation arena helps us not only to define the world we need to consider when studying innovation, but also to focus and define the scope of our innovation strategy and activities.

Although it looks from Figure 1.2 as if the four dimensions are independent of each other, we must be aware of the fact that there is not actually a clear line between technologies and applications, nor between applications and markets, between markets and (external or internal) organization, between exter-

---

[1] The TAMO combination is an extension of the well-known technology, product and market combination that reflects the holistic nature of successful innovation management.

nal and internal organization and technology. Furthermore, the four dimensions are dependent on each other, which means that a specific technology has a limited number of applications. It also means that not all points in this four-dimensional space are evenly possible. There exist certain constraints that make some TAMO combinations more feasible than others. Indeed, some combinations are even impossible.

case study

The development of the mini-mill business and its effect on the steel industry

The steel industry is characterized by large economies of scale. The larger the steel mills, the lower the unit production costs. The lower the production costs and the selling price, the larger the market share. The larger the market share, the larger the production facilities can be. This principle is of particular importance in mature industries where products are commodities and competition is, to a large extent, focused on price. This means that the concentration rate in such industries is high and the industry is dominated by a small number of large companies as entering such an industry is almost impossible.

All the above being true, innovations that change the economies of scale may have profound effects on the industry structure. In the USA, some have searched for other production methods and, as a result, mini-mills have been developed. In this way, Chaparral Steel has been able to achieve a prominent place in the industry and is now seen as one of the most innovative steel producers in the world. With mini-mills, it is possible to produce steel with lower costs because they use electricity instead of coal. This is because scrap is used as the raw material.

The introduction of mini-mills has had large consequences for the organization of production. Mini-mills are characterized by very simple, flat organizational structures. This enables companies to be flexible and react quickly to changes in the market. However, a disadvantage is that mini-mills can only serve limited markets. They cannot produce products that require hot rolling. This has a negative effect on the quality of the steel produced by mini-mills. For this reason, an additional process has been developed – the so-called thin-slab casting, which enables mini-mills to produce very thin plate steel. As a result of this, mini-mills have been able to develop new markets.

Because the demand for mini-mill steel has grown, the demand for scrap has also grown. As a consequence, there is a shortage of scrap metal. The search is now on for alternatives to scrap to use as the raw material for mini-mills. Alternative raw materials, such as iron carbide, have been found, which have the advantage that they increase the quality of the steel produced. However, iron carbide also has its disadvantages. This has led to the development of another substitute – namely, Fastmet.

The case study above illustrates how technology, application, market and organizational developments are related to each other.

Innovation can be the result of the introduction of new technology, a new product, processes or services, the development of new markets and/or new organizational forms. In most cases, it is a combination of multiple factors that are introduced partly simultaneously, partly sequentially. Because of the existence of mutual interactions between these factors, the systems change continually, following a typical trajectory. In short, innovation is not an isolated event, but, rather, a trajectory, consisting of many small events. Therefore, when analyzing *Innovation is not an isolated event, but, rather, a trajectory, consisting of many small events.*

an innovation, it is difficult to indicate the precise moment the innovation has arisen or to point to a single cause of the innovation. This means that to understand the development of a new business, we cannot study the different origins and participating organizations or stakeholders separately, but have to study the whole situation.

Analogies between warfare and management

From way back in history right up to the present day, innovation has played a central role in warfare. The first use of new weapons has often been a decisive determining factor in the outcome of the battle. Because warfare historically has been one of the most striking 'laboratories' for technological innovations, we may learn from it what the important parameters are that may determine the outcome of innovative efforts.

One of these parameters is that you need not only to have the technology but also to be able to use it in the right way. In other words, you have to fit your strategy and organization to the technology. Sometimes, armies can outperform adversaries that possess much better technology than they do by changing the rules of the game – as the North Vietnamese did during the Vietnam war by using guerrilla tactics. This means that, aside from the evolution of technical capabilities, it is necessary to have the right organization and strategies adapted to your capabilities in order to be successful.

Several books have been published that explicitly focus on the analogies between management and warfare, including *Sun Tzu: War and management* by Wee Chow-Hou, Lee Khai-Sheang and Bambang Walujo Hidajat, *The Innovation War: Industrial R&D ... The arms race of the nineties* by Christoph-Friedrich von Braun and *Marketing Warfare: How to use military principles to develop marketing strategies* by All Ries and Jack Trout. It is easy to find several analogies between these two areas, such as the existence of phenomena like 'arms races', 'industrial espionage', 'intelligence' and 'logistics'. Indeed, the field of strategy and tactics was developed in warfare and operational research was developed during the Second World War. These analogies help us to explore certain basic rules that play a role in both warfare and management.

The importance of technological edge or the constant development of new strategies and tactics that surprise the opponent is nowhere more evident than in warfare. The use of the longbow by the English during the invasion by William of Normandy gave the English an advantage – longer range – that proved decisive and resulted in their victory. The invention of the tank changed the way wars were fought. Other strategies such as the blitzkrieg became a favourite strategy and how armies were organized had to be adapted as a result.

The tragedy of the French defence during the Second World War is well known. They thought they had learned their lessons from the First World War. The French remembered the trench warfare only too well and so built the Maginot line to keep the Germans out. Alas new developments in the Second World War made the strategy useless.

The emergence of the tank led to the development of antitank weapons. These led to the development of tanks with thicker armour and stronger guns, which in turn led to the development of better antitank weapons and so on. Such arms races are clear examples of the co-evolution of technology and products, products in which the technology is embedded. However, it is not only the technology and products that co-evolve but also markets (or, rather, targets) and organizations.

Lesson one

The lesson we can learn from these military examples is that the full benefits of new technology and products can be reaped only when the other elements, such as target groups and ways of working, are adapted, leading to the co-evolution of technology, products, organizations and strategies. This can be done only when we understand the basic principles of the processes that are enabled by the technology.

Thus, when companies limit their innovative activities to the development of new technology and products, they will profit only partially from their innovative brilliance. In these cases, other companies may complete their innovative activities and they will profit most from the original company's endeavours.

It must also be remembered, however, that the battlefield changes. Although the battlefield is the place where the best combination of technology, product and organization is selected, it also co-evolves in an analogous way to the way in which the marketplace does. Therefore, the innovation arena can be compared to the battlefield. In situations where it is possible to get an overview of the innovation arena, the innovation efforts can be planned and incremental massive efforts will pay back. However, in turbulent and chaotic situations, a more guerrilla-like approach is recommended, using small, independent operating groups. In these situations, big plans worked out at department level are no longer sensible. Instead, the soldiers at the front line have to react to only locally present knowledge.

Lesson two

Organizations must be able to adapt to changing situations – relying on hierarchical planning in stable conditions and distributed decision making in ambiguous, turbulent situations. We have to build into our processes a certain amount of flexibility.

The approach of the many initiatives may be better in certain situations than the massive, carefully planned attack. Then, the distributed self-organizing forces in the innovation arena have to do their job. A well-known example of such an approach is the way Honda infiltrated the American market. Engineers were sent to the USA to study American habits. They travelled on their light motorcycles. In the process, they became aware of a market for these light motorcy-

In turbulent and chaotic situations, a guerrilla-like approach is recommended.

cles. After recognizing this opportunity, they switched their plans and entered the market with these motorcycles, for which there was no American competitor. After entering the market and building a basic service infrastructure, Honda started selling its cars in America, too. Such an approach is comparable to an attack on an unprotected area. After obtaining a foothold and building a base, you can start to attack the main area.

Lesson three

The lesson here is that management must have an insight into the dynamics of the processes in order to reach its goals. This insight helps in managing these processes as a number of parameters that affect these processes – such as the application of new, improved or adapted technology, the organization, employees acquiring the right skills by means of training and the use of the right coordination methods, forming the right partnerships and so on – can be adjusted accordingly.

Organizations with long lifespans

In his book *The Living Company* (1997), Arie de Geus discusses a study undertaken at oil company Shell looking at companies that have lasted for at least 100 years. He tells of the Stora company, a major Swedish paper, pulp and chemical manufacturer that was founded 700 years ago as a copper mine in central Sweden. After studying a couple more of these long-lasting companies, it was found that they had a number of common characteristics – that they were:

- sensitive to their environment;
- cohesive, with a strong sense of identity;
- tolerant;
- conservative with regard to financing.

It is interesting to note that these companies did not adhere to the well-known management principles, such as focusing on core competences, nor had they chosen one of the generic strategies, such as concentrating on cost leadership or using a differentiation strategy, and neither had they stuck to the middle path.

It is also interesting to apply these attributes to other organizations with long lifespans, such as universities. The university is an institution that has its origins in antiquity in the academe in Greece and Rome. In the fourteenth century, these became very popular in the city-states of Florence and Venice. From there they spread northwards and new academe were founded in Paris, Cambridge, Oxford, Leiden and so on. These academe, or universities, were places where the thinkers of the time were relatively free to speculate. The universities later embraced the liberal sciences, such as mathematics, mechanics, physics, chemistry, medicine and biology. They were tolerant places where professors and their students were free to develop new theories and new experimental methods to study their propositions. Up until now, the old universities have continued to exist and prosper – Oxford, Cambridge and Leiden carry on very much as they have always done. They have had their ups and downs, but have survived.

Almost all of the characteristics listed above can be applied to these organizations. They have been sensitive to their environment, but have always had a strong, very strong, sense of identity. They have been tolerant – that, indeed, seems to be their core value. Only the fourth point – conservative in financing – seems to be less applicable.

James Collins and Jerry Porras (1996), of the Shell study group, could not confirm the normal management rules of what they called visionary companies. They studied companies such as 3M, American Express, Boeing, Hewlett-Packard, Merck, Motorola, Wal-Mart and Walt Disney and compared them with similar, but, according to their definition, less visionary companies, such as McDonnell Douglas, GM, Burroughs, Colgate and Westinghouse. They formulated their conclusions as twelve shattered myths:

1 it does take a great idea to start a great company;
2 visionary companies do require charismatic, visionary leaders;
3 the most successful companies do exist first and foremost to maximize profits;

4 visionary companies do share a common subset of correct core values;

5 the only constant is eternal change;

6 blue chip companies do play it safe;

7 visionary companies are great places to work for everyone;

8 highly successful companies make their best moves by brilliant and complicated strategic planning;

9 companies should hire outside CEOs to stimulate fundamental change;

10 the most successful companies focus primarily on beating the competition;

11 you can't have your cake and eat it too;

12 companies become visionary primarily by means of vision statements.

These case studies make clear that successful companies distinguish themselves by having certain attributes, but these are mostly not defined in the well-known management lessons. Assuming that the management lessons given by the gurus are based on their practice, we must conclude that their propositions are time-dependent, applying only to a certain era, and cannot be transferred to another era. It is clear that we can learn from history but that the lessons cannot be applied directly in our own time. In contrast, copying the successful behaviour of our predecessors may be disastrous. The lessons we can learn from the past are more general, as the Lessons earlier show.

> *Successful companies distinguish themselves by having attributes not defined in management lessons.*

The non-linear behaviour of new product and new business development

The behaviour of a linear system can be extrapolated from knowledge about its previous behaviour in a restricted number of cases, but the behaviour of non-linear systems is, in principle, unpredictable and cannot be extrapolated from earlier observations. Moreover, the behaviour of linear systems can be derived from knowledge about the behaviour of the separate elements. For example, when we design a building or an engine, we can, within limits, derive the properties of the building from the properties of the separate building materials or the properties of the engine from the properties of its components.

The weather is a non-linear system, biological systems such as ecologies and the metabolism of the body are non-linear, and social and economic systems are non-linear too. Prediction of the behaviour of such systems is always hazardous and can be achieved only for very limited time periods, under certain restrictive circumstances and often only in qualitative, not quantitative, terms.

The examples of false predictions about success or failure of innovations in the marketplace are numerous. A number of these cases have been studied. A well-studied example is that of the success and failure of video cassette recorder (VCR) systems in the consumer market. In the early 1980s, three different, mutually exclusive VCR systems were introduced – the Betamax system by Sony, the Video 2000 system by Philips Electronics and the VHS system by JVC. Although most experts at that time agreed on the technical superiority of both the Betamax and Video 2000 systems, the VHS system won the battle.

Brian Arthur (1994), a well-known economist from Stanford University, has studied the causes of this outcome. The main cause turned out to be the availability of the video titles for the three systems. It happened by chance that more and better-appreciated titles were available for the VHS system than for the other two competing systems. The quality of the VCR systems, therefore, for consumers was determined not only by technical performance, such as image quality, but also by the number of titles available. The VCR can be referred to as the 'core product', the VCR and titles the 'extended or whole product' (Geoffrey Moore, 1995). Small initial changes in available titles stimulated the sales of the VHS VCRs and, in turn, the higher number of VCR systems sold stimulated producers of titles to bring out a new title first in the VHS

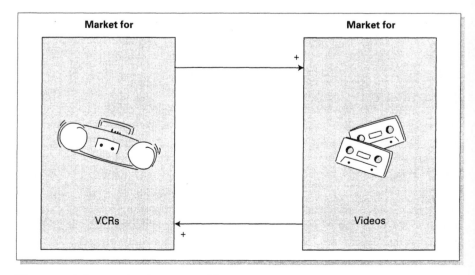

Figure 1.3 Interaction between VCR and video markets

standard. A small initial advantage in the marketplace ultimately translated into dominance of that system because of the reinforcing loop between the VCRs and video titles markets (see Figure 1.3). Computer simulation studies performed by Brian Arthur demonstrated this effect convincingly.

This example illustrates a number of things about the basic characteristics of new product and new business development (NPD and NBD) processes:

- we have to take the whole system into account, that one market can be coupled with another and influence the other;

- market shares influence the penetration process of the systems and this influences the market shares and competitive positions of the companies – an example of network economies, which we will discuss in more depth later on. Here, ultimately, both Sony and Philips abandoned their own systems in the consumer market for VCRs and licensed the VHS technology from JVC;

- history matters – a small event at the beginning can ultimately determine the whole sequence of events later on, so studying present events in isolation will never give us clues about a specific end result (this phenomenon is termed 'path dependency' in economics literature).

Path dependencies are common phenomena, associated with the existence of reinforcing loops and lock-in phenomena. A lock-in mechanism is the result of the existence of switching costs and can be considered to be part of the memory of the system – for example, money sunk into video titles or investment costs in terms of the time needed to learn and acquire the necessary skills to master a certain technique. We can guess, for example, what would have happened if the airship the Hindenburg had not crashed. Perhaps we would now fly in large airships instead of aeroplanes. At the time of writing, all attempts to revive airships have failed, because of the lack of infrastructure, industrial investment

Co-evolution is the phenomenon that the evolution of two or more elements influence each other.

capital and lack of designers with sufficient skills. Similarly, we can try to guess what would have happened had we not switched from the steam engine to the combustion engine. The technology might have followed a completely different route and, probably, we would be as happy or unhappy with that means of transportation as we are nowadays with the combustion engine.

Path dependency is associated with the co-evolution of linked elements in a system. It is the expression of the fact that history matters. Co-evolution is the phenomenon that the evolution of two or more elements influence each other. A well-known example is the co-evolution of the capacity and speed of microprocessors, memory elements and software in computers. The Wintel, Windows operating system and Intel microprocessors of the x86 series are an example of how this process may be used to keep competition away.

In summary, the non-linear behaviour of systems such as biological and socio-economic systems may be the result of the following processes:

- path dependency
- evolution
- co-evolution.

Besides these three processes, a fourth often occurs in these systems – namely:

- self-organization.

Not all possible structures are equally possible, as we discussed before regarding the innovation arena. Organizations have to follow certain rules to be feasible. Those in which the members do not communicate and where no agreements about the goals are reached do not survive for a long period of time. Biological organisms have to follow certain design rules, based on mechanical, physical, chemical and thermo-dynamic principles. Equally organizations have to fulfil the deeper psychological needs of their members and cannot violate the values and norms of society for long periods.

Although none of us can predict the future course of events of a specific non-linear system as a business, we are not totally handicapped. When we understand the processes of path dependency, evolution and co-evolution, and, last but not least, self-organization, we can make intelligent estimates about possible futures and consequences of our actions. These guesses will become less precise the more time passes, but our insight regarding these four processes may help us to decide which developments to monitor and what can be considered as early warning signals.

The evolution and co-evolution of technology, products, markets and organizations

Because the development of the four objectives of the innovation arena – namely technologies, applications and products, markets and organizations – is linked and they influence each other mutually, we have to take all these dimensions into account when studying NBD. This requires, first, the study of the underlying principles that govern these links and interactions.

Various authors have drawn our attention to these linkages. For example, Piet Bolwijn and Ted Kumpe (1990) have remarked that, during the last three decades, the dominant management practice has changed from a focus on efficiency to a focus on quality, flexibility and, ultimately, on innovation. According to these authors, the changes were driven by changes in the marketplace and shifts in customer wishes (see Figure 1.4).

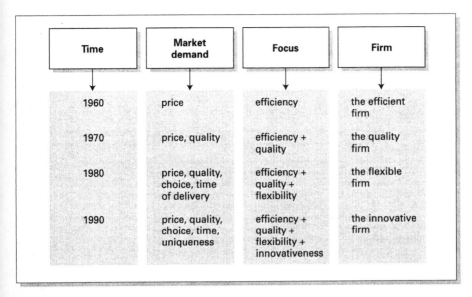

Figure 1.4 Bolwijn and Kumpe's evolution model

Philip Roussel, Kamal Saad and Tamara Erickson (1991), in their best-selling book *Third-generation R&D Management: Managing the link to corporate strategy*, recognize three different generations of R&D management. The generations were linked to a decrease in technological opportunities, restricted financial resources, more demanding customers and intensification of the competition in the marketplace.

Roy Rothwell (1992) even recognized a fourth and fifth generation of R&D management, driven by developments in IT and concentration on networking with suppliers and other partners. What all these authors make clear is that management evolves over time and that these changes are driven by changes in technology, the market and competition. What these authors do not say in so many words is that these changes in management change, in turn, the rules of competition, the marketplace, organization of an industry and so on. In other words, the many elements of the business co-evolve because they are connected to each other. These connections drive changes and changes in the environment drive changes in the internal NPD and NBD processes.

Studying the changes in the requirements of the outputs of the NPD and NBD processes, in the attributes of the inputs to these processes, attributes of the processes themselves and management of them will show that these elements co-evolve.

When we analyze the trends in the NPD and NBD processes, it is clear that, increasingly, more actors have to be taken into account. This occurs because more and more functionality is being put into products, leading to more complicated products. The increase in functionality is the result of the application of more technology to products. The technology is often less mature when it is applied than in the past because of faster developments in technology and the shorter lifespans of both products and technology.

In the early days of the Industrial Revolution, individual inventors were involved. These were legendary men, such as James Watt, one of the inventors of the steam engine, William Perkins, the inventor of the first synthetic colour 'mauve blue', Leo Baekeland, the inventor of Bakelite. The start of these inventions was often an idea originating from serendipity that was more or less elaborated by developing and testing prototypes. The available knowledge was very limited in those days. The NPD process consisted only of the generation of ideas and a prototyping process. Because only one or two people were involved, you could hardly speak of a development team or the application of NPD management. Those were pre-R&D days.

At the end of the nineteenth century, chemistry and physics had evolved to such a degree that it became profitable to use the available scientific knowledge and scientific methodologies in a more systematic way. This was first realized in the chemical and electrical industries in Germany and the USA. R&D labs were established. Scientists and their assistants developed new technology, making use of scientific methods, and exploited this knowledge by embodying their technology in new products in an equally systematic way.

The NPD process was gradually extended with the 'knowledge acquisition and exploitation' process as developed by the exact sciences of those days. In those labs hundreds of people worked and R&D management slowly became a discipline in its own right. However, R&D management at that time was concerned solely with what happened in R&D and only engineers and scientists were working in the area then. Roussel *et al.* (1991) named this first-generation R&D management. It was mostly concerned with hiring creative scientists and their staff and providing the right conditions to optimize outcomes. Many new products were developed and successfully commercialized, such as new materials – nylon and polyethylene – electronic devices – the telephone, radio, television, lightbulbs, automobiles, aeroplanes and so on. The 1930s and 1960s especially were the golden days for this type of product development.

In the 1960s and 1970s the number of opportunities for the new sciences, physics, and chemistry to develop new technology diminished, whereas, at the same time, competition increased, especially from the Japanese, who had improved their manufacturing capabilities in such a way that Japanese products became equivalents of quality products. As a reaction, marketing and production became more involved in the NPD process. More parties, introducing other types of expertise, also became involved. Project management became important as it was then necessary to plan the activities of all the parties involved and avoid wasting time and scarce resources. However, at that time, project management still consisted only of planning, work breakdown structures and allocation of resources. This is called second-generation management by Roussel and others.

In the 1990s, the NPD process became increasingly close to – indeed, linked with and integrated into – the strategic management process. Strategic management had become recognized as a separate management discipline in the 1970s and 1980s as a result of the work of Igor Ansoff, Russ Ackoff and Peter Drucker. Before then, strategy had emerged from operations. The 1970s and 1980s, however, were the hey-days of strategic planning and so more disciplined planning of the NPD activities and the allocation of scarce resources became essential. The integration of R&D management into the overall corporate strategy process is named by Roussel and others 'third-generation' R&D management.

Integration of R&D and strategic management led to the awareness that strategies may emerge during this process.

However, strategic management became increasingly synonymous with planning by extrapolation. The integration of R&D and innovation within strategic management makes clear that the planning processes are fundamentally different from production planning. During the development of new technology and products, new opportunities may become available that affect strategy. To grasp new opportunities, current strategies often have to be adapted. Integration of R&D and strategic management led to the awareness that strategies may emerge during this process. Henry Mintzberg has discussed this topic in his book *The Rise and Fall of Strategic Planning* (1994).

In the 1990s, time became the scarcest resource. This led to a redefinition of the role and focus of companies with respect to their NPD activities. As a consequence, feedback loops from customers were shortened by involving them in the earlier stages of the NPD process. Also, certain activities were outsourced to suppliers. This trend, towards integrating customers and suppliers in the NPD process, and to innovate in networks with other companies, led Rothwell (1992) to distinguish between a third, a fourth and a fifth generation of R&D management.

One of the driving forces – apart from the ones mentioned above, such as more demanding customers, more intense competition and so on – was the fact that products became more complicated, with more technology being embedded into them. In products that, traditionally, contained only mechanical or electrical parts were now also analogue and digital electronic parts, software and so on. This meant that more disciplines were involved in product development. Thus design, marketing and marketing research, production, purchasing, logistics, accounting and even sometimes psychology were given roles to play in product development. At the same time, specialization in the various disciplines increased further the number of people involved in the development of products. These people often had different backgrounds, values, goals and objectives, and time horizons. The composition and functioning of teams became more problematical. Teambuilding processes were recognized as being one of the most critical success factors in the NPD process and were considered to be an important separate part of the whole NPD process that needed special management attention.

In Figures 1.5 and 1.6, these trends have been represented schematically.

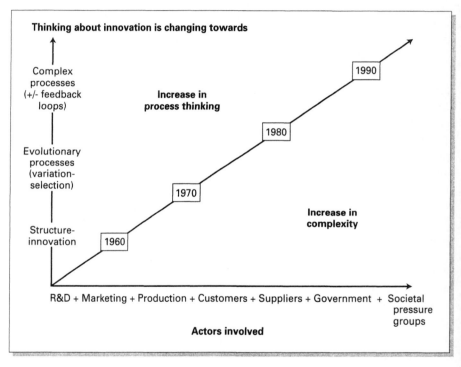

Figure 1.5 The evolution of paradigms in innovation management

Management teams became increasingly open to the environment, to what happened outside the walls of their own functions and companies.

In Figure 1.5, the increased involvement of a growing number of internal and external actors and stakeholders is evident. At the same time, the interconnectedness of the NPD with the NBD process has led to more complicated processes. Management of R&D has had to adapt to these (see Figure 1.6).

What is evident from these trends is that management teams became increasingly open to the environment, to what happened outside the walls of their own functions and companies.

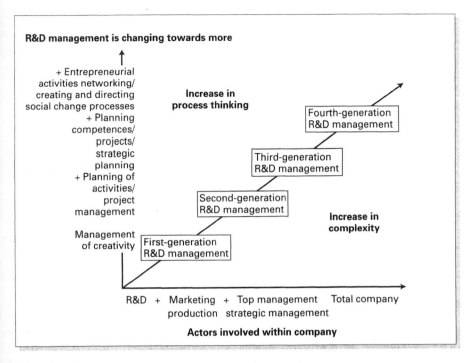

Figure 1.6 The evolution of the practice of innovation management

Shell is a clear example of this trend towards being more open to external signals. Shell had a very closed management system up until five years ago. It was seen as closed and arrogant. A number of incidents have changed this situation completely, especially the success of certain pressure groups for human rights and environmental issues in influencing management. South Africa, Nigeria, the Brent Sparr are all too well known. Shell is now in the process of becoming a more open and sensitive company.

Companies have had to do this in order to survive. Accompanying trends have been a change from R&D management as management of creative individuals and ideas generation to project management. In the 1990s, R&D management was incorporated into the general management process and an emphasis was put on knowledge management. With this change, the view of the organization as a machine changed to one of seeing it in more organic terms. Instead of mechanics, biology became the science that inspired management thinking. With the loss of a mechanical view of the world, the significance of planning became the major discussion point. This discussion was fuelled by Henry Mintzberg's book *The Rise and Fall of Strategic Planning* (1994). In the book, Mintzberg made it clear that plans are constantly adapted to environmental changes and initiatives from within the company. Strategy is, to a large extent, an emerging phenomenon and the planning format plays often only a modest role. It is interesting to remember the words of General Eisenhower that 'plans are useless, but planning is essential'. However, if plans are useless, what is the role of management? What is innovation management all about? What are the challenges for innovation management in the twenty-first century when, according to a large number of observers, innovation may become even more important than today? Will we need a sixth generation of innovation management? What will the important elements of this be? Without embarking on a discussion about the various innovation management disciplines, we will try to discuss the challenges of the coming decade for innovation management and what the consequences of this may be for the discipline.

The challenges of the twenty-first century for innovation management

Various authors have tried to relate environmental conditions and industry structure to organization and management issues and the dominant management paradigm. Above, Bolwijn, Kumpe and Rothwell were mentioned briefly. Other authors who have studied these relationships are, among others, Keith Pavitt, William Abernathy and James Utterback, David Teece, James Quinn, Tom Peters, Richard D'Aveni, James Moore, Ralph Stacey, Shona Brown and Kathleen Eisenhardt. We will discuss briefly first the contributions of Pavitt, Abernathy and Utterback, and Teece because, although we interpret their models differently now than ten years ago, these models have influenced our present-day ideas about the relationships between position, people and process. Subsequently, we will discuss the more recent contributions of the other authors to innovation management.

Pavitt (1990) distinguishes five classes of industries, based on the ways in which the innovation process is organized and managed.

1 **Supplier-dominated industries** such as agriculture, construction and the medical sector. The companies in these industries are mostly small- to medium-sized ones and their innovation originates, in the main, from their suppliers.

2 **Scale-intensive industries** such as the steel, petrochemicals, food and car industries. They generally belong to the class of mature industry and produce commodities. They compete on product differentiation and/or price. The main type of innovation in these industries is process-related, aimed at decreasing their production costs. Economies of scale and market share are the dominant driving forces of competition among such companies.

3 **Information-intensive sectors** such as most service industries – banking, consultancy, contract engineering firms. Knowledge is the main production factor. Innovations are mostly based on applications of information and communication technology.

4 **Science-based industries** such as electronics, pharmaceuticals, aerospace industries. R&D plays a dominant role as the emphasis here is on product innovations. In turbulent technological environments, a lot of technological breakthroughs appear in, for example, biotechnology and microelectronics.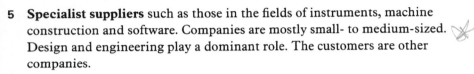

5 **Specialist suppliers** such as those in the fields of instruments, machine construction and software. Companies are mostly small- to medium-sized. Design and engineering play a dominant role. The customers are other companies.

This classification tries to explain the differences in the ways in which companies innovate. When studying product development in various companies, we have observed that the way in which innovation takes place is changing in the various industries. Industries that before were focused on process innovation are now becoming more science-based, and product development plays an increasingly important role. Science-based industries, such as pharmaceuticals, are outsourcing part of their research to new, dedicated biotechnology companies, and they aim to achieve economies of scale by focusing on development and marketing.

Other approaches to classifying industries in order to understand their ways of product development have been proposed. Abernathy and Utterback (1978) distinguish only three types of industries, based on an industrial lifecycle model.

1 Industries that are in the first, **fluid state** of their lifecycle. Examples are new areas of technology, such as certain software and biotechnology companies.

2 Industries that are in the middle of their lifecycle, called the **transitional state**. The technology is well recognized and evolving fast. An example is the microelectronics industry.

3 Industries that are in the mature, **specific state**, such as petrochemicals and steel.

In Table 1.1, an overview of the various characteristics of management in these three types of industries is summarized.

Table 1.1 Classification of the three phases of industrial innovation with their main attributes

Management issues	Fluid phase	Transitional phase	Specific phase
Innovation	Frequent, major product changes	Major process changes required by rising demand	Incremental for product and with cumulative improvements in productivity and quality
Sources of innovation	Industry pioneers, products' users	Manufacturers, users	Often suppliers
Products	Diverse designs, often customized	At least one product design, stable enough to have significant production volume	Mostly undifferentiated, standard products
Production process	Flexible and inefficient, major changes easily accommodated	Becoming more rigid, with changes occurring in major steps	Efficient, capital-intensive and rigid; cost of change high
R&D	Focus unspecified because of high degree of technical uncertainty	Focus on specific product features once dominant design emerges	Focus on incremental product technologies; emphasis on process technology
Equipment	General purpose, requiring skilled labour	Some subprocesses automated, creating islands of automation	Special-purpose, mostly automatic, with labour focused on tending and monitoring equipment
Plant	Small-scale, located near user or source of innovation	General-purpose with specialized sections	Large-scale, highly specific to particular products
Cost of process change	Low	Moderate	High
Competitors	Few, but growing in numbers with widely fluctuating market shares	Many, but declining in number after emergence of dominant design	Few, classic oligopoly with stable market shares
Basis of competition	Functional product performance	Product variation; fitness for use	Price
Organizational control	Informal and entrepreneurial	Via project and task groups	Structure, rules and goals
Vulnerability of industry leaders	To imitators and patent challenges; to successful product breakthroughs	To more efficient and higher-quality producers	To technological innovations that present superior product substitutes

The industry lifecycle can give us further clues as to why companies innovate in certain ways. However, it does not take into account the characteristics of certain technology. This point is addressed in Teece's (1986) model.

Teece distinguishes three important building blocks that determine innovation management.

1 **Appropriation regimes.** These are environmental factors exclusive to the company and market structure that determine the possibilities for the innovator to profit from their innovation. Examples are patents and other intellectual property rights, economies of scale, running down the experience curve, trade secrets and so on.

2 **Dominant design paradigm.** Teece distinguishes two phases and one transition phase in product lifecycles that determine this paradigm, namely a pre-paradigmatic phase, characterized by the co-existence of multiple types of designs and standards, and a lot of market trial and error to find out the market wishes. Market articulation takes place in this phase. The appearance of a dominant design (the transition phase) will thereafter determine the design paradigm. Examples are the DC 3, the IBM PC and Ford's Model T. Ultimately, there is a paradigmatic phase, when consecutive designs are variations on, and extensions of, the dominant design.

3 **Complementary assets.** These are assets that are necessary for full commercialization of the innovation. This is, for example, production, distribution, complementary technologies. They can make or break the viability and feasibility of a particular innovation if they are not present.

Based on these three building blocks, Teece has constructed a matrix that contains the most successful variations of innovation management (see Table 1.2).

All the authors above have tried to construct models that abstract from the specific events in a sector, but have a wider applicability over sectors and over time. Whereas Pavitt took as his starting point the structure of the sector, Abernathy and Utterback took the development process of a sector, expressed as the industry lifecycle, as their starting point, and Teece concentrated more on the behaviour of the various actors, expressed as the use of paradigms. However, Teece also incorporated attributes of the structure of the sector and technology into his model.

All these authors constructed their schemes in the 1980s, yet they contain points that are still valid today. However, one of the most conspicuous changes to have occurred since the models were devised is that both product and process innovation have become important in all industries. Not only hardware and software industries are innovating, service industries are too. In all industries, these innovations are linked to new technology. The development of information and communications technology in particular is a main driver of innova-

Table 1.2 The optimal contract and integration strategies for innovators

	Strong logical/ technical appropriability	Weak legal/technical appropriability	
		Innovator excellently positioned versus imitator with respect to commissioning complementary assets	Innovator poorly positioned versus imitator with respect to commissioning complementary assets
Innovators and imitators advantageously positioned *vis-à-vis* independent owners of complementary assets	Contract / Innovator will win	Contract / Innovator should win	Contract / Innovator or imitator will win; assets' owners will not benefit
Innovators and imitators disadvantageously positioned *vis-à-vis* independent owners of complementary assets	Contract if can do so on competitive terms; integrate if necessary / Innovator will win; may have to share profits with asset holders	Integrate / Innovator should win	Contract (to limit exposure) / Innovator will probably lose to imitators and/or asset holders

tion that transcends traditional industry borders. However, other types of technology, such as biotechnology and new materials, also have important impacts. Information and communications technology has not only increased the pace of innovation but also the interactions with the other parties as suppliers and customers. Biotechnology has changed dramatically the way new products are developed in the pharmaceutical and refined chemical and food industries. Also, new technology emerges from the fusion of specialisms such as genomics, bio-informatics and combinatorial chemistry. These were non-existent just ten years ago. Nowadays, though, such fields play central roles in the development of new medicines. The general expectation is that these trends will continue in the coming decade, with the result that various processes in the innovation arena will become even more linked together. This may increase the environmental dynamics to a state of turbulence, which means that projections from the past will be valid for shorter and shorter periods of time. The unpredictability of the future can only increase. D'Aveni (1994) has called this 'hypercompetition' and describes the new rules of the game. D'Aveni has developed a '7S's model to encompass the aspects that have to be covered by management:

The general expectation is that various processes in the innovation arena will become even more linked together.

1   stakeholder satisfaction

2   strategic soothsaying

3   speed

4   surprise

5   shifting the rules

6   signalling

7   simultaneous and sequential strategic thrust.

Stakeholder satisfaction – of customers, employees and shareholders – is needed for growth of the firm.

Sometimes small differences in development times can have large consequences on the profitability of products because of the multiplier effects of positive feedback loops. Furthermore, surprise and shifting the rules are constantly needed as older strategies, by definition, become useless after widespread imitation.

D'Aveni's 7Ss is a set of rules that may help to construct a proper strategy. The elaboration of it must be based on a deep insight into the processes and institutions of the business. It is perhaps superfluous to say that his 7Ss also seem to apply to devising strategies in warfare.

James Brian Quinn (1992) has summarized the characteristics innovations have in common. He notes that they are:

- needs oriented;
- deal with probabilities;
- complicated;
- time-consuming;
- prone to spurts, delays, resistance, setbacks;
- reliant on intuition and uncodifiable knowledge;
- found by fanatics or champions.

This list rings true for everyone who is acquainted with NPD.

Quinn has also classified the types of innovative organizations according to the specific attributes of the various functions, such as research, manufacturing, development, marketing, and the attributes of the customers. He distinguishes eight types of innovative structures, namely:

1   large systems producers;

2   basic research companies;

3   dominant market share companies;

4   state-of-the-art companies;

5 discrete, small product lines;

6 limited-volume fashion companies;

7 'one-off' customer designs;

8 expose the company to risk by producing simultaneous designs.

Quinn makes clear the variety of organizations that exist and, in this way, makes it evident that there is no one, unique, no-fail solution for innovation.

Tom Peters (1997) has summarized, in an eloquent and provocative way, the importance and main attributes of innovation. In his model 'the circle of innovation', Peters has included a number of issues that are also discussed in this book. Moreover, he has listed a number of the more psychological, or emotional, sides of innovation (see Figure 1.7).

James Moore, in his book *The Death of Competition: Leadership and strategy in the age of business ecosystems* (1996), describes a slightly different picture. He focuses on the fact that companies are always part of a number of networks. Competition is between networks or clusters of companies. A company may be a partner with another company in one cluster and another cluster may be a competitor. In other words, a large number of complicated and different types of dependencies may co-exist. Examples are abundant if we look at the consumer electronics industry, where, in some instances, Philips cooperates with Sony and, in other instances, they compete. It is important to have insight into these dependencies and in this way Moore supplements the approach of D'Aveni.

Authors such as Ralph Stacey, and Shona Brown and Kathleen Eisenhardt have applied the results of chaos and complexity theory to strategic management. Stacey (1993) distinguishes two types of management:

- ordinary management
- extraordinary management.

Most management textbooks deal with ordinary management, which is concerned with the control and development of an organization within a framework of assumptions and beliefs that is accepted and agreed on by people in that organization. Managers carry out their tasks of ordinary management by means of the formal organizational framework and this is perfectly adequate in conditions of predictable change.

When, however, an organization has to innovate and cope with the ambiguous, uncertain and unpredictable, managers have to change to extraordinary management. This management is based on chaos theory and theories about self-organization.

If we compare both these types of management with commanding armies, ordinary management can be compared with commanding an army outside the battlefield and extraordinary management with commanding during battles and

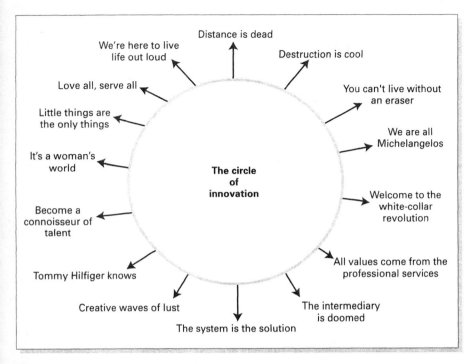

Distance is dead

We're here to live
life out loud

Destruction is cool

Love all, serve all

You can't live without
an eraser

Little things are
the only things

We are all
Michelangelos

It's a woman's
world

**The circle
of
innovation**

Welcome to the
white-collar
revolution

Become a
connoisseur of
talent

All values come from the
professional services

Tommy Hilfiger knows

Creative waves of lust

The intermediary
is doomed

The system is the solution

Figure 1.7 Tom Peters' circle of innovation

in guerrilla warfare when mostly chaos dominates. The most important contribution of Stacey is that he defines the two types of management in precise terms.

Brown and Eisenhardt's book, *Competing on the Edge: Strategy as structured chaos* (1998), goes a step further and tries to help management to apply certain principles developed within complexity theory to the field of management. The central principle in their book is the so-called 'edge of chaos'. This is an organizational situation between chaos and stiff structure. Research has demonstrated that organizational adaptability is greatest in this area and, by means of evolutionary processes, competing organizations drift towards this area.

The 'edge of chaos' is an organizational situation between chaos and stiff structure; organizational adaptability is greatest in this area.

Brown and Eisenhardt describe a range of business aspects or dimensions that it is important to consider when innovating, such as how to organize communication in the organization, capture cross-business synergies and take advantage of the past. The authors give a number of indications as to how to position the organization on the edge between chaos and stiff structures in the time and space domains. The authors end with a summary of strategy laws to be taken into account when competing on the edge. These are:

- advantage is temporary;
- strategy is diverse, emergent and complicated;
- reinvention is the goal;
- live in the present;
- stretch out to the past;
- reach into the future;
- change time and pace;
- grow the strategy;
- drive the strategy at the business level;
- patch businesses to markets and articulate the whole.

The authors we discussed before – Pavitt, Abernathy and Utterback, and Teece – looked at separate industries. Moore's thesis is that we have to think in ecosystems of clusters of companies.

Other authors, such as Brian Arthur, stress that products are used in combination with other products. This means that all kinds of products are related to each other in complicated ways. He speaks about product and technical ecologies. He also focuses his attention on business development processes and their underlying mechanisms. D'Aveni, Stacey, Brown and Eisenhardt start to develop management methodologies to cope with the unpredictability of business changes.

Conclusion

As a consequence of the changes in the business environment in the last few decades, management focus has switched from efficient operations via quality of products and service to innovation, which is now the dominant management paradigm. This has a number of consequences.

- There has been a switch from considering only isolated functions, such as R&D and marketing, to considering the whole business organization and integrating the various functions.
- There has been a trend away from analysis of structure and towards an analysis of processes and process management.

- There is a growing awareness that innovation and business development do not exhibit linear behaviour, but, rather, behave in a non-linear way.
- There is a growing awareness that we cannot predict events, but that it is important to have insight into the various processes inside and outside the company.
- The consequence of this growing awareness is that we cannot rely on expert systems, especially not in NBD, but have to introduce and improve the management of knowledge.

When managers understand the basic processes underlying NPD and NBD and the rules that govern these processes, they can better anticipate potential consequences of their present-day decisions. Therefore, it may be expected that their innovation efforts will be more successful. They will create more value for their stakeholders, such as their customers, and, consequently, their shareholders.

To understand business dynamics we need to make more use of biological metaphors.

We will discuss the state of the art with respect to knowledge of the various processes and underlying rules in Part 1 of this book, and present ways in which this knowledge can be used and applied to the business situation. There are no easy rules of thumb for success, but we will present tools that help us to analyze the NPD and NBD processes and to formulate new business models and communicate these to other important stakeholders. We call these instruments 'dynamic business modelling', or 'DBM', and will discuss these in Part 2 of this book.

In Part 3, we will explain how these instruments can be applied and used to support various business functions, such as business intelligence, scenario planning when making decisions and NPD and NBD management.

From this chapter it is clear that to understand business dynamics we need to make more and more use of biological metaphors. The analogy of business models to models developed in biology seems to be close and worth exploring further. Evidence for this is the popularity of concepts such as lifecycles, evolution and co-evolution, ecologies and ecosystems and self-organization.

In the next chapter, we will briefly explore these analogies and study in a little bit more detail what we can learn from biology. On the other hand, we also will discuss the difficulties with putting too much emphasis on the value of biological models for business.

2 | The age of biology

Introduction

One of the central issues in biology has been the origin of life and the process of evolution that has produced the multitude of species that exist today. The publication of the evolution theory by Charles Darwin was a major landmark in biology. After this theory was accepted as the best explanation of the origins of the various types of uni-cellular and multi-cellular organisms, plants and animals, the search was on for the proof for this theory. Almost one century on, archeo-paleontologists have gathered large amounts of circumstantial evidence to support the theory of Darwin. However, a large number of questions have remained unresolved. One is that there were periods of fast evolution and speciation followed by periods of slower evolution. Another is how life on Earth started.

The use of computer simulation has speeded up enormously the process of building theories about the origin and evolution of life on Earth. Scientists have been able to model and simulate evolution using a multitude of approaches. The Santa Fe Institute in New Mexico in particular has become a centre for students of computational biology.

The simulation studies reveal the various contributions the mechanisms of inheritance – such as mutation, crossover and sexuality – have on the speed of evolution. They have increased our insight into how agents that follow only simple decision rules and possess only local information can build large, complicated structures. Also, how simple molecules that possess autocatalytic properties (that is, they can stimulate their own chemical transformation) can form entities that possess all the attributes of living organisms. They have demonstrated that, by evolutionary processes, a certain state – namely the edge of chaos – is occupied by organisms that are characterized by fast adaptation to outside challenges.

From these studies a number of new principles of evolution and self-organization emerged. These could be generalized to other systems that consist of a number of agents, molecules, cells or individuals that are loosely coupled –

that is, they influence each other but have to be considered as independent entities.

The organization of molecules into cells, cells into tissues and individuals in ecologies, and the behaviour of these higher-level organizations, can now be better understood from the attributes of the constituent elements.

This understanding of fundamental biological principles has enriched the traditional approaches in biology, the study of structures in morphology, anatomy, histology and cytology, the study of processes in physiology, genetics and biochemistry, and the study of individual and group behaviour in ethology and ecology.

A large number of books about business and management have appeared that explicitly refer to biology and biological concepts in their titles. For example, *The Death of Competition: Leadership and strategy in the age of business ecosystems* by James Moore (1996) and *The Living Company: Growth, learning and longevity in business* by Arie de Geus (1997). The titles of these books echo a longer tradition of using biological concepts as metaphors in management, such as 'the lifecycle' of technologies, products, markets and industries, 'evolution' and 'co-evolution' of technologies, products, markets and organizations, or self-organization and 'ecologies' of products and organizations. The applicability of these biological concepts indicates an analogy between business and biology, as noted in Chapter 1.

A large number of books about business and management have appeared that explicitly refer to biology and biological concepts.

Biology, in contrast to large parts of physics and chemistry, is not an exact science in which the behaviour of systems can be described by 'relatively simple' mathematical formulae that enable us to predict the trajectory of such systems when we have enough information about their initial conditions. In biology, it is hazardous to extrapolate the results of studies of parts of the system to the whole. Isolated enzymes, cells or tissues behave differently in isolation than they do when they are part of the whole. This is because the behaviour of biological systems is the result of many individual elements – so-called 'agents', be they molecules, cells, tissues or individuals – that are weakly coupled and react to each other in complicated ways. This results in non-linear behaviour and the emergence of completely new phenomena at higher hierarchical levels. We cannot predict the behaviour of cells by studying the behaviour of the constituent molecules, such as proteins, DNA, RNA, sugars, amino acids, salts and so on. Also, we cannot predict the behaviour of bodies by simply studying the behaviour of cells, or of ecologies by studying only the behaviour of individual animals and plants.

Essential here is the notion that such systems consist of a number of agents that react on local information and it is the reactions of all these agents that give rise to the emergence of global effects that cannot be extrapolated from knowledge about the local behaviour of the agents. Likewise, phenomena such as life, consciousness, innovation and business development are phenomena at a higher level of the hierarchy that result from the local behaviour and interaction of many molecules, cells or producers and users respectively.

Everyone knows that groups behave differently from the individuals that make up the groups when they are on their own. Equally, the behaviour of any given market is different from the sum of the behaviours of the separate buyers. This is most evident when we try to predict the performance of a completely new product from tests of individual preferences, as the Coca-Cola company experienced when introducing its new Coke about ten years ago. Akio Morita, formerly Chairman of Sony, was right when he did not follow the advice of his marketers, based on market studies, *not* to introduce the Walkman. Many identical examples can be found in literature or are well known in particular industries.

Complex adaptive systems

The development of non-linear science, or complexity theory, by researchers from different parts of the world during the last decade has greatly enhanced our insight into the behaviour of such systems. By means of computer simulation, researchers have been able to demonstrate how it was possible for insects such as termites or ants to build complicated nest structures and form highly complicated social organizations by following a very few simple behaviour rules (see John L. Casti, 1997).

Four different tasks of the adult harvester ant worker have been recognized, namely foraging, patrolling, nest maintenance and midden work (building and sorting the colony's refuse pile). It is the (local) interactions among ants performing these tasks that give rise to what is called emergent (global) phenomena in the ant colony.

Research has revealed that task allocation depends on two kinds of decisions made by individual ants. First, the decision as to which tasks to perform and, second, the decision as to whether or not to be active in these tasks. These decisions are based only on local information; there is no central decision maker. The factors that influence what decision is made are an increase in food availability, detected by the individual ants and by means of interaction with other ants, detritus on the surface of the nest mound and intrusion by foreign ants. In his book, Casti summarizes the characteristics of the behaviour of complex adaptive systems as follows:

- inconsistent phenomena – that is, the existence of paradoxes;

- large effects of small changes – that is, instability;

- behaviour transcends rules – that is, incompatibility;

- behaviour cannot be decomposed into parts – that is, connectivity;
- self-organizing parts – that is, emergence.

Researchers have made models of societies and demonstrated the emergence of behaviour such as trade, wealth creation, networks of friends and so on. These are called 'complex adaptive systems'.

Other researchers have made computational models of societies and demonstrated the emergence of behaviour such as trade, wealth creation, networks of friends and so on in these artificial societies. These resulted from individual entities following simple (local) rules (see Joshua M. Epstein and Robert Axtell, 1996).

These types of systems are called 'complex adaptive systems', or CAS, and one of the founding fathers of the study of these systems – John H. Holland (1995) – has noted a number of characteristics that they share:

- aggregation of similar things such as 'ants' that can perform four tasks or people who can be either 'buyers' or 'sellers' of a certain type of product;
- tagging mechanisms – the individual agents recognize others, so buyers recognize sellers and sellers recognize the buyers, for example;
- non-linearity – means that the behaviour (output) of the system cannot be extrapolated in a simple way from its earlier behaviour;
- flows – such as flows of materials, information, cash;
- diversity – no two situations are ever exactly the same;
- internal models – the agents react in a certain way to environmental stimuli, so the basis of these reactions to signals from the environment is 'models' of the environment, which may be very simple, as with the example of the ant discussed above, or quite complicated, such as those used by humans;
- a limited number of building blocks, such as buyers, sellers and middlemen.

It is not difficult to recognize these properties in the business systems we are familiar with.

There are several students who have modelled financial markets or e-commerce using these types of modelling techniques.

In the book *How Hits Happen: Forecasting predictability in a chaotic marketplace* (1998), Winslow Farrell describes his results with computer models of markets based on CAS theory. Based on his efforts, he advised various companies, such as Macy's Aventuras, how to staff and arrange the set-up of their shops.

Stuart Kauffman

A biologist who has drawn the attention of business consultants and managers is Stuart Kauffman. Kauffman studies biological evolutionary processes by means of computer modelling and simulation. He applies a certain type of physical model – the so-called 'spinglass' model – to evolutionary processes. Briefly, the spinglass model has the following characteristics. Spinglasses consist of small magnetic dipoles that can adopt two positions – upwards or downwards. The magnetic dipoles are weakly linked, which means that they have a tendency to align themselves. When a dipole is upwards, it exerts a certain force on its neighbours to adopt the same direction. When the number of dipoles in a certain direction increases, the force to switch to the same direction also increases. These forces are created by the tendency of materials to settle in the state of lowest energy content. The interactions between the dipoles vary according to material, temperature and so on and these influence the speed with which they find their lowest energy state because a higher temperature disrupts this process and the system settles at higher energy levels.

Kauffman adapted this model to evolutionary processes in the following way. Instead of defining energy states, he defined a fitness landscape. The model settles in a state of highest fitness. The speed and way in which the highest fitness state is reached is dependent on a number of characteristics of the system. In his model, the individual elements are not small magnets but the individual building blocks of genomes (genes) or of proteins (amino acids).

When genes can exist in just two forms (one with maximum fit for a certain function in a certain environment and one with a minimum fit) and the genes are independent of each other (meaning that the fitness of one form is independent of the forms and thus fitness of the other genes), there is just *one* optimal state of maximum fitness for the total genome. However, when a certain form and fitness of gene is dependent on the form and fitness of another gene, there is no longer only one optimal state for the whole genome – there are *several*. When the fitness of a form of gene is dependent on subsequently two, three and more genes, the number of fitness states increases and so the ultimate fitness that can be reached will be reduced.

In this way, the fitness landscape changes and starts to consist of many peaks divided by valleys. When, through evolution, a certain genome has reached a certain fitness peak and will no longer change, it will be imprisoned on that peak. It no longer changes, because every change will result in reduced fitness. Thus, it cannot jump to another, higher fitness peak that is separated by a deep valley.

A second thing is happening at the same time. When the number of interactions between genes increases, the speed of evolution decreases, because improvement is the result of the simultaneous change of a number of genes.

Highly connected genomes will only slowly become fitter and the ultimate fitness they will obtain will be less.

A complication may arise when the environment of the genome changes. In this case, the fitness landscape will change and, in a certain environment, a fit genome may now be less fit. In connected genes, that live in a so-called rugged landscape, this may result in the situation where a genome cannot change and climb a hill with a higher fitness peak because it will have to go through a valley of lower fitness. In nature, there are several strategies to overcome this problem. One is the crossing over of genes that may combine parts of genomes existing in different sets of genes sitting on faraway peaks. A related strategy is that of sexual propagation. In this way, faraway sets of genes can be combined, overcoming fitness valleys.

By compartmentalizing products into components, the technological dependencies decrease and the speed of progress increases.

Kauffman has applied his findings regarding these types of evolutionary models to business situations in his book *At Home in the Universe* (1995). In it he makes clear that by compartmentalizing products into components, the technological dependencies decrease and the speed of progress increases. Standardization of the interfaces between components may support this process. Also, compartmentalization of organizations – into departments, divisions or business units – that have a certain freedom to change may increase the speed with which companies adapt to new situations.

The ways in which the departments are linked and the coordination mechanisms are critical in determining how much room there is to experiment and change in each individual department. Also, the types of linkages there are will determine to what degree better performance of one department may result in improvements in the other departments, ultimately leading to improvement of the whole organization.

The fitness landscape of biological organisms, technologies, products or organizations is the result of the properties of other organisms, technologies, products or organizations. The evolution of one organism, technology, product, company or market influences the evolution of others. In this way, co-evolution can be modelled.

Kauffman also demonstrated that, in particular circumstances, organizations that ignore certain market information might be better able to innovate and develop completely new products for new markets. An example of this is the development of the Walkman by Sony, as mentioned above.

As in the case of the CAS models discussed earlier, a number of researchers are applying the model developed by Kauffman to a variety of business situations. The change of core *competences* into core *rigidities* after some time and environmental change, as described by Dorothy Leonard-Barton (1995), can also be explained by this model. Again, current business practices that have proven to be best in various situations can be explained using these principles. A whole range of ways in which organizations may cooperate, depending on the intended timeframe of cooperation, frequency and commitment, ranging from simple market transactions, outsourcing, joint manufacturing, joint ventures and acquisitions, has pros and cons with respect to profitability, costs, risks and speed of development.

Trajectories of non-linear systems

Systems or organizations of agents evolve over time and follow certain trajectories. Sometimes these trajectories follow a clear path to a certain equilibrial state after some sort of disturbance. In other situations, they follow a fixed cyclical pattern or systems may follow a chaotic path that cannot be predicted and never will be the same again (this is defined as 'deterministic chaos'). Depending on the type of trajectory, we speak of the presence of a 'point attractor' to a global or local equilibrium, a 'cyclical attractor' or a 'strange attractor' respectively. The attractors are coupled to certain spaces – sets of system parameters – in which the system is present. With fluctuation, the values of the sets of system parameters might change a little bit. This may result in one or another trajectory that the system follows. Splits in trajectories are called 'bifurcations'. The presence of bifurcations and various types of attractors are also characteristic of non-linear systems.

The transitions from one state to another are termed 'phase transitions'. An example is the transition of a normal beating heart into a fibrillating heart or the transition of normal propulsion of the gut into chaotic movements of the lower gut, resulting in stomach pain, or the normal brain patterns that suddenly transform when a person has an epileptic attack.

In business, small variations may have drastic consequences. Innovation, in general, may start with a small event that leads, ultimately, to a completely different situation. Time to market is equally critical. Being a little bit later than the competitor or missing a critical market window may result in a drastic other, worse, situation.

In Parts 2 and 3 of this book, we will apply these concepts to a large number of business situations and describe how management can deal with these opportunities and threats.

Self-organized criticality

Some very complicated phenomena seem to follow simple rules. Per Bak (1996) has formulated a theory – self-organized criticality. It demonstrates the similarity between a wide variety of phenomena such as the formation of sand piles, earthquakes, forest fires, bankruptcies in the economy and so on. When

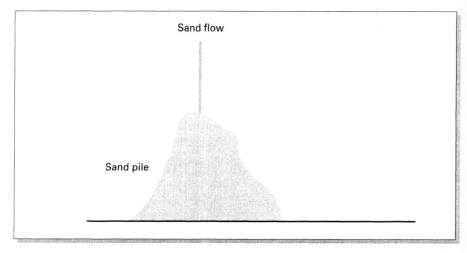

Sand flow

Sand pile

Figure 2.1 The formation of a sand pile

we have a pipe from which sand is streaming at a constant rate, below the pipe a sand pile is formed (see Figure 2.1).

When the pile becomes too high and the slope too steep, avalanches occur. Bak did this simple experiment and measured the amount of sand that was removed by every avalanche. Subsequently, he made a graph in which the size of the avalanches was put along the y axis and the number of avalanches of a certain size was put along the x axis. The result was a pair of graphs that follow a power law (see Figure 2.2).

The graphs prove that the power 'a' remains the same in all types of experiments. Somehow, some regularity is hidden in this process. Since this simple experiment has been published, Bak and his group have studied a large number of other phenomena and have always found that the same simple formula describes the phenomena. It has been proven, for example, that when you examine the size of earthquakes in relation to their number, a similar power law becomes apparent. Also whichever earthquakes have been studied, the power remains the same. There are long, relatively static periods punctuated by crises of various sizes. The simple power law can describe all these phenomena. This indicates that the same forces are causing earthquakes, forest fires or avalanches wherever they occur.

These concepts have been applied to, for example, the bankruptcies of financial organizations during the last century. It was demonstrated that the number of bankruptcies in a defined period could be described by a similar simple power law. This indicates that the mechanisms causing bankruptcies were comparable during the last century. It also indicates that we always will

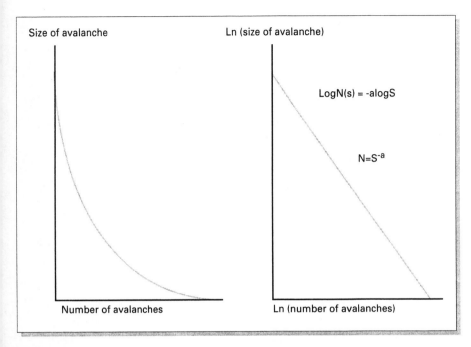

Figure 2.2 The sizes of the avalanches versus the number of such avalanches

have periods of high and low numbers of bankruptcies, independent of all new technology or instruments to control the financial transactions of the banks.

So far, a study of this kind on inventions and innovations in a certain area has not been published, but we may expect that these too follow simple power laws. Where a system exists in space, it is similar on all scales. This is called 'fractal geometry'. All these phenomena are fractal. It may be expected that inventions and innovations are also fractal. What does this mean for management? It means that upsets in business are unavoidable. Now and then, innovative movements – disruptive technologies – will be so large that an industry changes dramatically. We cannot control this. What we can do, however, is carefully monitor things and take the right measures when something is going to, or does, occur (Bak, 1996).

> *It may be expected that inventions and innovations are also fractal. What does this mean for management?*

System dynamics

Last, but not least, we will discuss another type of modelling of non-linear systems. It was developed outside the biological arena, but is also applicable to biological situations, such as the behaviour of ecosystems and all kinds of body processes. This is 'system dynamics', as developed by Jay Forester in the 1950s.

The similarities between system dynamics and the other approaches used to describe and understand the non-linear behaviour of systems are:

- an emphasis on the whole system;
- the fact that the behaviour of the system cannot be extrapolated from knowledge of the behaviour of the individual parts;
- the often counter-intuitive results that may occur;
- the recognition that small events may have large consequences and the emphasis on various non-linear mechanisms, such as reinforcing loops.

From its start, system dynamics has been applied in an effort to understand the dynamics of the economy – that is, industry dynamics – and social systems – that is, urban dynamics. System dynamics has always remained removed from mainstream economics. One of the possible reasons for this relates to the fact that, in the early days, the claims for it were too high – namely, that system dynamics would result in predictions about the course the economy would take. At that time, the characteristics of non-linear systems were not recognized. The objective of better prediction of the dynamics of economic systems could not be proved for reasons we became aware of only during more recent decades. The fundamental unpredictability of the behaviour of non-linear systems made that objective unrealistic.

This claim is no longer made by system dynamists. Instead, they emphasize other benefits, such as the increase in insight into the processes that are relevant and shape the behaviour of the system. System dynamics is now widely recognized as a tool that supports learning and knowledge management and facilitates the learning organization. It is, in general, less suitable as a methodology for building expert systems.

System dynamics focuses on processes instead of the behaviour of individual agents that interact with each other.

Peter Senge's book *The Fifth Discipline: The art and practice of the learning organization* (1990) made this modelling approach well known in the business community. An increasing number of consultants and companies are applying this methodology to support their decision making.

The penetration of the system dynamics methodology may be partly due to the use of archetypes – simple models of non-linear systems that can easily be

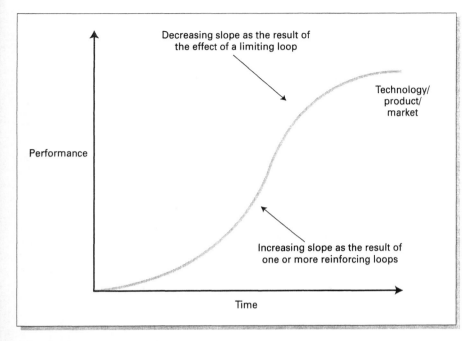

Figure 2.3 The well-known 'S' curve representing the product lifecycle

recognized and understood. One of the archetypes is 'limits to growth'. This refers to the well-known product lifecycle concept, as depicted in Figure 2.3. The limit to the growth archetype consists of two coupled non-linear processes or mechanisms – namely one growth process consisting of a reinforcing loop and one limiting process consisting of a negative feedback loop. In total, Senge distinguishes 11 archetypes with names such as 'success to the successful', 'tragedy of the commons', 'fixes the backfire', 'escalation', 'drifting goals', 'shifting the burden', 'growth and underinvestment'. In Figure 2.4, these archetypes are summarized and briefly described.

The various archetypes are simple combinations of a limited number of non-linear mechanisms, such as reinforcing loops, limiting loops and time delays.

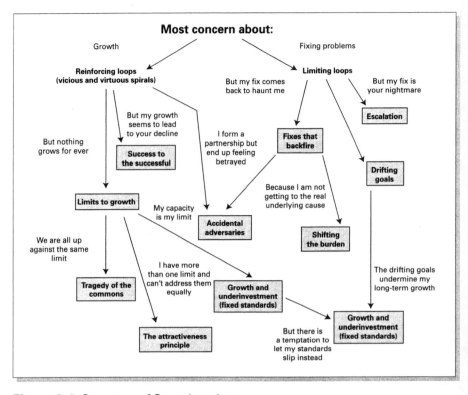

Figure 2.4 Summary of Senge's archetypes

An introduction to dynamic business modelling

Dynamic business modelling (DBM) can be defined as the iterative process of analyses of the three Ps of innovation – position, people and process – which helps to translate tacit knowledge into explicit knowledge, integrate the knowledge of the various experts, increase the understanding of the dynamics of the innovation arena (encompassed by the four objectives of innovation – technology, applications, markets and organization), facilitate the formation of a shared model of the innovation process and support the decision making for innovation management.

> *Dynamic business modelling can be defined as the iterative process of analyses of the three Ps of innovation – position, people and process.*

Another definition of DBM is as follows.

DBM is a knowledge management instrument that supports business intelligence, strategic decision making, management of the innovation network, project management, communication and training. It consists of the inventorization, analysis, integration, modelling and simulation of the internal business processes and/or external innovation processes. It helps in the codification, integration, storage and exploitation of existing knowledge and the generation of new knowledge. DBM is a process and can be viewed as part of the management process.

DBM can be divided into a number of steps. We can distinguish three stages, the first consisting of three different steps, the second of two steps, and the third being of a more continuous character.

1 Analysis of the position, people and processes.

  - **Position** the analysis of the present and possible future position of the company.
  - **People** analysis of the forces that inhibit or help to move the company from the present to the wished for future position – that is, analysis of the people involved, or, in other words, the internal and external stakeholders.
  - **Process** analysis of the business processes and external NPD and NBD processes.

2 Analysis of non-linearities of the business system.

  - **Non-linear mechanisms** analysis of the non-linear mechanisms that determine the overall behaviour of the business system.
  - **Behaviour** construction of a computer model, structural and behavioural validation of this model, investigation of the model sensitivities and determination of the white spaces in the model.

3 Application of the model to:

  - our understanding of the innovation process and monitoring the environment;
  - strategic decision making and scenario planning;
  - management of the NPD and NBD processes.

As these consecutive actions demonstrate, an evolution of the model from static to dynamic, from qualitative to quantitative and, consequently, from simple to complicated will take place. During the process, we will get an increasingly deeper insight into the business system that helps when we study the various ways in which the system may react to possible actions, the critical success factors and bottlenecks for the various strategic options for NBD. However, it is not an expert system; predictions cannot be made. The modelling efforts rest upon the principles of chaos and complexity theory, as described earlier in this chapter.

The analytical techniques start with the inventorization of existing information and knowledge about the business that is stored in the heads of the different managers and experts and so is partly not yet codified (tacit knowledge), partly codified and may be present in the available business reports. In this first step of Stage 1, therefore, the emphasis is on static and qualitative modelling techniques that describe the position of the company (this step will be discussed in more depth in Chapter 3).

In the next step of Stage 1, the model will take the form of relational diagrams and influence matrices. Existing frameworks, such as Porter's five forces market model, may facilitate the analysis and other stakeholder analysis frameworks (see Chapter 4).

During the analysis of the processes in the next step of Stage 1, flow diagram techniques, activity matrices and cognitive mapping techniques, as developed by Eden (1989), are used. In this step, we analyze the (generic) processes within and outside the company, such as the generation of ideas, knowledge generation, acquisition and exploitation, product realization, implementation, teambuilding, decision making and cash flow, market penetration and competition processes (Chapter 5).

The causal and flow diagrams that are the output of the last step are the inputs of Stage 2, the analysis of non-linear mechanisms, such as reinforcing loops, limiting loops, lock-in mechanisms, selection mechanisms and so on. These methods are widely used in qualitative system dynamics and described by, for example, Peter Senge (1994) in his book *The Fifth Discipline Fieldbook: Strategies and tools for building a learning organization* (we will describe the various non-linear mechanisms in Chapter 6; the modelling, validation and analysis of the computer model via simulation will be described in Chapter 7).

In this way, a number of different types of business modelling techniques are used and integrated.

The various applications of DBM – such as in business intelligence, strategic management and scenario planning, innovation network management and management of the NPD process – are described fully in Part 3, but here Figure 2.5 presents the main elements schematically.

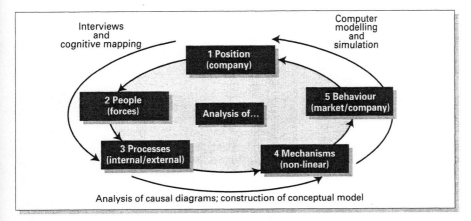

Interviews and cognitive mapping

Computer modelling and simulation

1 Position (company)

2 People (forces)

Analysis of...

5 Behaviour (market/company)

3 Processes (internal/external)

4 Mechanisms (non-linear)

Analysis of causal diagrams; construction of conceptual model

Figure 2.5 Schematic representation of the DBM process

Conclusion

In this chapter, a number of modelling approaches developed during the last decade for studying complex systems have been discussed.

The modelling approach in the NPD and NBD processes that will be described in Part 2 of this book is based on the application of the system dynamics methodology. The reason for this is that it remains closer to daily management practice than other methodologies because of its focus on processes. However, it has the drawback that the processes have to be defined beforehand. When, in a business system, other types of process evolve, this requires a new (variant) model. This limits its use to a medium level of business system change. However, whereas in decision making a period of two to five years is a relatively long time, this approach is presently more easily applicable than other modelling methods of non-linear system behaviour, such as the CAS (multi-agent) modelling techniques. The different modelling approaches, however, must be viewed as complementary instead of substitutes for one another. Further developments of the CAS type of models may make these approaches more feasible in the near future.

To understand the evolution and self-organization of the innovation arena, we must try to understand the mechanisms underlying evolution and self-organization.

To understand the evolution and self-organization of the innovation arena, we must try to understand the mechanisms underlying evolution and self-organization. The route from events to the three Ps – position, people and process – to the non-linear mechanisms follows a certain abstraction path that is facilitated by the right modelling approaches. In management, already a multitude of different models are used to analyze various aspects of the business and generate new strategic options. In Part 2, we will discuss this methodology in more detail.

Part 2

The steps of dynamic business modelling

3 | Determining your present position and setting goals

Introduction

Deregulation, new technologies, the blurring of industries, the emergence of the Internet and e-business, globalization of markets and internationalization of competition, the growing importance of sustainability – all are trends that strongly affect the business environment. Because these trends are often, in one way or another, connected to each other, extrapolation of these trends is hazardous. Companies such as the electric power companies have to react properly to these environmental changes if they are to survive. From being inward-looking bureaucracies they have to change into outward-looking, much more entrepreneurial ways of management. They have to develop competences in the analysis and interpretation of markets and competition. Moreover, they must become able to react appropriately and adjust their business processes.

Looking for new business models in a changing world – deregulation in the electricity sector

case study

The electric power industry is changing rapidly. Because of huge investments in infrastructure, the existence of large economies of scale and the notion that this industry has been the motor for the rest of industry, governments have been highly involved in determining its fate.

All over the world, the industry had a monopoly. Because of this, companies did not study the market. They were very much focused on the internal technical processes and were ramparts for the engineers.

In the 1990s, governments became more keen on the functioning of markets and realized that competition was needed to improve this in such a way that the customers would profit via the creation of net value in the form of lower prices. Deregulation of the market started first in the USA, then Britain and other European countries followed.

The position of the electric power companies changed drastically and they lacked knowledge of markets, customers and product innovation. From being bureaucratic and technocratic organizations, they had to transform into entrepreneurial mode. Some were able to make the transformation, others were not. New organizations got their chance and started growing and prospering.

One of the successful companies is the Florida Power and Light Company. It is one of the fastest-growing electric utilities in the United States. The company recognized that the key factor for future success in a competitive market would be to become a low-cost provider of electric services. The company adopted a multidisciplinary approach to design a new strategy to face future challenges in such fields as technology, customer demand, competitive pressure and regulation.

Several innovations were introduced. For example, the combustion turbine manager spent $15 million a year on gas turbines alone. He saw as his principal goal to drive down costs. He therefore looked at operational costs and budgeting in a different way. Normally, he looked three years in advance. Now he started to look instead at lifetime costs. When you pay two times more for an engine that lasts three times longer, in the long run you actually save money. What he did was to look for investments that resulted in the least dollar per service hour – everything was reduced to that. In this way, for example, he started to build his own combustion liners instead of purchasing them because he figured out that buying the components himself and the necessary materials saved large amounts in terms of costs and provided him with better machines. The cost savings were so large that he could afford to amortize the tooling costs.

It also proved to be more economic to start and stop large coal power plants more often, even up to 200 times a year, whereas before it was only done, at most, 10 times a year.

The Florida Power and Light Company is in the process of transforming itself into a more customer-driven and cost-focused company.

The change in the environment resulted in a change in its market position and this demanded that the organization adapt its competences. The Florida Power and Light Company realized this and prepared itself better for the future than a number of its competitors. This has enabled it to grow and prosper.

In Part 2, we will describe dynamic business modelling (DBM) that supports the inventorization, analysis, modelling, validation and simulation of the new product development and new business development (NPD and NBD) processes.[2] DBM supports the development of innovation strategies and integrates a large number of new and commonly used methodologies. It can be divided into three stages consisting of, in total, five steps of increasing complexity.

---

[2] The NPD and NBD processes encompass both the internal business processes, leading to the development of new technology and its applications to products, services and processes, and the external processes, taking place in the supply chains, markets, competitive processes and so on. It excludes the purely technical processes that belong to the area of the various scientific and technical disciplines. The modelling and simulation of these processes are sophisticated and well developed. These processes belong completely to the technical system of the innovation arena. In our modelling efforts, we look at the consequences of these processes.

- **The first stage** has as its purpose analysis of the existing business systems. This consists of three steps:

  1 definition of the scope of the modelling effort by determining the present and desired future position of the company, defining the business boundaries and setting the business goal(s);

  2 analysis of the stakeholders that play a role in the positional move – that is, in the development of the new business;

  3 analysis of the processes that are part of the business development process, both inside and outside the company.

- **The second stage** consists of the analysis of the (non-linear) mechanisms that affect the potential dynamics of the NBD process and the behaviour of the innovation system.

- **The third stage** consists of building DBMs that support the validation of the present knowledge about the business to which new knowledge can be added and used to train new managers and communicate strategies to other partners and employees. Such a model will also support the business intelligence process and the process of 'strategic conversation' as Kees van der Heijden (1996) called it. This is the process of experimenting with possible new strategies and operational interventions to make these strategies work.

In Figure 3.1, the steps of DBM outlined above are presented. In this chapter, we will discuss the first step – analysis of the position of the company.

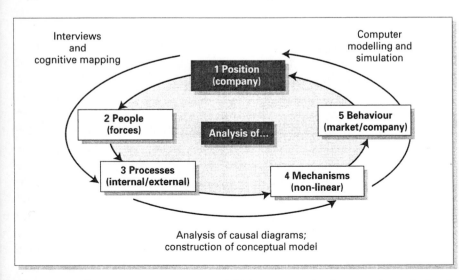

Figure 3.1 The steps involved in the DBM process – the first step is analysis of the position of the company

This consists of the analysis of the external position of the company *vis-à-vis* its customers, competitors, suppliers and so on, and its internal position.

The analysis of the external business and its internal position – that is, the assets and competences of the organization – is one of the areas of management that is now well established. Many books have been published about analysis of markets, the competition and industries, as well as resources, assets and core capabilities of the company. Therefore, in this part of DBM, a number of proven approaches are applied. In the strategic management literature, two separate approaches are often recognized as being effective in analyzing the external and internal positions of a company. The so-called structure-conduct-performance school provides analysis tools for the external market position. One of its most well-known representatives is Michael Porter.

Companies with much market power can appropriate more of the value they create for their customers than other organizations in the sector, such as their competitors, suppliers and distributors.

The second approach is that of the resource-based school. Its most well-known representatives are Gary Hamel and C. K. Prahalad (1994), who focus on analyzing the internal position of a company as determined by its resources, competences and abilities, and how these affect its competitive advantage.

Both schools of thought realize that competitive advantage depends on both the external position and the internal capabilities. In this chapter, we combine both approaches, seeing them as being equally important in determining the position of an organization.

Analyzing the position of a company starts with an analysis of its external position in comparison with its competitors, followed by an internal analysis of the assets and abilities of the company. The market power of the company is determined by its position. The power of a company determines its ability to control its environment and assemble valuable resources. Michael Porter (1985) has made it clear that companies with much market power can appropriate more of the value they create for their customers than other organizations in the sector, such as their competitors, suppliers and distributors. This is because they can ask higher prices. Also, the financial resources they can assemble can transfer into higher-quality products and services. In this way, a reinforcing loop is created. Because they can control their environment to a larger extent than less powerful companies, they become less vulnerable to disturbances, which decreases their business risk. This also generates value for their stakeholders such as shareholders and employees. In this way, the reinforcing loop is strengthened further – the external position of such a company enables it to accumulate more resources and its internal resources strengthen its external position.

Many tools have been developed to support the analysis of organizations' resources and market and network position. Let us briefly discuss and evaluate these tools. Table 3.1 gives an overview of the various elements of positional analysis.

Table 3.1 Elements of the analysis of the position of a company

Company's resources	External position
Technology – applications	*Applications – market*
◉ Capital assets	◉ Position in business system: competitive
◉ Knowledge: technology, market and	position, market position, interaction
customer knowledge, competitive	with other markets, position in financial
knowledge	markets
Organization	*Technology – applications*
◉ Organizational assets: structure,	◉ Position in technical system: key
systems, culture	technologies, technology interactions,
◉ Management assets: experience,	technology position
style	*Organization*
◉ Financial assets	◉ Network position and position in the
◉ Reputation	supply chain
	◉ Institutional position

Table 3.1 distinguishes two parts of the analysis – that of the external position of the company and of its resources (assets). The analyses of the separate elements of both these parts is well established and part of all strategic planning activities. There are three reasons for dedicating a separate chapter to this analysis. First, the analysis of a number of the elements has become more sophisticated over time and new concepts and tools have been added. Examples are instruments for determining market segmentation and product positioning and valuation tools for tangible and intangible assets.

Second, whereas in most strategic management approaches the analysis ends with the analysis of the position of the company, in DBM it is the start.

Third, most strategic management approaches are normative, putting emphasis on certain elements – for example, choosing the right market and obtaining high market share, concentrating on a limited number of core competences and focusing on throughput times and development speed. The analysis concentrates on certain aspects of the positional analysis. Instead, we will focus more on the dynamic capabilities and opportunities for NBD. As the rules of competition change constantly, we cannot say beforehand what the essential elements of a successful strategy will be. We can say only that a thorough understanding of the business system and the NPD and NBD processes is essential for developing strategies that may surprise the competition and provide competitive advantage.

The assets of a company determine its abilities to perform certain tasks. In this book, we will concentrate on the NPD and NBD abilities of the company. Its external position and the dynamics of the environment determine the opportunities for such development. A widely used instrument to confront internal and external analysis and inventorize the various options is SWOT analysis.

The opportunities for NBD are a function of both internal abilities and external opportunities. This means that the options of a company can be increased by looking for more interesting markets to operate in or by stretching the capabilities of the company. The first can be defined as looking for a better fit between abilities and markets, the latter as looking for strategic stretch. Both ways have to be explored, but can be explored only when sufficient insight into environmental opportunities and internal abilities is available. This insight cannot be based solely on knowledge of the present situation by static analysis of the business, but must also be based on insight into the dynamics of the business development process and the forces that affect its potential future position. This understanding of system behaviour is obtained by studying the underlying processes and mechanisms.

Study of the internal and external positions of the company makes use of desktop research as well as interviews and field research. All three types are complementary to each other and have to be used.

The innovation arena and technical and business systems

Before the start of any analysis, we need to define the scope of the study and the system boundaries. In other words, we have to start by defining the best combinations of technology, applications, markets and organization. A tool that helps to define the scope of the study – that is, the optimal combinations of technology, applications, market and organization – and visualize the present and desirable future position(s) of the company is the 'innovation arena' as presented by Robert G. Cooper in his book *Winning with New Products* (1993). Figure 3.2 shows a schematic representation of Cooper's vision.

We have to start by defining the best combinations of technology, applications, markets and organization.

Cooper's innovation arena has three dimensions – technology, applications and customer groups. An innovation arena encloses both a business system and a technical system. Where these three meet, there is the present combination of technology, applications and market(s).

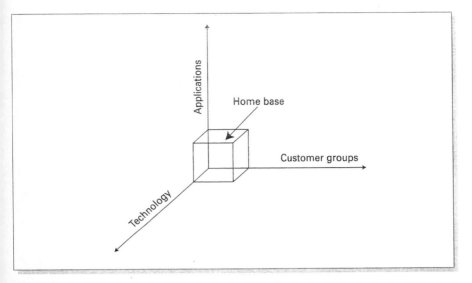

Figure 3.2 The innovation arena according to Cooper

After determining the present position we have to depict along the axes of the three dimensions subsequent developments of technology, applications and customer groups. In this way, a number of points in the three-dimensional space are filled, together forming a selected innovation trajectory.

The development of an innovation

A nice example of an innovation trajectory is the development of the mobile phone. Fifteen years ago, mobile phones did exist, but they were very user-unfriendly and far too heavy. Besides, supporting (analogue) networks were very limited geographically. As a result of technological progress, things have changed dramatically. Today's mobile phones are easy to handle and lightweight. Besides, digital networks are ubiquitous. The developments in miniaturization of the technology have resulted in products that customers actually do buy on a large scale, even if they already have a phone at home! Now, as technological developments progress even further, the possible next step in mobile telephony will be the use of the mobile as an entry terminal to the Internet. Applications such as ordering a soft drink from a vending machine using your mobile phone as a remote control device for ordering, payment and operation of the machine are already feasible in some countries. At the same time, as a result of economies of scale, mobile telephony prices decrease continuously. In this way, yet another market has been created that will attract even more customers. New ways of selling, such as prepaid subscriptions, will further boost mobile telephone sales.

case study

We can also apply this framework to the example of InCyte, discussed in Chapter 1. Incyte's technologies are based on:

- biotechnology, the unravelling of DNA codes;
- the industrialization of what was originally a laboratory technique;
- information technology, the creation of databases and the creation of new information by datamining.

The application of this technology platform is the commercialization of the information accumulated in the databases for the development of new targets for drug development.

The customer groups are the innovating pharmaceutical companies all over the world.

In the case of InCyte, we can imagine that further development of datamining techniques and those used to translate the information obtained from the databases into the best biological targets for further drug development may improve their position in this market.

Another opportunity would be to develop other markets, such as agricultural ones, where similar information about crops may be used to improve them or genetic information about micro-organisms may help in the development of better antibacterial or antifungal drugs.

Such a trajectory can be considered as a three-dimensional road map. In these road maps, however, parallel timelines need to be drawn – one representing the subsequent technology the company wants to develop and the other the markets. Timelines of a certain duration represent the course of the development of the technology, applications and markets/customer groups. Lines between these development projects indicate the relationships between the various projects, as shown in Figure 3.3.

Development of new technology, applications and markets/customer groups often calls for organizational adaptation to be made. A fourth dimension of the innovation arena, therefore, must be 'organization'. By 'organization' we do not only mean the internal organization, but also the external organization of innovations (see Figure 3.4). This we call the extended innovation arena.

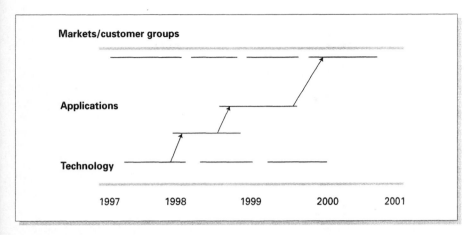

Figure 3.3 The timelines on a road map plotting an innovation trajectory

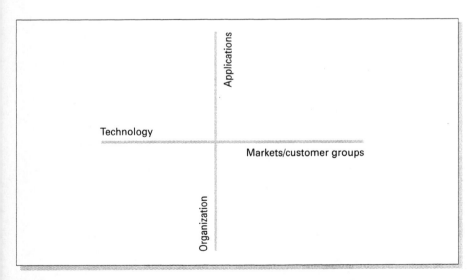

Figure 3.4 The extended innovation arena, defined by the technology, applications and market/customer group and organization dimensions

Innovation and the organization dimension

To come back to our example of InCyte, the organization of the internal business processes, operation of the many DNA decoding machines in parallel and the processing of the information into the databases, as well as the external networks with the various physicians so as to obtain the material, and the communication of this information to the customers, is all part of its organization dimension. Part of the innovation rests on developing new types of external organizational forms, of which information and communications technology is the enabler.

Technological and product innovation often requires adaptation on the part of the organization. For example, it has been demonstrated many times that the introduction of information and communications technology and automation have to be combined with organizational adaptation. Also, NPD is often facilitated by adaptation of the organizational parameters. As it is often the result of cooperation between networks of organizations, the external network is as important for innovation as the internal organization. Development of a new market is often impossible for individual companies but can be successful when a number of companies cooperate.

An example of this that most of us will be familiar with is the introduction of new models of cars. Many times, new cars are developed (which is quite an achievement) that include a little bit of new technology and are introduced to the market with great spectacle, shows and advertising campaigns. The customers rush to their dealers to purchase the new car. When the deal is closed, the salesperson tells them, almost inaudibly, that the expected delivery date will probably be eight months. Then the customer explodes and the salesperson may need to do a lot of talking to prevent the customer from cancelling the purchase.

This is a great example of sound technology and product development, excellent market development and poor organizational development. The factory isn't ready to deliver the new models! This is a pattern seen over and over again and it strongly damages product and company reputation. In the worst case, it may even mean that the product has to be taken off the market until it can be delivered properly.

Let us take two further examples of the contrast between good and poor organization and the effects of this. The problems involved in the development and commercialization of high-definition television were due partly to the lack of commitment of the industry to one global standard. The success of mobile phones in Europe is due partly to the agreement between the producers on the use of GSM as the standard protocol.

The various two-dimensional planes of the TAMO (technology, applications, market and organization) combinations are often used to analyze present and desirable future positions. Well known are Ansoff's product and market, technology and market, and technology and product matrices – see Figure 3.5.

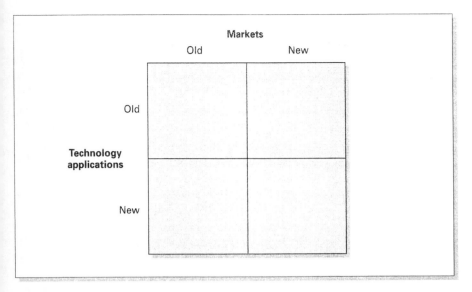

Figure 3.5 Ansoff's well-known product, technology and market matrix

As mentioned earlier, increasingly innovations are no longer the work of individual, isolated companies. Most innovations are the result of cooperation between a number of organizations in a network. Organizing these external networks is as necessary as organizing the internal operations. The positions of the companies in these networks determine, to a large extent, the openings they have to develop, implement and exploit their innovations. Analysis of partnerships, the quality of these partnerships and the position in these networks or value systems are important company assets. Next, we will discuss in more detail market, technological and product and network positions and partnerships.

The various two-dimensional planes of the TAMO combinations are often used to analyze present and desirable future positions.

The extended innovation arena, with its four dimensions, integrates both the internal company part of the innovation arena and its external part.

Analysis of external position

A lot has been written on the analysis of a company's external position. Therefore, we will restrict ourselves to a number of topics we feel are of key importance or the value of which may have been underestimated in the past.

We will discuss technology, applications, markets and external organization combinations and the institutional position of the company.

Technology and applications combinations

This brings us to the topic of technology analysis. A discussion about products applies also to technology. Most technology analysis focuses on the analysis of a separated technology, isolated from the other technologies it is combined with in products and processes. However, the performance of a technology is always a function of other technology, such as material technology, it makes use of and of the other complementary technology that is embodied in the product. Drawing up technology trees, webs or maps and impact matrices to make the interactions between the various technologies explicit is an essential first step.

The interdependency of technology and applications can be seen, for example, in the introduction of new materials in the making of propellers and turbines. As they can resist higher temperatures than before it is possible to increase the rpm. This affects the power to weight ratio that can be delivered. The use of CAD (computer-aided design) techniques has resulted in better and thus lighter construction in which less material is used.

A next step is to determine what opportunities exist for further development of a technology. Here, lifecycle analysis plays an essential role. Analyzing the interactions between the technologies in a certain product or process environment may reveal the technology whose further evolution is most central to the evolution of the others. It may be the first technology you submit to more elaborate lifecycle analysis. This may be followed by an analysis of the attraction of this technology for the company, its position in this field and/or the possibilities that exist to improve its position *vis-à-vis* competition. (Porter *et al.* (1991) have described a number of methods in their book *Forecasting and Management of Technology* that can be used in technology analysis, Rias van Wyk (1996) has published a number of articles on the lifecycle analysis of technology, and in Roussel *et al.*, *Third-generation R&D Management* (1991), the impact of lifecycle analysis for R&D management is discussed at length.)

Applications and markets combinations

We will focus on the analysis of a company's competitive position, market position, customer preferences and perceived product quality.

Analysis of competitive position

Michael Porter's (1985) five forces market model is still one of the tools most frequently used to determine the competitive position of a company in a market. In the model, the market strength of a company is determined *vis-à-vis* its competitors, suppliers, customers, new entrants and substitutes. The strength of the model is its simplicity. However, it also has some drawbacks. In a world

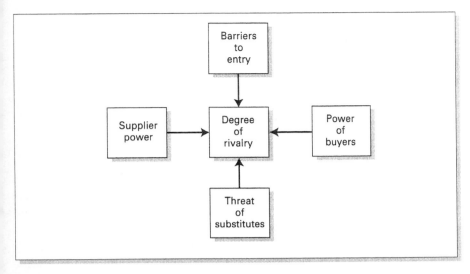

Figure 3.6 Porter's five forces market model

in which partnerships are essential, the results derived from the model are less easily interpreted. Figure 3.6 shows Porter's well-known framework.

The competitive position of a company is determined by five forces that are all highly complicated constructs, determined by a number of interrelated factors, such as the number of buyers, suppliers and substitutes, which depend on the market segment it serves – that is, the company's market position, uniqueness, imitability and so on.

The five forces market model is also used to determine the relative power distribution in value systems. This is done in an analogous way to analyzing isolated markets.

Analysis of market position, customer preferences and product quality

A large number of market segmentation and product positioning techniques exist. Glenn Urban and John Hauser (1993) give an overview of a number of these in their book *Design and Marketing of New Products*. In these techniques, two elements are important in order to analyze correctly.

● Finding the best dimensions along which the customers can be aggregated in more or less homogeneous groups. The question is thus, 'Along which dimensions can we classify the customers in more or less homogeneous groups with respect to their buying behaviour?' The fewer dimensions needed and the more homogeneous the groups, the better this is for planning. We must, of course, be aware of the dynamics of these dimensions. Market segmentations change over time, as was demonstrated by the classic market disaster of the Ford Edsel.

⦿ Finding the parameters and attributes that play a role in the buying decisions. How do the different customer groups distinguish between the various products and how do they set their priorities? The fewer attributes are used and the better these attributes can be operationalized, the more accurate the analysis will be.

Quality in the eyes of the customer is sometimes defined as the sum of the various attributes multiplied by a weighting factor, which reflects their preferences. We think that this way of analyzing quality is useful in mature markets and static environments, but it can be disastrous in emerging markets and dynamic environments.

When we qualify the value of the various attributes and preferences by comparing similar products, we forget that products are used in combination with other products and services. Thus, the value of an attribute often depends on the characteristics of other products. As a result, some authors distinguish core products and whole products in reference to this situation. The value of cassette recorders, TV sets, computers and so on is determined by the availability of music cassettes, TV programmes and software programs. The value of a telephone is determined by the number of other telephones – if you are the only one possessing a telephone, it is useless to you. When customers buy soup they prepare the soup using certain utensils, in combination with other ingredients. They store the soup in a certain way and so on. The attributes that are preferred by the user are therefore determined by how the product performs in combination with the other products needed in the process, the skills of the user and how well the whole meets any expectations of the outcome. When the complementary products change, the preferences of the user and buyer may also change. Marketing research is therefore becoming more important.

How do the different customer groups distinguish between the various products and how do they set their priorities?

The consequence of all this is that, in order to understand market trends, we have to learn more about how products are used and their interaction with other products. In summary, we must consider the ways in which the markets of complementary products and services interact with each other. The relationships between products can often be successfully analyzed by taking into account what happens in the process of customers using them. For example, the cassette recorder referred to above is the instrument that enables the process of music and cassette production to deliver the inputs for its use.

The importance of these interactions will be discussed in more detail in

Chapter 6, where we will explain how interacting markets may create reinforcing loops, which influence the importance of time to market.

Especially at the beginning of the lifecycle of a new product, a lot of innovations are performed by the customers and so classical ways of determining market needs and wishes are risky (von Hippel, 1988). In these situations, marketing research, involving studying the use of a new product type by innovative users, is essential.

When the VCR for private use by the general public was marketed at the beginning of the 1980s, manufacturers thought that it was only going to be used to record programmes from TV. It was not visualized that users would like to hire titles from a video shop to watch films at home. This use can be viewed as an application invention, created by innovative users, some of whom started their own businesses as a result. However, most of these types of innovation are discovered by professional users, as has been demonstrated by von Hippel.

The evolution of dominant designs is tightly linked with the application of new technology. Such 'disruptive technology' enables new companies to dominate the new or altered industry.

Market and product lifecycle analysis helps to estimate the relevance of these topics. However, although interpreting the lifecycles afterwards is easy, in real time it is difficult to estimate which phase of the lifecycle we are in. One aspect that may help in interpretation is the appearance of a dominant design. James Utterback (1994) defined as dominant designs such things as the DC3 of the late 1930s. The IBM PC from the beginning of the 1980s can also be easily recognized as being a dominant design.

Although the concept of dominant designs is an important one in determining the maturity of a product class and the strategic options, it also has its drawbacks. Even dominant designs do not last for ever and can change during the product's lifecycle, as can be seen in, for example, the aerospace industry where the propeller aeroplane was substituted by the jet aeroplane, or in photography where, slowly, traditional cameras using film are being substituted by digital cameras and so on.

These changes in dominant designs are driven by changes in the products' environment. The evolution of dominant designs is tightly linked with the application of new technology. This leads to drastic changes in the structure of industries, causing the closure of some companies or even whole industries. Such 'disruptive technology' (Christensen, 1997) enables new companies with different competences to improve their position and dominate the new or altered industry. However, most design architectures are changing in an evolutionary, rather than revolutionary, manner and so the industry concerned has enough time to adapt. For example, although the introduction of the IBM PC is seen now as a dominant design, the PC has changed dramatically since it first appeared. The same can be said of aeroplanes from 1938 and 1998 or cars from 1920 and 1990.

Market and external organization combinations

We will focus here on technology and the analysis of network positions.

Analysis of network positions (external organization)

Companies are part of networks that deliver essential resources for their processes, such as finance, knowledge and materials, and transform these inputs into products for their customers until they reach the end users. The relative positions companies have in these networks may give them certain advantages, because of earlier access to new information and knowledge, new types of material or services or access to cheaper money to finance new operations.

Networks can restrict the manoeuvring space of companies. Partners expect certain behaviour, otherwise the benefits of the partnership vanish and they will leave. How much manoeuvring space they have depends on the influence or power a company has over its partners in the network. Network analysis, therefore, consists not only of inventorization of the partners, their relationships, and the critical dimensions of these relationships but also of the various sources of power (this point will be elaborated on in the next chapter when we discuss stakeholder analysis).

The configuration of networks is a reflection of product architectures. Because networks provide advantages with respect to access to new information, improved technology and products, they facilitate and force the development of products along existing lines. Because of the constraints on movement to alternatives, they may create inertia, blocking the development of new architectures, which may form the basis of new dominant designs (Sanchez, 1996).

There are several books on network analysis and the effect of networks on NPD. Their authors often belong to different schools of thought. Here, we want to mention H. Hakansson (1987), M. Callon *et al.* (1992), Wiebe Bijker (1991), James Moore (1996), Gary Hamel and C. K. Prahalad (1994) and Adam Brandenburger and Barry Nalebuff (1996). All these authors have concentrated on different types of networks and the different roles they play in NBD.

The institutional position

The institutional position of companies relates to their legal position in terms of rights and liabilities. In NBD, patents are the most conspicuous institutional rights, giving the owner a monopoly to commercialize certain technology in a certain region and during a certain time. Other intellectual property rights relate to the authorship and the growing of certain plant varieties. However, it may also be important to consider other institutions, such as tax regimes, employment and environmental legislation, unions, political (in)stability and so on.

Good access to governmental bodies almost always is an important asset, the value of which cannot be underestimated.

Internal analysis of resources or assets

Here, we will briefly discuss ways to analyze the assets of a company, such as capital, knowledge, organizational reputation, financial and management assets.

Technology and applications

Capital assets

Capital assets are important because they are necessary for all the various operations of a company. However, as noted above, they have lost their monopoly as the main driving force in the valuation of a company. Sometimes capital assets combined with a specific location can give a company that has them competitive advantage. For example, being situated close to suppliers and having access to a large reservoir of scarce talent is very valuable. This can be seen in, for example, Silicon Valley, where the prices of land and property rose sharply during the growth in Internet start-up companies.

Place is still an important asset. However, these days, it is the availability of knowledge and specialist skills that is critical. Especially in high-tech areas, knowledge is often a considerable tacit component that cannot be transferred in the normal ways.

Knowledge

Knowledge has become the most important production factor in most industries. However, the value of knowledge differs widely, depending not only on the type of knowledge and its uniqueness, but also on organizational contingencies that determine whether or not the knowledge can be applied and exploited profitably.

Knowledge management is a management discipline that is still in an early phase of its development. It encompasses the activities of monitoring, acquisition, maintenance and exploitation of knowledge. One of the critical aspects is the classification, inventorization, codification, storage and accessibility for the relevant people and inaccessibility for unqualified people to the knowledge present somewhere in the company.

Furthermore, the comparison of present knowledge with needed knowledge is essential. As technology still embodies the largest part of the present and needed knowledge, a large number of the methods of knowledge management closely resemble the methods used in technology management.

One of the bottlenecks that occurs in the process of codifying and making this knowledge accessible does so because of unique knowledge co-workers have and their position in the company. Knowledge means power and so these workers fear that making it available to others may diminish their power as specialists. Although sharing knowledge may increase the possibilities for using and applying it and may even form the basis of new knowledge, these possibilities are often underutilized.

Although sharing knowledge may increase the possibilities for using and applying it and may even form the basis of new knowledge, these possibilities are often underutilized.

The bottlenecks and other factors make valuation of knowledge hazardous. The value of knowledge depends on the options for using it and how easily these options can be exercised. It depends on the context. For example, Novartis paid $1.2 billion for Plant Genetic Systems – a company that hardly made any profit at that time – because the knowledge it had, protected by patents, was very valuable when combined with the knowledge within Novartis.

A difficulty is that when, after acquisition of an organization, the most valuable and skilled workers leave the company, it may be hard to exploit the acquired assets and so they will not live up to expectations.

Last, but not least, the value of knowledge depends on opportunities that are often not yet known. This adds to the difficulty of valuation. The real options theory seems to be the most promising approach in such situations. We will discuss this point in more depth in the chapters about the application of DBM and in the epilogue.

Organizational assets

General organization

The value of the various assets discussed above depends on a number of organizational conditions. There are three sets of organizational attributes that have to be discussed in this regard:

- structure
- systems
- culture
- flexibility.

The structure of organizations is changing constantly, reflecting new insights into organizational behaviour, the dominance of new management fads and the changing environment. Dynamic environments demand structures that consist of loosely coupled groups, such as business units. On the other hand, the importance of both quality and costs requires that we make maximum use of economies of scale and scope.[3]

Economies of scale and scope are not only to be found in manufacturing, but often also in product development, marketing and sales. Enabling technology in the field of information and communications technology has a large impact on these economies of scale and scope. Therefore, it is an important driver of organizational change.

Because each situation is more or less unique, generally applicable best solutions do not exist; you cannot just copycat the organization that is the best in your field. Moreover, organizational change is inhibited by the existence of inertia within companies. Every change affects the position of a number of people negatively, making them less willing to cooperate. This applies to the implementation of almost all innovations that are the subject of this book. Therefore, this topic will be discussed in more detail in Chapter 4.

The next set of factors – management systems, such as quality, reward and budgeting systems – can be both enablers and causes of bottlenecks for innovation and NBD. Excess numbers of procedures stifle organizations, making them bureaucratic and efficient in narrowly defined areas, but, when demands are changing, less effective. On the other hand, they may enable organizations to cooperate and for many tasks and activities be correctly adjusted to each other.

Innovations are not possible without a certain level of stability. Systems, especially management ones such as quality systems (quality function deployment, design for manufacturing, failure mode effect analysis and so on), improve the communication between functional specialists and the integration of knowledge. Therefore, they have a positive effect on development speed, product quality and development costs. Moreover, the use of these systems also affects group dynamics and may help in teambuilding (see Peter Hinssen's thesis 'What difference does it make? The use of GroupWare in small groups', 1998).

At the same time, what happens when these systems are introduced is critical to their success or failure. They may affect the positions of individual group members and so result in strategic use of the system by some group members and resistance to it from others. Therefore, large numbers of systems are never used after their introduction and a brief period of use or else are abandoned sometime later. Thus, if systems are being used, this may not automatically translate into their having positive influence on the operations or product development (see Rinus van Breukelen *et al.*, 1996).

---

[3] Economies of scope is a simple but powerful innovation tool. Economies of scope is the competitive advantage we get from applying the same technology in different products, selling the same product in different markets, using the same production plant for different products and so on.

Last, but not least, culture often determines the success or failure of NBD efforts. The culture, which is the values and norms in a company, business unit or team, affects the way opportunities are sensed and exploited. It determines the freedom individual members have to experiment, and the way in which outside knowledge is judged. A 'not invented here' attitude may originate from the prevailing culture in the company.

Cultures will change over time, but this may happen very slowly and not always in the way management feels is appropriate. Everyone agrees that an entrepreneurial culture is essential for NBD, yet to

Culture often determines the success or failure of NBD efforts.

change a conservative, inward-looking culture into an entrepreneurial, innovative culture often means that you have to change staff, management systems, such as accounting and reward systems, and the structure to shorten communication lines. This is often impossible or at least takes considerable time.

Although culture is a very soft variable, diagnostics have been developed to classify the different types. Peter Scott-Morgan has described ways in which you can study and diagnose prevailing values and norms in a company in his book *The Unwritten Rules of the Game* (1994).

Because of the interrelationships between the various organizational aspects, a number of archetypal organizations can be distinguished. Often these are classified as innovative or entrepreneurial, bureaucratic, focused on efficiency of the internal processes, flexible and so on.

Valuation of organizational flexibility – options
Options, in stock market parlance, are rights to buy or sell assets at a predetermined price for a predetermined period of time. Options have value because they give flexibility to their owners. When a company acquires a certain type and level of knowledge, it can exploit this knowledge. Often, at the start of the acquisition or generation of knowledge, the organization has little knowledge as to whether or not it can be applied profitably in one or another product, process or service. Often, it becomes clear that the knowledge can be used in another area than that originally thought of. Furthermore, a certain level of prior knowledge is needed to be able to acquire specific knowledge that can be used directly. In other words, the possession of knowledge can be thought of as being like an option that costs some money but may create new opportunities for the company.

All of this determines part of the value of knowledge. Just as knowledge is like options, simply having a presence in a market may create opportunities that may be used for further business development.

In short, assets that increase the flexibility of an organization can be thought of as options. These options have value only when uncertainty about particular aspects of future developments exists. An option is created only when opportunities are realized. In other words, only when we have ideas about the various ways in which we can exploit flexibility can we speak of an option, because only in such situations are the various alternatives considered systematically. The valuation of the various options is slowly realized. Some companies, such as Merck, have already used option theory to valuate the extra opportunities that are created by flexibility.

The exploitation of knowledge is dependent on how well a team performs. High-performance teams and good management will generate and test more options to exploit existing knowledge than teams performing badly. It is well known that a good team may even succeed with an average idea, whereas a poor team may fail with a good idea.

Reputation

Reputation is increasingly recognized as being a very important asset in certain industries – even more important than specialist knowledge. Reputation is always linked with certain attributes or a bundle of related attributes of a firm and a certain group of stakeholders. A good reputation with investors can easily translate into a good rating, lower capital costs and, therefore, a higher shareholder value.

The expectations of investors and a company's reputation are critical to its success. Managing these expectations is a vital management process and determines the company's reputation. We will discuss this hugely important process in more depth in the next two chapters.

> *Reputation is increasingly recognized as being a very important asset in certain industries – even more important than specialist knowledge.*

Another important type of reputation is that of brand names. For companies such as Coca-Cola, brand names are their main asset.

A good reputation with potential employees can also be a very valuable asset, especially in times of shortages of certain types of people. We will therefore discuss this asset in more detail in the next chapter about stakeholder analysis.

Financial assets

Financial assets take four main forms:

- financial reserves;
- cash flows of the various present and future businesses;
- access to the various financial markets;
- relative costs of capital.

These assets are tightly knitted together. Information about the financial reserves and strength is partly derived from the balance sheet. Various financial ratios, such as the liquidity ratios (current ratio and quick ratio), capital structure ratios (long-term debts to equity ratio and total debt to equity ratio), profitability ratios (return on total assets, return on equity and turnover ratios – total asset turnover), give a quick idea of the financial position of a company. More important are cash flow analyses.

One aspect will be discussed here – gap analysis. In a financial gap analysis, you calculate the estimated future turnover and cash flow for the next three to five years from the products presently on the market and those in the pipeline. A decrease in total cash flow indicates the necessity for developing additional new business.

In high-tech fields, such as biotechnology, in which new companies do not have a regular income from products on the market, the burn rates in relation to the cash position are critical performance indicators. Also, for high-tech companies that merely have products in the pipeline and do not receive enough cash from operations or selling their know-how, access to financial markets is essential and can mean the difference between success and failure.

Lastly, the relative costs of capital play a critical role in defining whether a certain project can be started or not. This is especially important for long-term R&D projects. It is also the most important driver of shareholder value.

Management assets

In the evaluation of new businesses by venture capitalists, the quality of management often makes the difference between providing the financial resources and refusing to do so. The best indicator to use when evaluating the management is prior experience. The same applies for project and NBD management in large companies (see C. Gordon Bell, 1991).

In his book *High-tech Ventures*, Bell describes most of the assets that are valuable for a company when assessing its capability to innovate and develop new businesses. He introduces a number of instruments that may help in this assessment. He describes the so-called Bell-Mason diagnostic – a relational graph that consists of four main dimensions, each of which is subdivided into a number of elements, as follows.

1 Marketing and sales:
   - marketing
   - sales.
2 People:
   - CEO
   - team

- board of directors.
3 Finance/control:
  - cash
  - financeability
  - operations/control.
4 Technology/product:
  - technology/engineering
  - product
  - manufacturing.

In this diagnostic, all these factors are evaluated, which results in a score on the spider's web diagram. During the development of a start-up, these scores must increase in time, otherwise a problem area may exist that must be dealt with. Each of the individual factor scores is based on a number of issues that can be pinpointed using certain precise questions, but often it is estimated intuitively by the investor.

We think that the best way to choose how to assess, and what priorities to give to, the various factors is to call on the expert knowledge of experienced managers in the business, completing the process with an inventorization of the attributes of past successful and unsuccessful projects.

In Figure 3.7, we have presented the various key assets in a spider's web diagram.

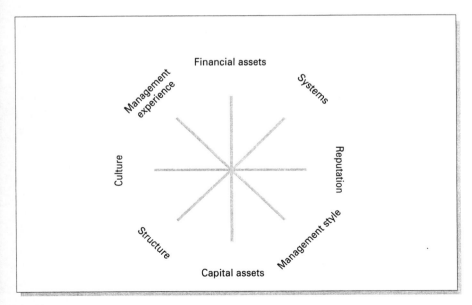

Figure 3.7 Spider's web model of the assets of a company

During development of a company, all the assets have to grow in balance. How-ever, all eight resources have their contribution to make to the business success of the company. Some are used as inputs in processes, such as the financial resources; others must be considered as enablers of the primary processes of a company because they are not used during the processes themselves. These include organizational, management and knowledge resources. All these resources are the outputs of other supportive processes, such as know-ledge acquisition, teambuilding and management development. Most of these supportive processes are linked to external processes, such as knowledge generation, dissemination and education.

During development of a company, all the assets have to grow in balance.

Although certain resources are not used in the primary processes, other processes may cause devaluation of these resources. Knowledge devalues because it is diffused over time, making it less exclusive. Equally, skills may become obsolete as practices evolve. Therefore, doing nothing will slowly devalue the company and worsen its position. To improve a company's posi-tion and growth, these supportive processes have to be managed carefully after a more exact definition of the resources and prioritization of the various devel-opment options have been worked out. The supportive processes will be pre-sented in greater depth in Chapter 5.

Discussion

In this chapter, we have discussed the various parameters that determine the internal and external position of a company. The key internal parameters can be mapped to the inputs and enabling factors of the relevant business processes that take place within a company. These determine the competences and capa-bilities of a company.

Technology is the input, output and enabling factor in the various processes that belong to the NPD and production processes, along with the other assets of the company, such as financial, capital, organizational, management assets and reputation. The assets that determine the internal position or the resources of the company (summarized in Table 3.1) can be mapped onto this analysis of a business process. Capital assets and knowledge are the enablers of the process, as depicted at the top of Figure 3.8. Organizational and manage-ment assets are depicted as enablers at the bottom of the figure. Financial assets are related to the input and output sides of the figure.

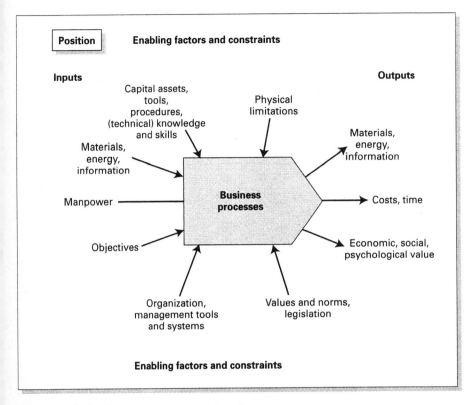

Figure 3.8 Business processes analyzed

By means of these business processes, resources are transformed and value is created for the customers. This value creation enables the company to improve its position in the marketplace. This may enable the company to increase its control over internal and external resources. As long as it is able to use this increased control over resources to create customer value, it may improve its position and this drives the reinforcing growth loop.

The parameters that determine the external position of a company also determine how far the goals or strategies can be transformed in terms of value for the company.

The parameters that determine the external position of a company also determine how far the goals or strategies can be transformed in terms of value for the company. This is also dependent on the roles, goals and position of the other stakeholders in the company, and the value that the company creates for those stakeholders. In the next chapter, this will be discussed in more detail.

4 | People – internal and external stakeholder analysis

Introduction

In this chapter, we will discuss the people who play a role in the NBD process and in some way or other may influence the outcome of innovation (see Figure 4.1).

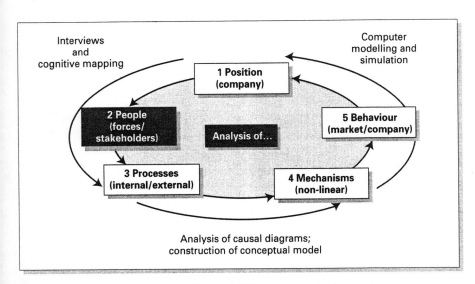

Figure 4.1 The steps involved in the DBM process – the second step is analysis of the people aspects of the company

In the last chapter, we discussed the factors that determine the internal and external position of a company. Using the innovation arena as a starting point, we can describe its present and desirable future positions. The position of a company depends on its control over internal and external resources and how able it is in transforming these resources into successful products and/or services.

The control a company has over resources is closely linked to its position in its networks of stakeholders. This means that its control over resources and ability to transform these into higher-valued products determine its power in its network and its position, which in their turn determine its control over scarce resources.

The agricultural sector in The Netherlands

Over the years The Netherlands has built a strong agricultural sector with exports to many countries. A strong sense of cooperation has developed over many decades in the agricultural community, starting with the care for the dikes and waterways in the Dutch polders.

This culture of cooperation and decision making based on consensus is often used as an explanation for the economic success of The Netherlands in the 1990s. This model is therefore called the 'Polder model'.

The results of this cooperation are the many auctions for agricultural products. These auctions are the common property of, often, large numbers of producers. They meet the small shop owners who buy vegetables, fruits and flowers, but also the purchasers or large retailers. The auctions are so successful that many foreign producers also bring their trade to them. In this way, billions of dollars of agricultural products are traded each year.

Another benefit of this cooperation is the effective knowledge network that has been created. Small and large producers, universities, consultants and governmental institutes work together to improve plant variants, breeding procedures, fertilizers and new tools and instruments.

However, new global developments are threatening this strong position. Growing agricultural products in The Netherlands is expensive because of high land prices, high levels of pay, high energy prices and the big investments made in glasshouses, warming systems and, more recently, in automated climate regulation, watering and transportation systems.

The most popular way of dealing with these threats has been to continuously introduce innovations and make use of economies of scale by enlarging the crop areas. Scarcity of competent labour and land and costs of capital, however, have blocked efforts to use these strategies to the full. It has also been realized that it will become more and more difficult to reap the profits from exploitation of the opportunities offered by new developments in research and biotechnology because foreign competitors make up for their weaker areas. There is also a very real threat in the form of the ever more powerful retailers that increasingly control the market.

As a reaction to these threats, the cooperation between the independent auctions was taken a step further. A mega-organization was founded in which these auction and their breeder members would cooperate. The name of this mega-organization was The

Greenery International. At its headquarters, a new type of manager appeared who introduced modern logistical and marketing techniques. After a short period, the organization was in bad shape, for a number of reasons. Most importantly:

● the interests of the various producers were, in certain respects, equal but, in other respects, conflicted with each other, so producers sometimes had to accept much lower prices for their products than they could obtain on the open market;

● a large gap in culture existed between the producers, who thought and operated in an independent way, and the managers, who were used to the values and norms of large corporations.

At a certain point, producers started to leave the organization, making it more expensive for the ones staying behind as there were fewer of them to pay the overheads of The Greenery International. The financial problems of The Greenery International became worse and managers left the organization. The reputation of The Greenery International suffered as more producers left the organization and the organization threatened to become a vicious loop.

H. Hakansson (1987) has described the relationships between the actors, activities and resources in networks (see Figure 4.2).

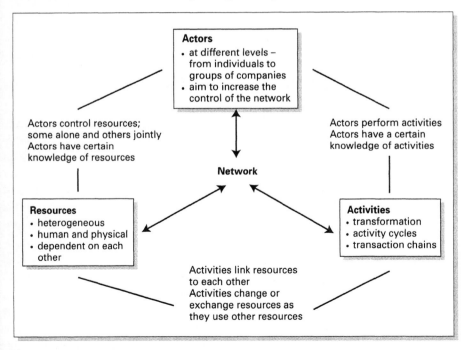

Figure 4.2 Hakansson's network model

Whereas Hakansson focuses mainly on external networks of actors, the model can be extended to internal networks of stakeholders.

In contrast to Hakansson, Sumantra Ghoshal and Christopher Bartlett, in their book *The Individualized Corporation: Great companies are defined by purpose, process and people* (1997), focus on internal networks of actors and stress that the era of the corporate man has gone. Today, for a company to grow, it is essential that it mobilizes all the creativity and knowledge it possesses. This can only be done by using all the creativity and knowledge of all the employees. Mobilizing these internal driving forces and directing them towards clear goals in such a way that forces are not neutralized but add to each other is the great challenge of management. Great companies, such as 3M and ABB, are building their strength on this capability. Bruce Pasternak and Albert Viscio (1998) call this the triumph of people power. They bring the mobilization of people power down to five principles, namely:

Today, for a company to grow, it is essential that it mobilizes all the creativity and knowledge it possesses. This can only be done by using all the creativity and knowledge of all the employees.

- commit to employee wellbeing as a core value;
- ensure that open communication forms the foundation of day-to-day relationships;
- have employees manage their own careers;
- ensure employees gain employable security by building key skills;
- ensure that accountability for performance extends to all levels of the organization.

However, it is not only mobilization of the driving forces inside the company that is important, but also of those outside the company. It is essential to do this with customers, by involving them in this process, as InCyte does and as do many other companies, with suppliers, too, as companies such as Nike do, and with governments, as pioneered by the Ministry of International Trade and Industry (MITI) in Japan, or even with competitors when we want to develop a new business and cannot do so alone, as the telecoms companies Ericsson and Nokia did by agreeing on a common standard in the mobile phone industry.

While we are mobilizing the driving forces, there are other, inertial forces that we have to circumvent or neutralize. Inertial forces are those relating to switching costs of customers, suppliers, retailers, as well as the counteracting forces of competition from other companies experiencing a deterioration of their position as a result of the innovation. There are also inertial forces inside the company. These may stem from the reactions of internal stakeholders who may feel that their position is threatened by the changes, switching costs relating to money spent on plant, other machinery and raw materials, switching costs relating to procedures being changed and employees needing to change their ways of working.

Inertial forces are the analogues of core rigidities as defined by Dorothy Leonard-Barton (1995), who mentioned a number of these as inhibiting innovation. Core rigidities are the variations from old values and norms, knowledge, skills and management systems that are the most difficult to change. Leonard-Barton describes how these four core rigidities are also core capabilities. Core capabilities can change into core rigidities when the environmental situation changes. Innovation, by definition, changes the situation inside and outside the company.

In Chapter 3, we analyzed the internal and external position of a company. The goal of this analysis is to determine how we can improve our position, defining a trajectory the company can follow. Having defined a preferred and feasible trajectory, the driving forces that have to be mobilized and inertial forces that have to be neutralized or avoided will be inventorized. In social systems, these forces originate from the roles, motives and goals, positions and behaviour of the various stakeholders involved during the realization of the positional change.

'Stakeholders' are all actors, individuals, groups or organizations that, in one way or another, are affected or potentially affected by the innovation. Included are both internal and external stakeholders. They are involved in the NBD process because they may play a role in the value system by means of some exchange of resources. They may be involved in the exchange of materials, energy or work, information, knowledge and/or money.

Stakeholders may have enabling or inhibiting roles in the process. This last group includes governments, interest groups (consumer organizations, unions, environmentalists and so on), the media. Also, competition can be classified as an inhibitor. An example of what can happen is the effect the actions of environmentalists have had on biotechnological innovation in several European countries. Regulation of the types and ways in which experiments can be carried out has hindered the level of innovation in biotechnology. Also the possibilities, or, rather, impossibilities for patenting transgenic animals has influenced the level of innovation taking place in this area in some European countries.

On the other hand, legislation with respect to safety or environmental friendliness and efficacy of innovations has stimulated the emergence of many new products that have often given companies where such legislation exists a lead over companies in less progressive countries. For example, pharmaceutical companies in North America and the UK where the registration process for medicines has become stricter than is the case in a number of other developed Southern European countries are now much stronger than such companies in these other countries.

All stakeholders have some interest in the outcome of the NBD process. Value is either created or destroyed during the process. Furthermore, the behaviour of the stakeholders is influenced by their expectations of the process. The reputation of the company in the eyes of stakeholders determines their expectations and, thus, their behaviour. Last, but not least, the effect of their behaviour on the outcome of the NBD process is determined by their power and position in the business system.

Thus, in summary, there are five important attributes of stakeholders – their:

- role in the NBD process;
- position in the business system;
- motives, goals and objectives;
- expectations of the value that will be generated or destroyed;
- perception of the reputation of the company.

These five attributes are based on the notion that the behaviour of agents in a system depends on their position in the network, the power they have within it, their goals, what they value and their models of the world around them (John H. Holland, 1995, p 6).

Networks of stakeholders translate into networks of business processes.

Figure 4.3 sets out the parameters that are central to the analysis of stakeholders in relation to our general scheme of business processes.

The stakeholders can be related to the business processes of the company in a large number of ways – they can be suppliers, customers, partners. The stakeholders are also the owners and actors in their own business processes. In this way, networks of stakeholders translate into networks of business processes (see Figure 4.4).

To inventorize the external stakeholders, tools such as the PEST or September frameworks and Michael Porter's five market forces framework are frequently used. Porter's five market forces framework was discussed in Chapter 3. The PEST or September frameworks are both acronyms of the first letters of parts of the environment:

- political
- economic
- sociological
- technical.

These parts are also referred to as the macro environment.

Network analysis is most directly linked to stakeholder analysis. In the PEST analysis, general factors are inventorized, but in the network analysis, the stakeholders that have direct links with the company are inventorized.

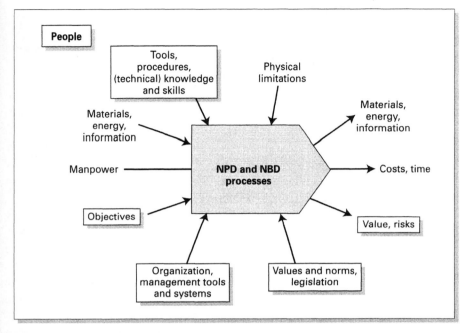

Figure 4.3 The relationships between parameters that are determined during stakeholder analysis and their role in business processes

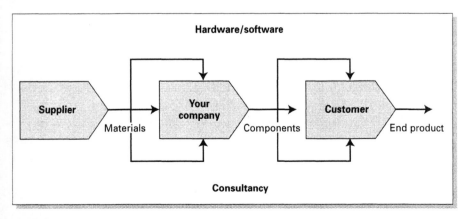

Figure 4.4 Networks of stakeholders can be translated into networks of processes

Last, but not least, the external stakeholder analysis covers all stakeholders in the market – customers, retailers, competitors, customer groups and so on.

Next, the internal stakeholders must be inventorized. After years of neglect, it has become evident that a large number of bottlenecks and causes of failure of innovation efforts have been due to incomplete involvement of internal stakeholders. This may still be one of the weakest points in innovation management. In particular, stakeholders downstream of the innovation trajectory who become involved during the implementation phase may behave differently than anticipated because of a lack of involvement in the process, resulting in the innovation, from their point of view, having a lower priority than other things, which means that the necessary organizational changes in production and sales do not occur as planned.

The most important lesson that has been learned over the years is that early involvement of the internal as well as, if possible, the external stakeholders in the NBD process increases the chances of success dramatically. However, there is a limit to this. Involving more and more stakeholders will also significantly increase the complexity of the process to be managed. So, we need to find the optimal balance between involvement of stakeholders versus complexity of the innovation process. Do keep in mind that different stakeholders may have different, sometimes even conflicting, interests. Stuart Kauffman therefore proposes in his book *At Home in the Universe* (1995) that to achieve innovation, it is better for companies to ignore the voice of the customer to a certain extent. He states that new developments are hindered by too tight a coupling between organizations and, therefore, loosening up these linkages will increase the pace of development.

External stakeholders

Customers

Who are our customers, what are their motives and goals, and what do they value in the types of products we deliver? These are still the main questions businesses have often not answered satisfactorily.

We have discussed earlier that the connectivity in our economy is increasing, resulting in more people being involved in, and affected by, new developments. Networks seem to become more extended and complicated all the time, resulting in more complicated and unpredictable behaviour of business systems. This seems to be true for suppliers, partners and, downstream, for customers.

Almost always, there are multiple customers. In the pharmaceutical sector, patients, physicians, pharmacists and life insurance companies are all customers in some way. Even today, customer value is almost exclusively determined by studying the preferences of customers for the products in defined markets or market segments. By relating these preferences to the attributes of the competing products an impression of which attributes are preferred by whom and to what extent is obtained.

Who are our customers, what are their motives and goals, and what do they value in the types of products we deliver?

This type of study does provide essential information, but it is often not sufficient in new and emergent markets because it is based on the assumption that the circumstances in which the customers use the product do not change. These circumstances are determined by the ways in which the customers use the product – that is, the process that ultimately delivers the users the desired benefits. Because every product or service involves at least two processes – a physical one, producing certain results or certain outputs, and a social and/or psychological process that affects the groups the users are a part of and the positions of the users in those groups – these have to be taken into account when developing new products. Engineers and marketers involved in the NPD process may estimate the relative weight of these two processes and their outcomes differently. However, stressing only the physical side or only the emotional side will give a biased view and is hazardous for the company.

When we realize this, we have to analyze both processes and their possible developments in more depth. This asks for detailed customer research. The physical qualities of a product depend on the other complementary products our product is used with, as well as on the delivery of services related to the product and the skills of the customers using the product.

Changes of these complementary products and services affect the value of our product. Ignorance of these complementary products and services and developments of or relating to them have frequently been a cause of NBD failures. On the other hand, successes can often be attributed to unforeseen changes. Geoffrey Moore (1995) describes how, during development, the focus switches from the first customers for a new type of product to the techies, focused on the technology, to the visionaries, who have a vision and see the new technology as instrumental in realizing their dreams, to the pragmatists, who are looking for a product that can improve performance, to conservative customers, who just want a product that works. The first customer group tests the technology, the second customer group helps to define the applications. The third group supports the development of the core product into the whole product. For the last customer group, this whole product must be in place. It is evident that each of the markets needs an appropriate, often completely different marketing approach.

Whereas the physical values of a product are relatively easy to test, the emotional values are much more complicated. Both tradition and fashion play a role. Winslow Farrell has studied how fads and fashions may arise. He describes in his book, *How Hits Happen: Forecasting predictability in a chaotic marketplace* (1998), a number of fundamental mechanisms that may help in tracing the potential for hits. His conclusions agree with ours, that interactions between actors in the market may result in self-reinforcing loops. These loops are the basis of the development of fashions and fads.

As the emotional values of products are as important to customers as the physical values, the emotional reactions to a company or its brands are as relevant as the physical ties of customers to that company. The emotional ties customers have relate to the reputation the company has with them. Reputation is built up over time, customers are confronted with the company and buy its products. Reputation building is a social process that involves not only the interactions between companies and customers, but also the interactions of both actors with other actors in the field. Although everybody recognizes its importance, our understanding of the process itself is limited.

Suppliers

We can distinguish several groups of suppliers, providing companies with the traditional means of production:

- financial resources – from shareholders, banks, governments (in the form of subsidies) and so on;
- raw materials and components;
- capital goods;
- knowledge – from institutions, consultants;
- ideas – from customers, partners, consultants;
- staff.

The roles suppliers play in the innovation process vary from industry to industry. Keith Pavitt (1990) has classified sectoral innovation processes partly on the basis of the role of suppliers in the innovation process. He has distinguished supplier-dominated industries, industries in which suppliers play a dominant role in the innovation process. Examples are the medical sector and the construction industry. In general, it can be concluded that, in all industries, suppliers play an increasingly important role in the innovation process. This makes the problem of appropriation of the value generated by the innovation an urgent one.

David Teece (1986) has addressed this problem in his model, discussed in Chapter 1. Because of the links required between several organizations in a value system during the NPD process and the alternatives that are available to suppliers for exploitation of their innovations, the reputation of the company with suppliers and its willingness to give up part of the yield to them may increase the chances of success. The increase in value for the suppliers will ultimately pay back in the form of extra goodwill and a greater chance of being involved in future innovation attempts. Thus, options for new innovations in the future will be created by virtue of such benefits all round.

Competitors

Competitive forces are both driving forces of innovation and NBD in general and a source of inertia, a force working to prevent the success of NBD efforts of other companies. From research in the field of economics, it is known that the rate of innovation is highest in oligopolistic markets. In markets where complete competition exists, entry barriers are low and protection from innovation in the form of imitation is impossible. This results in the return on investment in innovations being too low. Innovation is then the province of suppliers (supplier-dominated industries).

Competitive forces are both driving forces of innovation and NBD in general and a source of inertia.

In monopolistic markets, the need for innovation is minimal, meaning that, again, the return on investment in it is too low. On the other hand, creating new markets is often impossible for individual companies.

In situations of market growth, imitation of innovations by competitors may be less problematical. Innovating together in these situations is an even better option as developing a market might be next to impossible for a single company. Also, when the market is attacked by substitute products, partnerships with competitors may be profitable. For this reason, increasingly, competitors are cooperating in some of their markets.

The increase in competition has resulted in what is now known as hypercompetition. Richard D'Aveni (1994) distinguishes four areas of competition:

- cost and quality;
- timing and know-how;
- the creation and destruction of strongholds;
- the accumulation and neutralization of deep pockets.

Whereas traditional approaches to strategy stress 'creation of advantage', D'Aveni stresses the importance of the 'creative destruction of the opponent's advantage'. D'Aveni argues that we must look much more for dynamic strategic interactions – that is, the rapid series of moves and countermoves that propel the competitive game forwards. To survive in this hypercompetitive arena, he advises that companies meet the seven Ss, which are all factors that have to be taken care of in competitive arenas:

- stakeholder satisfaction
- strategic soothsaying
- speed
- surprise
- shifting the rules
- signalling
- simultaneous and sequential strategic thrusts.

For partners, the company must be predictable and trusted so that they are inclined to invest in the knowledge that they will earn their investments back. For competitors, the opposite applies. For competitors, the company's behaviour must be unpredictable, so that their strategies based on anticipation do not work. Surprise and shifting the rules are instruments to this end. Here, a close similarity between business and military strategy exists. The driving force of competition results in a speeding up, resulting in the 'Red Queen effect', as discussed in Part 1.

Institutional stakeholders

Institutional stakeholders are governments and controllers of infrastructures, as seen in regulated industries. Deregulation of a number of sectors has a profound effect on the whole industry structure. Clear understanding of the scope of the deregulation and its significance for business operations is an important topic for NBD in these sectors.

New regulations may also become important causes of innovation. The stricter the environmental rules are in a number of industries, such as the chemical, steel and car industries in Europe, the more they can act as important stimuli for innovation. For example, without tighter governmental regulations regarding car exhaust emissions and fuel economy in Europe, newer lighter materials, such as aluminium and plastics, would have had a hard time becoming routinely designed into cars. Under the old situation they simply would have been assessed as too expensive.

Society

We can imagine that discussing society here could be seen as a mistake. After all, society is not a stakeholder in the sense that employees, shareholders, customers and competitors are. These are real people or organizations and we can inventorize them in terms of the five attributes of role, position, motives, value, reputation. Society, however, is an abstraction and so is difficult to define.

This is all true, but for companies to prosper over long periods of time, they must be seen to be contributing to the society they are a part of. This society is personalized via the media. Companies such as Shell have recognized that thinking that you know best what is good for society ultimately works like a boomerang. Defining society's values and trying to improve things is good for the company. It creates goodwill with more recognizable and definable stakeholders, which creates opportunities with regard to future situations that may be unknown at present but may be very valuable at some later date.

Internal stakeholders

Shareholders

Apart from customer value, the creation of shareholder value is one of the most important driving forces for growth of the company. Cash is king, according to Tom Copeland *et al.* (1990) and the management of present and future cash flow is one of the foremost goals of general management. Shareholder value is achieved via two routes – dividends and increases in share prices. The prices of shares result from the aggregation of the expectations of shareholders and the value of the company, which is the result of the present value of the present and future cash flows and a certain rest value of the company minus its debts. Therefore, four components determine the value of a company:

> *Apart from customer value, the creation of shareholder value is one of the most important driving forces for growth of the company.*

- cash flow
- rest value
- discount rate
- debt.

Three of the four value components are dependent on value drivers. The fourth – debt – is dependent on companies' financial and investment policies.
   The value drivers for cash flow are:

- growth of sales;
- exploitation of the profit margin;
- tax percentage.

The rest value has as its value driver investment in working capital and fixed capital goods, while the discount rate is dependent on the cost of capital.
   Insight into these various value drivers and the relationship between these drivers and shareholder value and the ways in which these drivers can be influ-

enced provides management with the means to increase shareholder value. Because of the interactions between the various processes that influence the value drivers and the feedback between the creation of shareholder value and creation of customer value, the creation of shareholder value cannot be extrapolated from previous actions. Computer modelling and simulation of the processes and their complicated interactions, therefore, can be of much help here.

Past performance is the most important element in determining the reputation of a company with investors and their willingness to invest. How willing they are to invest determines the amount of financial resources available to the company, and the relationship between available and required amounts determines the cost of capital. A company's position in relation to these variables affects shareholder value and so a second feedback loop is created.

In high-tech industries, many new companies that have no products yet on the market and no past performance history are demanding finance for investment in NBD. In such cases, other signals become important for investors as they decide whether or not to give companies their money. These include their attractiveness – that is, the size and growth of markets, competition and signs of monopoly power over certain technology, partnerships with well-known companies that have good performance records, low burn rates and the keeping of promises, for example in meeting project milestones.

Such companies can best be treated as you would a portfolio of options and potential investors look for a limited downside risk and high upside benefits. The valuation of companies and projects as options is a fast-moving and promising new field of research.

An important factor here is that the loss of investors' trust can bring new and established companies to the edge of bankruptcy. Good communication with investors is therefore vital.

Employees

Every innovation has effects on internal processes and demands adaptation within the organization. Organizational change affects the positions of the employees. Change can be considered by employees as either an improvement or as a worsening of their positions. Change may also create extra work, the credit for which generally goes to others. This may result in work relating to implementing changes being given lower priority by employees than their other tasks.

Ultimately, this may end up with the various people in the company whose involvement is essential for its success evaluating the innovation as positive, neutral or negative. These people may be the company's own employees, employees with temporary assignments (on a project basis) or support staff hired from consulting firms.

When these elements are recognized and properly analyzed, management can correct the situation in various ways so that it becomes closer to a win–win game for everybody. A good example is the institution of so-called 'skunk works' outside the mainstream organization.

A still better option is to design the project in such a way that it works out positively for everybody involved. Including them from the beginning or recognizing their goals and requirements can have this effect. Again, it is not only physical requirements that are important, emotional ones are too – the so-called 'soft factors', such as workload, status, authority and power relations.

Especially at the start of a new project and in the realization phase, the ways in which employees can become involved in the innovation project may be critical to its success. It is not only the project leader who plays an important role in this process, it is also the product champion. The product champion is the person in the team who 'sells' the project to other members of the team and within the company, and, ideally, is a top manager within the organization.

Predicting stakeholders' behaviour and its effects on the NPD and NBD processes

Trust and reputation are as important roles in obtaining cooperation with internal stakeholders as they are with external stakeholders. Communication and past performance, keeping promises and the like, are central issues here too. Ultimately, we get a very simple reinforcing loop in which the three groups of stakeholders – customers, shareholders and collaborators – play similar essential roles. This is depicted schematically in Figure 4.5.

Figure 4.5 depicts a central single reinforcing loop that drives growth. However, it is too simple. Other stakeholders – especially suppliers of components, capital goods and knowledge – play essential roles that let the loop work. Moreover, partners that develop and deliver complementary goods and services and retailers are equally essential. We will discuss this issue at greater length in Chapter 9.

Research into micro-economics has made enormous contributions to the study of the operation of markets by first defining the roles of the stakeholders, producers and users, their motives – maximization of profit and utility respectively – and what they value – lower prices, keeping quality constant. Researchers assumed complete knowledge of the market and prices. In such a situation, reputation is not an issue. They could express this by using two simple mathematical formulae and then solve the equilibrium situation. In this way, they obtained insight into global behaviour of markets, starting with simple behavioural rules of the stakeholders. With the mathematical tools available at that time, this was as far as they could get. However, from the beginning

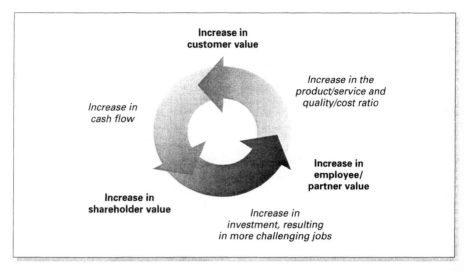

Figure 4.5 Reinforcing loop of customer, shareholder and collaborator value creation

it was obvious that the simplifications that were made were enormous, limiting the applicability of the approach.

Two new ways of analyzing the consequences of the behaviour of stakeholders for strategic management have been developed since then, namely by applying game theory to business strategy (Brandenburger and Nalebuff, 1996) and agent-based modelling. Both approaches were stimulated by the ongoing increase in computer power.

The need to look at transient states, not simply equilibrium, has intensified because of increasingly dynamic industries, resulting in states that are becoming, for longer periods, further removed from equilibrium.

Today, we have the tools to deal with much more complicated problems by using the power of modern computers. We can banish simplifications such as perfect knowledge of the markets, use more complicated decision rules, solving the situation not only in the equilibrium phase but also studying transient states and so on. We can even introduce learning by the agents. This makes the models much more realistic.

The need to look at transient states, not simply equilibrium, has intensified because of increasingly dynamic industries, resulting in states that are becoming, for longer periods, further removed from equilibrium. The constant introduction of innovations is both the cause and the result of this situation. Examples are the introduction of one new generation after another of microprocessors, improved software programs, new materials and new applications of information and communications technology, such as intelligent transport systems that are able to position your car extremely accurately, monitor a number of car functions, inform you about traffic situations and so on. More and more businesses are permanently out of equilibrium because of this push effect.

In the past, products could be seen as commodities with more or less similar qualities. This was the result of the Industrial Revolution, which introduced mass production.

As the connectivity of an economy increases, the economy is behaving more like complex systems with emergent properties that cannot be predicted by analyzing the isolated parts of that economy. To study such a system, computer modelling techniques and simulations have to be used. In the chapters that follow, we will discuss modelling techniques for the various linked processes in the system. Before using these techniques, stakeholder behaviour has to be translated into well-defined processes. This will be discussed in Chapter 5. In Chapter 6, we will analyze these processes in relation to nonlinear mechanisms that influence system behaviour. In Chapter 7, we will discuss the system dynamics approach that we have used to construct the computer models for studying the behaviour of these systems.

However, techniques also exist to model the behaviour of the various stakeholders – that is, agents – directly and study the evolution of the system over time using computer simulations. Various programming software have been developed that help this modelling process. Swarm is an example. It is a program developed by a group at the Santa Fe Institute. Joshua Epstein and Robert Axtell (1996) have built artificial societies using such programs that demonstrate a number of behaviours that are familiar in real life. These similarities indicate the value of such approaches. Also, applications closer to real-life situations can now be modelled, such as the behaviour of consumers in shops, indicating which are the best places on the shelves for the various products.

Although the progress in this area has been enormous, most situations are still so complicated with so many stakeholders involved, complicated rules of behaviour that may even change in time because of learning processes, that, at the time of writing, it takes too much effort to develop reliable models. However, we would recommend monitoring progress in this area closely, as the techniques become easier to apply.

We would also like to stress that the approach we have chosen to follow in this book – modelling the processes driven by the stakeholders and that may take place to a certain extent between stakeholders by using system dynamics – has its pros and cons. Two of the pros are that complicated situations can be modelled and that the models produced are closely related to the way managers view these processes. The cons relate to the fact that the processes cannot be changed fundamentally during the simulation. Single-loop learning processes can be modelled easily; double-loop learning, in which the rules change, can only be modelled with much more difficulty. The actions and reactions of companies to each other's moves are hard to model, too, but can be simulated to a certain extent in business games with two or more groups. Also, all the processes have to be modelled beforehand – the system itself is not smart. This makes this type of modelling suitable for middle range times. Hypotheses over the emergence of new processes can be modelled in special variants, and within these the consequences can be studied and verified by empirical field research.

5 | Analysis of the NPD and NBD processes

Introduction

In the last two chapters we discussed two commonly used approaches to studying business systems – the structure (position) and stakeholder (people) approaches. The structure approach treats business systems as static systems composed of actors and factors with specific attributes, which are related to each other. These types of studies are focused on the determination of the strength of the position of a company in its environment and the factors and attributes that determine this position.

In this chapter we will complete the triptych by focusing on the innovation processes in business systems. In Figure 5.1, we have presented this in the DBM steps model of this part of the book (Part 2).

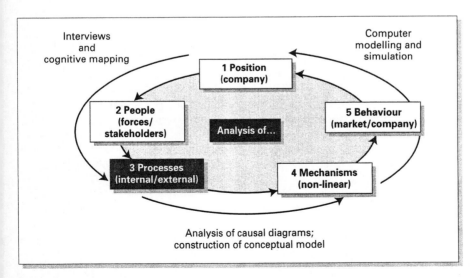

Figure 5.1 The steps involved in the DBM process – the third step is analysis of the NPD and NBD

Innovation at Philips consumer electronics

Philips is one of the few consumer electronics companies left in Europe. It was founded at the end of the last century as a company that produced lightbulbs. The company made use of the absence of a good patent system before 1910 in The Netherlands and of copied technology from abroad. Physics and electronics flourished at the beginning of the twentieth century and Leiden, an old university town in The Netherlands, was one of the main centres for physics. At the same time, the new technical university in Delft, another old historic town in The Netherlands, prospered.

The founders of Philips – Gerard and Anton Philips – were visionary entrepreneurs. In 1914, the first scientist at Philips, Gilles Holst, a physicist, founded a laboratory that would grow in a couple of years to become the famous Philips Research Lab. In the lab, in Eindhoven, there were very many breakthrough inventions that helped Philips to become one of the main innovative electronics companies in the world.

Although the Philips Research Lab remained an important source of new technology in the 1980s and 1990s, the company became less able to profit from these technical highlights. The Japanese, especially Sony, were much better able to translate technology into saleable products.

The Japanese proved to be better at integrating the various development processes with the production, logistics, purchasing and sales processes – they were better at making use of the knowledge that was internally available. The quality revolution that started in Japan in production was translated into product development and two Japanese – Nishimura and Takaynagi – introduced quality charts in 1972. In 1978 in Japan, Yoji Akao's book on quality function deployment was published, and it included many case studies describing this approach. QFD helped to integrate the various product development functions. Certain Japanese traits proved to be an advantage in product development, such as the emphasis on teamwork, and propelled Japanese companies to the forefront of innovation. The ways in which Japanese companies create knowledge has been described in a book by Ikujiro Nonaka and Hirotaka Takeuchi (1995).

Western companies such as Philips in highly competitive industries where the Japanese held a strong position were the first to be confronted with their new ideas about product development. Since that time, companies such as Philips have learned a lot. Whereas in earlier times the timescale for developing new television sets was years long, now they are able to do it in less than half that time. They do it with fewer people without compromising on product quality and innovativeness. They have achieved this because they understand the various processes that are part of the product development process much better and they know how to integrate them better too. At the same time, competitors are also learning their lessons and competition, increasingly, is concentrated on product development in combination with speeding up the time to market. Those companies that are able to achieve developments in the shortest possible time – producing the best designs, the highest quality TV sets with the best features and the most stable technology – win the most customers.

Although the development process has become much, much more complicated than in the days of Anton and Gerard Philips, insight into these processes has become essential. Understanding them and knowing how to integrate and manage them makes all the difference.

In the past, several models of NPD and NBD processes have been proposed. We will now review a few of them.

NPD and NBD can best be characterized as very ambiguous processes full of uncertainties. These uncertainties are diminished and transformed into well-known risks by the acquisition and exploitation of knowledge. This is shown in Figure 5.2.

This new knowledge can reveal new opportunities. These often start as weak signals from technology or the market that may facilitate the generation of new ideas and may direct further research for additional information and generation of new knowledge. During this process, earlier options may be turned down. Other options may become more feasible and new options may appear. For example, in a company I worked for more than ten years ago, antidepressants were developed. One of the compounds that demon-

NPD and NBD can best be characterized as very ambiguous processes full of uncertainties. These uncertainties are diminished and transformed into well-known risks by the acquisition and exploitation of knowledge.

strated some interesting antidepressant actions was tested broadly for unwanted side-effects. In one of these tests, a very pronounced antihypertensive effect was found. This was the basis for a project on a new type of very effective antihypertensive. After a couple of years of optimizing, a few compounds with the most interesting activities were selected. One of these com-

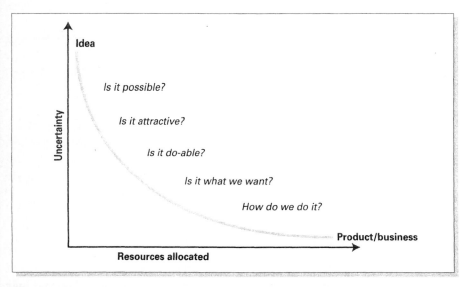

Figure 5.2 In the NPD and NBD processes, ideas are transformed into products or new businesses by diminishing the uncertainties as knowledge is acquired and utilized

Source: W. H. Matthews, IMD, Lausanne, Switzerland

pounds demonstrated unwanted central nervous side-effects in some tests. Studying this compound more closely demonstrated that it could be a good lead for new types of antipsychotics. This was the start of a new project on a new type of antipsychotic.

Such technical opportunities cannot be planned but may lead to new business opportunities. We speak of serendipity – the process of noticing small things that later on may lead to unexpected breakthroughs. Many examples are documented, such as the discovery of penicillin by Fleming, the structure of benzene by Kekule, mauve by Perkins, nylon by Carothers, the transistor by the group of Shockley and so on. The Post-it Note from 3M is one of the most famous examples. A chemist developed an adhesive with properties that were not interesting in terms of the original project as two objects could not be glued permanently to each other with it. However, they could be removed from each other easily. This led ultimately to a completely new application and the development of a totally new and very profitable business for 3M. That business would never have been developed if they had simply pressed on with their original aims. There are most probably companies where, in the R&D departments, there lie compounds that have similar properties to Minoxidil and Viagra. However, who in a pharmaceutical company would dare to develop drugs for baldness and erection problems? Only some really entrepreneurial people would have seen the possible markets, and only in companies such as Upjohn and Pfizer would management teams have dared to consider business outside the traditional pharmaceutical markets as being worthwhile investing hundreds of millions of dollars in.

Examples of new market options can appear in a similar, serendipitous way. The Walkman was developed because of a new need that could be fulfilled by the combination of a cassette player without a recording function and small headphones. It made it easier to listen to your favourite music during all kinds of activities without disturbing other people too much. Again, the concept was originally based on an unexpected observation – that engineers developed this apparatus and labelled it as unsuitable for the well-known and defined markets of that time.

In Figure 5.3, the NPD process is depicted as a process in which options are created and developed. In this process two parameters are important:

- the estimated return on investment, or what the value will cost;
- the volatility, or what the range of possibilities includes.

An option – for example a new idea – that seems to be costly and the value of which seems so low that the costs will probably not be recouped but that may have huge potential is still interesting to study. Eventually, more promising possibilities may come up. Now, a number of possibilities that are not interesting are cut. The volatility decreases, but the value to cost ratio increases. After further

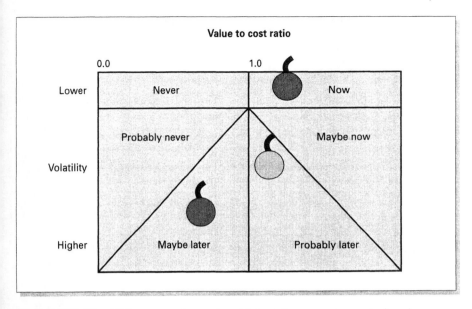

Figure 5.3 The NPD process is one in which options are generated and developed

Source: Adapted from Luehrman, 1998

development, the project has narrowed down further to the highest value to cost ratio possibilities. At a certain time, the project is ripe for execution.

To promote the discovery of such opportunities, R&D people need the freedom to perform extra experiments in their slack time, the so-called 'Friday afternoon' experiments. Until now this has been the only way to ensure that certain ideas are not killed by using too stringent checklists. A tool that may support the Friday afternoon experiments, instead of cutting off prematurely, is obviously an improvement.

Kim B. Clark and Steven C. Wheelwright (1993) have focused on the screening process in their funnel model of the NPD process. You start with a large number of ideas, then, by screening, you throw out as fast as possible those ideas that never will become interesting projects. This is done in the first phase of the funnel. Some ideas, however, stay longer in this first part to ripen. When the ideas are ripe enough, the projects are defined and, in the second half of the funnel, the scarce resources are focused on these projects (see Figure 5.4).

Whereas Clark and Wheelwright focus on quantitative screening – that is, you start with many ideas and end up with a small number of highly focused projects by screening and separating the bad from the good ideas – Robert G. Cooper (1993), in his stage-gate NPD model, focuses on the decision-making process (see Figure 5.5).

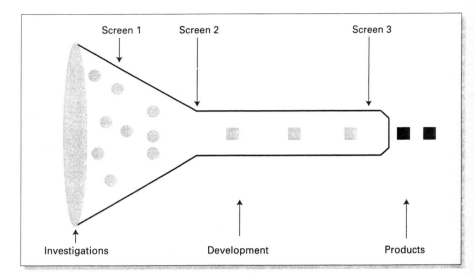

Figure 5.4 The NPD process as a funnel

Source: Reprinted with permission of The Free Press, a division of Simon & Schuster, Inc. from *Managing New Product and Process Development* by Clark, Kim B. and Wheelwright, Steven C. Copyright © 1993 by The Free Press.

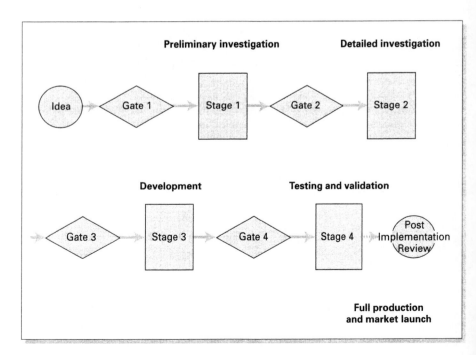

Figure 5.5 Cooper's stage-gate NPD process

These gates are like valves, allowing projects to move in one direction only and preventing the backflow of projects into earlier stages in a way that is comparable to the valves in the heart ensuring blood travels along the veins. It prevents stagnation of projects. Projects have to move forward or else stop moving and be removed from the funnel. In such a case, a clear decision has to be made to either stop a project or invest more time and money.

There are also models that focus more on the transformation of an idea into a product via a number of prototypes, ranging from global to detailed design. Figure 5.6 shows an example.

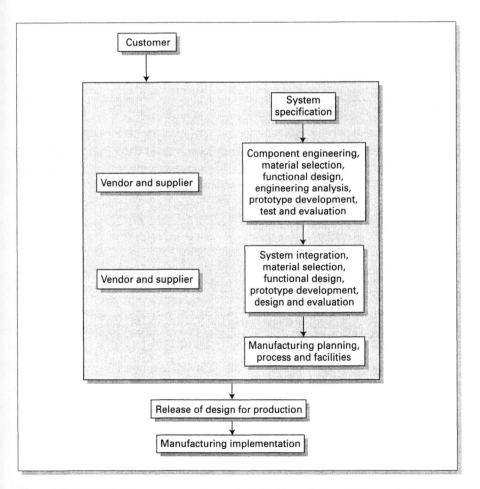

Figure 5.6 The NPD process as the materialization of ideas into products

Source: Adapted from Compton, 1997

The kind of model shown in Figure 5.6 has been modified by others who have added all types of feedback loops (Kline and Rosenberg, 1986; Roy Rothwell, 1992). In Figure 5.7, the model proposed by Rothwell is presented.

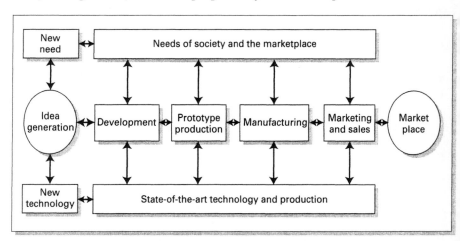

Figure 5.7 Rothwell's coupling model of innovation

Last, but not least, models of teambuilding processes have been proposed. In Figure 5.8, we have depicted team performance as a function of the four team-building phases of forming, storming, norming and performing.

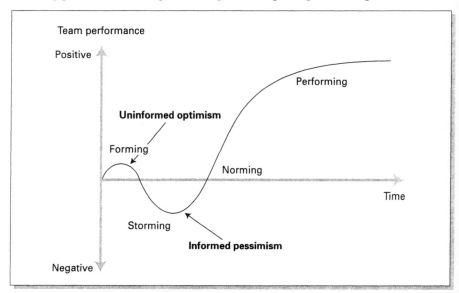

Figure 5.8 Team performance as a function of the four teambuilding phases of forming, storming, norming and performing

Source: Adapted from Ayas, 1996

In the stage of forming, the identity of the team is established. During storming, members seek to prove their expertise and establish dominance. Coalitions between parties may arise to ensure a secure position. In the next stage, norming, the team begins to establish its identity as a functioning and productive unit. Ultimately, in the performing stage, the team members collectively monitor the accomplishment of tasks. Mutual trust is established (Ayas, 1996).

What we have observed has been that various authors have stressed different aspects of the NPD process.

All the models described focus on phases of certain activities or the outputs of certain processes and on the various performance indicators of the NPD process, such as the:

- number and quality of ideas entering the process;
- number, quality and risk associated with the outputs of the NPD process – products and services;
- efficiency of the process with respect to the scarce resources of manpower, money and time.

However, these models do not describe the processes themselves and the ways in which they interact with each other. Neither do they consider the building up of skills, competences and options for the future.

In this chapter, we will discuss business systems in terms of networks of processes. By means of these processes inputs are transformed into outputs. Enabling factors, such as a variety of tools, may accelerate these processes, but they are not changed by them. Also, knowledge must be viewed as instrumental in the model, because it enables the process but is not used up. Organization and the use of management systems and tools are also considered enabling factors. Fulfilment of certain restrictive regulations, such as safety, health and environmental regulations, the existence of physical and technological restrictions, such as the temperature sensitivity of certain materials, and the existence of group values and norms can be regarded as constraints. All the elements that determine the internal position of a company are thus linked to the model of a business process.

Stakeholders have goals and create value when these goals are fulfilled via their business processes.

In Figure 5.9, the general process model we have seen earlier returns. We will apply it to both internal NPD processes and external NBD processes.

Thus, the positional and stakeholder analyses of earlier chapters are useful steps towards the process analyses discussed in this chapter because the various inputs, outputs, enabling factors, constraints and bottlenecks are inventorized.

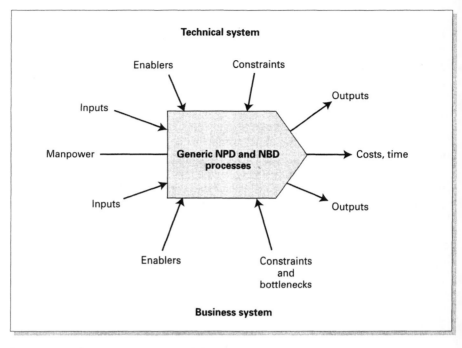

Figure 5.9 Generic process model

When appropriate, we will define the attributes of specific business processes in this chapter in more detail and will add some further attributes, such as process phases and performance indicators. We will concentrate on the various processes that are part of the NPD and NBD process.

Processes are more or less linked to each other. In serial processes, the output of the preceding process is the input of the next. In parallel processes, the outputs of two or more processes are the input of the next process. However, often, not only is the output of process A the input of process B, but the output of B is also the input or an enabling factor of A. This gives rise to various kinds of non-linear behaviour. In this chapter, we will demonstrate that, especially in NPD and NBD processes, these types of interactions are common and add to their non-linear dynamics. Management can profit from these, but only when they understand the basis of the underlying non-linear mechanisms. In Chapter 6, we will discuss the various non-linear mechanisms.

Based on literature studies and our own research, we may classify the processes that are part of the NPD and NBD processes under seven headings:

- management and decision making;
- prototyping;

- knowledge generation, acquisition and exploitation;
- generation of ideas;
- teambuilding;
- implementation I – ramp up and production;
- implementation II – product launch and roll out.

Although in this chapter we will discuss only general models of the various generic processes, we must realize that, in real life, these processes may vary considerably.

The seven generic NPD and NBD business processes

Introduction

We will only discuss those intra-company processes that are part of the NPD and NBD process. These are the processes that take place in research, development and engineering, marketing and implementation in production and sales. The word 'product' is used here in a broad sense, and includes services – even the introduction of a new process.

The processes that take place during NPD and NBD are hardly described in publications and books about the management of these developments.

Although a large number of books and articles deal with process management, the processes they cover are mostly restricted to operations – production and logistics. The processes that take place during NPD and NBD are hardly described in publications and books about the management of these developments. Almost all these books deal extensively with the various organizational structures, management tools and other critical factors, such as the composition of teams, culture and management style, that enable the process but lack a careful description of the characteristics of the process. That is a pity, but understandable as the complexities of the development processes are enormous compared with those of the processes that are part of normal operations.

More recently, however, attention has been given to certain types of processes that are part of the overall development process, such as the acquisition and exploitation of knowledge and the learning, teambuilding and decision-making processes. In more technically oriented literature, the design and generation of ideas processes have been described.

Here, we will discuss the seven intra-company processes separately. Afterwards, we will study in more detail how these processes interact and what this means for the management of NPD and NBD.

We think that by having a better understanding of the generic processes and their interactions during the course of a project, we can construct better process and performance indicators and, at an earlier stage, receive, recognize and interpret weak signals that may give clues as to how to manage the project for optimal results.

We will start with the decision-making process because it affects all other generic processes and, because of the management of NPD and NBD, is the central theme in this book.

The management and decision-making process

The management process consists of a number of separate activities, such as planning, organizing, leading and controlling. During all of these, decisions are made. However, all team members constantly make decisions during the development process. At certain specific moments, during milestone reviews, these decisions are made in a more formal setting.

Inputs of the decision-making process are goals, available resources – that is, skills, financial resources and options. Outputs are plans of the activities that have to be undertaken to reach the goals set, the requirements for the outputs of these activities, allocation of resources, skills, finance and time to the various activities, and an inventorization of any uncertainties or lack of knowledge to fulfil the various tasks. Enabling factors are knowledge and the dependencies among the team members – that is, the hierarchical and power relationships between the team members. Various tools are used, such as spreadsheets, graphics, SWOT analysis and so on. In Figure 5.10, this process is depicted.

It is important to realize that, during decision making, it is not only the organizational goals that are inputs but also the personal goals of the team members. Further, it is important to realize that a lot of decision making not only takes place in the NPD or NBD team context but also in smaller groups during the execution of individual tasks. In other words, within companies there exist hierarchies of decision-making processes. Three levels of such hierarchies are of importance here:

- the work floor – the group of engineers, scientists and their technicians who are performing the real work;
- the project level – the core project team;
- top management – where the requirements of the various projects are determined and resources allocated.

These three levels interact with each other – decisions made at a lower level may influence higher levels, and vice versa. Especially in NPD, the lowest level can greatly influence the course of events. In this way, strategies are not only decided on at top management level but also emerge during development activities.

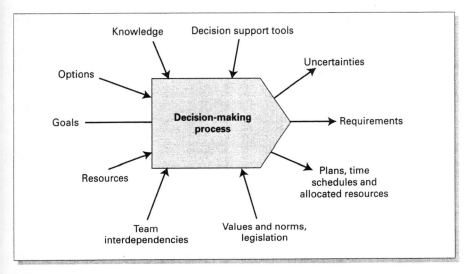

Figure 5.10 The decision-making process, with inputs, outputs, enabling factors and tools

Whereas the allocation of resources and goals are typically top-down inputs, where decision making at higher levels of the hierarchy determines the lower-level decision-making process, options are inputs where lower levels influence higher levels of decision making. Also, knowledge is an enabling factor that works, at least partly, from the bottom up. Hierarchical dependencies, on the other hand, are typical top-down enabling factors. In decision-making situations where the knowledge and options dominate, the *Strategies are not only decided on at top management level but also emerge during development activities.* higher-level decision-making processes are strongly dependent on the lower-level decision-making processes. This is the case in high-tech sectors where technology, products and/or markets are at the beginning of their lifecycles. Also, in the first, fuzzy front end of product development, low-level decision making plays an important role. In these cases, the authority to make decisions is delegated to much lower levels than in situations where this is not the case.

Where budgets are low, the locus of control often switches automatically to the higher hierarchical levels. Also, when goals are clear and well defined, the locus of control is at the higher levels, as it is in the later phases of NPD and NBD.

The outputs of the decision-making process are the inputs of a number of other generic processes. The requirements and allocation of resources are inputs of the prototyping process. The uncertainties are the inputs of the knowledge acquisition process. Uncertainties are also the inputs of the idea-generation process. Allocation of resources will influence the teambuilding process.

The inputs of the decision-making process are partly the outputs of the higher-level decision-making process, such as goals and resources, but are also the outputs of lower-level decision-making processes. For example, the goals are partly the result of group decision-making processes and teambuilding at the lower levels. Options are the outputs of the generation of ideas process.

Knowledge, as an enabling factor, is the output of the knowledge-generation process, and dependencies are partly the result of the teambuilding process, partly of decisions made at a higher level.

Mostly, but not necessarily, the decision-making process can be divided into a number of subsequent phases, such as definition of the problem, decisions about the criteria for the potential solution, inventorization of options, selection of the best option and planning the implementation. The decision support tools often help to structure the decision-making process, by setting the agenda and facilitating communication.

Prototyping

In NPD, the prototyping process encompasses the design and testing of a series of prototypes that become increasingly detailed and real. It starts with rough sketches that later become more detailed drawings, schemes and computer models. Ultimately, these slowly become more and more detailed and sophisticated physical prototypes that resemble the final product.

The sequence and types of prototypes and tests differ, but, in most industries, the process of prototyping has been speeded up considerably and become less costly as a result of using computer modelling and simulation techniques for this. Also, various physical, mechanical, chemical and biotechnological procedures have speeded up this process.

Fast prototyping techniques and testing procedures, such as combinatorial chemistry and microchips tests, have changed the research process in the pharmaceutical industry dramatically. The tests are the filtering mechanism in the development process that ensure that the technical, commercial and economic requirements are met.

Because of the increasing complexity of products in general and specialization of many of the experts involved in prototyping, the process is modularized. This means the product is broken down into its parts – components that can be developed and produced separately. Compartmentalization of a product is one of the ways in which the complexity of the whole process can be diminished. By decreasing the number of links between the various parts, the amount of communication can be reduced, increasing effective development time and increasing the speed of innovation (see Stuart Kauffman, 1995).

Critical success factors in the process of compartmentalization of a product are defining the right interfaces and designing these interfaces in such a way that they leave maximum freedom for future developments. Compartmentalization must not only take into account those boundaries that are most logical for product development, but also those for production, assembly, logistics and service.

Because of the relationships between the architecture of organizations, supply chains, networks of organizations and product architecture, making changes to the architecture becomes increasingly difficult in the later phases of the lifecycle. This may be one of the factors that synchronizes lifecycles of technology, products and industries, as was discussed in Chapter 2 (Abernathy and Utterback, 1978; Teece, 1986).

Also, the standardization of the design of the interfaces between components influences the product and the product architecture and, concomitantly, the structure of industries, and, thereby, the position and power of companies in these industries, so the process of standardization is institutionalized. Influencing the outcome of this standardization process is therefore strategically important.

Whereas the product realization process consists of a series of more and more detailed and more real prototypes, a number of processes can be run in parallel. This concurrent engineering speeds up the process. Often these various types of prototyping are phased. The phases run then from global design or architectures to detailed designs. It also makes good fine-tuning between the parallel activities and communication between the experts more important. A number of tools, such as CAD/CAM techniques, DFM, FMEA and other quality management techniques, support this fine-tuning and communication process. By smart modularization and standardization, taking smaller steps between subsequent product generations and using general product architectures, the product realization process can be shortened further (see Smith and Reinertsen, 1998). In Chapter 10, we will discuss the ways in which the prototyping process can be accelerated. Figure 5.11 shows a general model of this prototyping process.

The cyclical nature of the process of prototyping consists of four activities:

- design and construction of prototypes;
- testing of the prototypes;
- data handling;
- modelling.

Inputs of the process are allocated resources and requirements. Both these inputs are outputs of the decision-making process. Outputs of the process are prototypes that perform better and better, and information on the relationships between attributes of the prototypes and gap between the requirements and performance of the prototype. Enabling factors are tools, skills and knowledge.

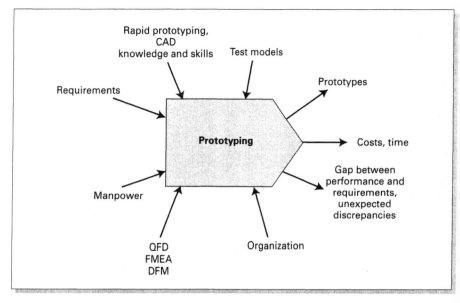

Figure 5.11 The prototyping process

The knowledge-generation, acquisition and exploitation process

The knowledge-generation, acquisition and exploitation process is linked with the prototyping process. Essentially, the information flows from the tests are the inputs for this process and, after the interpretation of this information using the available and newly generated knowledge, the outputs of this process can be used to redesign and refine the prototypes. In certain situations, this process is separated from the prototyping process, by using existing knowledge as much as possible – that is, proven technology. Separation also takes place, if possible, by acquisition of the necessary knowledge before the start of the prototyping process in the research and pre-project phase.

Knowledge management has become popular as a tool for acquiring and exploiting the knowledge present inside and outside a company in a more effective and efficient way than before.

By separating these processes, it becomes easier to use the knowledge that is available outside particular projects, in other parts of the organization. Determining which knowledge is necessary and which is missing limits the possibilities for separating the process of knowledge acquisition from the prototyping process. Knowledge management has become popular as a tool for acquiring and exploiting the knowledge present inside and outside a company in a more effective and efficient way than before.

Inputs of the knowledge-generation, acquisition and exploitation process are information from the product realization process, allocated resources, uncertainties from the decision-making process, ideas and hypotheses, and models and schemes derived from the outside world. Outputs are also knowledge. Enabling factors are the existing knowledge base of the team members, tools and methodologies, such as information and communications technology and scientific methods. In Figure 5.12, this process is schematically represented.

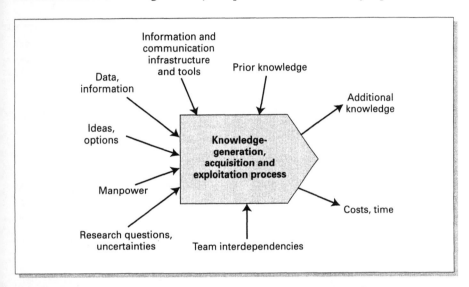

Figure 5.12 The knowledge-generation, acquisition and exploitation process

Knowledge generation is a very special process because the outputs – new knowledge – are the same as its enabling factor. New knowledge can only be acquired when there is a base of prior understanding.

Generally, two types of knowledge can be distinguished:

- codified knowledge;
- tacit, uncodified or intuitive knowledge.

Ikujiro Nonaka and Hirotaka Takeuchi (1995) have proposed a cyclical model, consisting of four phases. In their model, most knowledge starts as tacit knowledge that is later codified. After codification, this knowledge can be combined with other knowledge. Then, it can be applied and is internalized within the organization. In the explication process of knowledge, prototyping plays an important role. Prototyping, testing and modelling are therefore tightly linked to the codification of knowledge and, based on this codified knowledge, new knowledge can be acquired. Often it is acquired from published sources.

Communication is another important way to codify tacit knowledge. It helps in the articulation of tacit knowledge. Because communication is highly dependent on the quality of the team, team performance and the teambuilding process have close links with the knowledge-generation, acquisition and exploitation process.

We have restricted ourselves here to the generation, acquisition and exploitation of disciplinary knowledge – that is, technical, market knowledge and so on. In the literature, a distinction between individual and organizational learning is made. Both types of learning are closely linked. In Nonaka and Takeuchi's model mentioned above, some phases are more related to individual learning than others, and some are more related to organizational learning. Other cyclical learning models are proposed by David Kolb (1981) and Peter Senge (1990), who adapted and extended Kolb's model to make it suitable for use with organizational learning. In later chapters, we will discuss these models at more length.

The generation of ideas process

The generation of ideas process can best be considered as being separate from the knowledge-generation, acquisition and exploitation process. Reasons for considering this process as a separate process are that:

- coming up with ideas demands creative skills, whereas knowledge generation requires you to be analytical and synthesize. Often, different types of people are talented in generating ideas or knowledge – generally people cannot do both;
- generation of ideas is optimized in different situations than those in which knowledge generation and acquisition is – ideas come forth most abundantly when criticism is postponed; knowledge generation and acquisition are promoted by a critical attitude;
- new ideas can be necessary in situations where the availability of knowledge is not the bottleneck.

Often the generation of ideas precedes knowledge acquisition. On the other hand, discrepancies between knowledge about processes and realized outcomes are inputs of the ideas process. However, the generation of ideas can be separated from knowledge generation and acquisition when we only look for options to solve certain problems where lack of knowledge is not the critical factor, but other constraints, such as cost or time, are.

Other inputs for the generation of ideas process are weak signals from, for example, technology or market trends. Outputs of this process are ideas, options and hypotheses. Enabling factors are the skills of people, existing knowledge (although this may also hinder the generation of ideas) and diversity of approach and knowledge. Other important enablers are team attributes such as the tolerance of differences in behaviour and beliefs. These factors are themselves dependent on the ways in which team members deal with each other – in other words, the dependencies among the team members. Figure 5.13 illustrates this process.

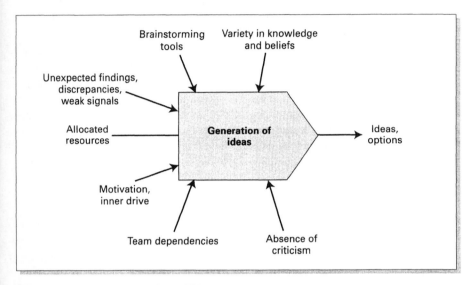

Figure 5.13 The generation of ideas process

The generation of ideas process often occurs at the start of a new project. Especially in the beginning or fuzzy front end, high-quality ideas ensure the success of the project. In later phases, the generation of ideas should play only a subordinate role to the other generic processes, such as knowledge acquisition, prototyping and realization. It is necessary to come up with ideas during the whole of the project to solve problems as they occur. However, if this situation dominates in the later phases, the project will never be able to achieve a clear focus. Knowing when to start, stop and use it as a supportive process for other processes is essential for the success of the project.

A large number of books have been published about brainstorming. Most of them deal with methods that facilitate this process. It is generally accepted, as noted earlier, that the ideas process must be separated from the evaluation of ideas. It is also widely accepted that part of the process is unconscious. So, after identifying the problem, it may help to perform simple, repetitive activities, such as walking, digging or taking a shower. During the borderline time between sleeping and waking, a dream-like state exists that seems to facilitate the generation of ideas.

Generation of ideas can be planned in organized brainstorming sessions, but unorganized times for this process are of the utmost importance. One type of unorganized, spontaneous generation of ideas is serendipity. Serendipity is a process that plays an important role during the whole process and often sows the seeds of a new project. As we saw earlier, it has been the basis of many breakthrough discoveries, such as penicillin, X-rays, nylon, transistors, Post-it Notes and so on. It originates from observed discrepancies between empirical facts and knowledge – that is, from unexpected outcomes during experimentation. Serendipity is still one of the main sources of completely new ideas for radical product innovations.

Serendipity is still one of the main sources of completely new ideas for radical product innovations.

Some companies know how to make use of this process. For example, at the Belgian pharmaceutical company Janssen Pharmaceutical, co-workers in the labs were encouraged to look out for unexpected findings in particular and study the causes of these deviations carefully.

Teambuilding

The teambuilding process is widely recognized as being one of the most crucial for a project's success. It is, however, a process that is difficult, if not impossible, to manage, as is the generation of ideas process. The role of management cannot be more than that of facilitator of the process.

Teambuilding encompasses the definition, codification and legitimization of common goals, norms and values that coordinate the behaviour of the members. The output of this process can therefore be defined as being the emergence of certain interdependencies between the team members.

The process consists of ensuring common understanding of the environment by the various team members. This needs to be coupled with open communication between the team members. Communication can therefore be viewed as one of the critical aspects of the process.

Inputs of the process are the goals, beliefs, norms and values of the individual members, the organizational goals of higher levels of management and the resources and allocation of resources among the team members, because this determines the distribution of power in the team.

Enabling factors are tools that support the communication and clarification of beliefs, values and norms and communication infrastructure. Also, it is well known that the physical location has a dominant effect on communication and on teambuilding. Another enabling factor is product architecture. This determines the ways in which the members deal with each other and determine their interdependencies. In Figure 5.14, we have depicted the process with its inputs, outputs and enabling factors.

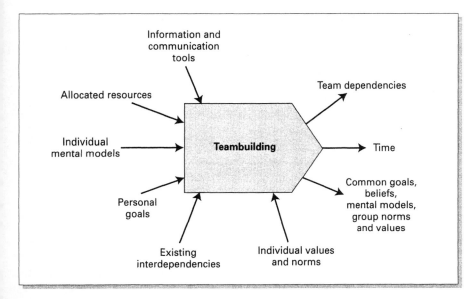

Figure 5.14 The teambuilding process

Although many other parameters may play a role in teambuilding, a number of the most important have been included in Figure 5.14.

Team formation can be seen to occur in several phases, as you may recall from earlier:

* forming
* storming
* norming
* performing.

Whereas in this and other schemes a rather linear process of project team formation is envisaged, it can also be seen to be a complicated process with two stable outcomes and one meta-stable one. The stable ones are a hierarchical team structure, where one member dominates over the other team members, and a chaotic team, where all members act independently of each other. The meta-stable one is the network team, where individual team members dominate only for short periods and switch places with each other for dominant position as long as the situation demands. This kind of team is located at the so-called edge of chaos. The edge of chaos is characterized by its flexibility (see Brown and Eisenhardt, 1998). Such teams are the high-performance teams.

A prerequisite for high-performance teams is the presence of a well-balanced number of team roles.

A prerequisite for high-performance teams is the presence of a well-balanced number of team roles. Several classifications have been proposed, one of which is R. Meredith Belbin's (1993). He has defined the essential team roles as being the following:

- chairman
- shaper
- plant
- monitor evaluator
- company worker
- team worker
- resource investigator
- completer.

The fulfilment of these team roles makes sure that the various necessary activities are properly executed.

The fulfilment of these team roles makes sure that the various necessary activities are properly executed. Later in this chapter we will discuss the relationships between Belbin's team roles and the various generic NPD and NBD processes in more detail.

To measure the quality of teams, various maturity indices have been developed. In these indices, four or five levels are distinguished – level 1 is no cooperation, level 4 or 5 teams are where members cooperate smoothly and support each other.

Implementation I and II

The process of implementation encompasses both the introduction of a new product, service and/or process inside the company as well as extra-company processes, such as introduction of these to the supply chain and market. The realization or implementation process in a company is rather complicated and, in reality, is composed of a number of separate processes, such as adjustments to the physical layout of the production plant, logistics, organization, the preparation of sales activities and so on. Because it depends on the type of new business or product being implemented, how similar it is to normal operations and so on, the amount of adaptation required will vary enormously.

Often, the effort and time needed for the implementation process is underestimated, resulting in costly delays and frustrations. For this reason, starting with an inventorization of the critical points for implementation and preparation as early as possible is important. One of the ways in which this can be done is by involving one or more of the people who will be key to the implementation process in the project right from the very beginning. Various total quality tools have been developed that support these processes, such as design for manufacturing (DFM), quality function deployment (QFD), and failure mode effect analysis (FMEA).

Integration of the various intra-company processes

Before we start discussion of the integration of the separate generic processes, a number of general remarks need to be made.

All seven generic processes generally occur more or less concomitantly in the NPD or NBD process. During this time, ideas are generated for solving problems, knowledge is generated, acquired and exploited, prototypes are made and tested, small and large decisions are made and, of course, cash is obtained and used to pay for the various activities. Also, at an early stage, ideas are tested to see how the organization will react. In other words, all the processes are operating from the start to the end of a project. However, the intensity of these processes varies widely during this time. The generation of ideas is dominant at the start, followed by knowledge acquisition and team-building. Then, during development, product realization becomes dominant, ending with the implementation within the organization. Decision making is interspersed between the various phases and dominates at the times of mile-stone reviews.

All the processes are interlinked and, as we will demonstrate, they also affect each other. By deliberately defining the project phases in such a way that during each phase one generic process clearly holds the central position and the others support it, the development process becomes more manageable.

From the literature in this area we know that successful teams include members who adopt certain critical roles (see 'Teambuilding' section above). When looking at these critical roles it becomes clear that most of them coincide with one of the generic processes. As mentioned earlier, successful teams possess a:

- chairman
- shaper
- plant
- monitor evaluator
- company worker
- team worker
- resource investigator
- completer.

The chairman is important for the management and decision-making process, the plant for the process of generating ideas, the resource investigators for the knowledge-generation, acquisition and exploitation process, the team worker is important for teambuilding, while the completer is the one who looks at the executability of the plans, guarding the realization process and often the implementation process too. Table 5.1 shows the relationships between certain team roles (the roles of internal stakeholders) and the generic processes.

Table 5.1 The generic processes and the roles of the various internal and external stakeholders they relate to

Generic NPD and NBD processes	Team process owners
Management and decision making	Chairman
Prototyping	Shaper
Knowledge generation	Resource investigator
Generation of ideas	Plant
Teambuilding	Team worker
Implementation I and II	Completer

Integration of the various isolated processes may result in unexpected behaviour of the overall process – that is, virtuous loops may be formed that support the growth of the company or, conversely, vicious loops may occur that could lead to the downfall of the company. Although in the next chapter we will discuss in more detail the various non-linear mechanisms and their consequences, in this chapter we will study the consequences of integration of these processes for management and the ways in which management can deal with it.

The generic processes are connected to each other via their inputs, outputs, enabling factors, constraints and bottlenecks.

As already stressed in the separate discussions on the generic processes, they are connected to each other via their inputs, outputs, enabling factors, constraints and bottlenecks. In this way, the decision-making process is closely linked to teambuilding, the knowledge-generation process with generation of ideas and prototyping, and the prototyping process with teambuilding. Further, all the processes are linked to the decision-making process. Figure 5.15 shows these interactions.

We will now briefly discuss a number of management conventions that can be illustrated using this rather complicated diagram of the NPD and NBD processes. Before looking at the various consequences for NBD separately, a few general remarks can be made.

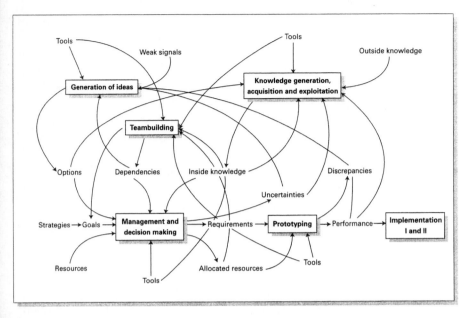

Figure 5.15 The interactions between the generic NPD and NBD business processes

● Although the diagram looks impressive and complicated, it does not take into account the repetition and hierarchy of the processes. As discussed before, most of the generic processes are present in iterative cycles during the development process. Prototypes are constantly designed and redesigned until they fulfil all the requirements. Because of the complexity of most products, many disciplines are working in parallel on the development of parts of the product. We have simplified the diagram here and presented the generic processes only once.

● For the generic processes to be performed well, they have to be performed more or less simultaneously. When designing and testing a prototype or part of it, knowledge has to be acquired and information is collected that may lead to old knowledge being adapted and the generation of new knowledge. Also, problems are met that cannot be solved directly. Ideas and new options have to be generated and decisions made on how to continue. During these processes, the team assumptions and beliefs, norms and values are constantly expressed, confirmed and perhaps adapted slightly, changing perhaps the team member dependencies little by little. In other words, the complicated process of development affects the organization and, in reality, it must be viewed as an evolving phenomenon, as discussed in Chapter 3. Arie de Geus (1997) has likened organizations to living systems, and this seems to apply most to NPD.

● Although the various generic processes are tightly linked together, all of them have their own optimal conditions that are often in conflict with each other. The generation of ideas is promoted by using a variety of approaches and focusing on the requirements that need to be met by the product. Whereas teambuilding is enhanced by an equality among the group's members, decision making needs someone with authority and knowledge generation is encouraged by open minds and hindered by the 'not invented here' syndrome and so on. Implementation needs a more closed mind, which helps others to be convinced of the product's advantages.

● Emerging systems such as development cannot be managed in a Tayloristic or bureaucratic way. The process cannot be predicted completely beforehand. A lot of decisions have to be made on a continuous basis at all levels and the organization must therefore adapt itself constantly. On the one hand, subtle control and tolerance with respect to the solutions found are important and, on the other, the overall performance indicators for all the projects – such as speed, quality, costs and risks – must be closely controlled.

The following are solutions innovation management has developed to deal with these complications and paradoxes.

● The phasing of the development process is the first solution. By compartmentalizing elements of the process in a number of phases, in each of which one process is dominant over the others, the complexities of the overall process are reduced. We have already indicated that the phases of prototyping, generation of ideas, knowledge generation, acquisition and exploitation, teambuilding and implementation I and II, interspersed with well-defined periods during which decision making, milestone reviews and so on take place, demonstrate this. In this way, the conditions during each phase can be adjusted in accordance with the requirements of the dominant process to optimize its outcome.

● The existence of various critical team roles that coincide with the various generic processes we have distinguished can be understood when we assume that these critical roles are performed by process owners, who ensure the proper execution of the various generic processes. This can also occur in phases where certain generic processes are not dominant – they survive and, when necessary, can be activated.

- The use of various tools to support the various generic processes stimulates communication and therefore facilitates teambuilding. A bad team spirit hinders the proper use of these tools. Teambuilding as well as decision making are, at all times, critical processes. However, team demands may change depending on the requirements of the dominant process. It is important that this adaptation process takes place continuously. The tools used during the various phases play critical roles in this teambuilding process.

- One of the critical success factors is a high-performance team. In such teams, decision making is more effective. Instruments such as the team maturity index may be used to measure team performance. High-performance teams are characterized by an atmosphere in which there are equal opportunities for every member to contribute. In very hierarchical teams, where one person dominates, or chaotic teams, where no real communication between team members takes place, this attribute of high-performance teams is violated.

- Success breeds success. Prototypes that perform well facilitate the acquisition of financial resources and increase team spirit. The objectives of the project, time schedule and available resources must be in balance. If the goals and expectations are set too high, this is frustrating to everyone and, ultimately, kills innovation.

- Product architecture is often difficult to change because it influences and depends on the various positions of, and dependencies between, the team members. For the development of a completely new product, you often have to break away from the normal organization, forming so-called 'tiger teams' or starting a new venture.

A number of actions that can be taken to shorten development times can be better understood using this model of the interactions between the generic processes. Working with multidisciplinary teams stimulates the generation of ideas and, therefore, increases the quality of the design. It is better to start as early as possible with the design and testing of cheap prototypes to facilitate the articulation of tacit knowledge, support the communication of ideas and the inventorization of critical bottlenecks in the design. Each stimulates the knowledge-generation process.

Success breeds success. Prototypes that perform well facilitate the acquisition of financial resources and increase team spirit. If the goals and expectations are set too high, this is frustrating to everyone.

Changing the composition of the team only slightly from project to project speeds up the teambuilding process and, at the same time, does not stifle ideas and innovation.

One concluding remark has to be made here. The delineation of the seven generic processes is general and contains elements from the literature in this area and our own research. However, the diversity of development processes is enormous and varies depending on the key technology, type of product, service or process to be developed, type of innovation (breakthrough, new generation, incremental improvement, line extension), characteristics of the company (style, organizational structure, system used, skills present, resources available), type of market (business to business, consumer market, several related markets), characteristics of the supply chain and so on. Therefore, every company needs to analyze its own processes and the specific conditions present within the company and its industry. The general descriptions of the generic processes included here may help this process, but are not meant to be equally applicable to every situation. Also, certain processes that have not been discussed may be important for your particular development process, such as the acquisition and training of essential staff, and so these will also need to be taken into account.

Discussion

In this chapter we have discussed the last of the three Ps. All three – position, people and processes – are closely linked with each other. The relationships between the intra-company generic NPD and NBD processes, resources and internal and external stakeholders are depicted in Tables 5.2–5.4.

Table 5.2 The relationships between intra-company generic NPD and NBD processes and the company's resources

Generic NPD and NBD processes	Company's resources/assets						
	Cash	Capital	Options	Knowledge	Structure	Systems	Culture
Management and decision making	Input/ output		Input	Enabler	Output/ enabler	Output/ enabler	Enabler
Prototyping	Input	Enabler/ output	Input	Enabler		Enabler	
Knowledge generation	Input		Input	Input/ output		Enabler	Enabler
Generation of ideas			Output	Enabler		Enabler	Enabler
Teambuilding			Enabler	Enabler	Enabler	Enabler	Input/ output
Implementation I and II	Input	Input/ output	Input	Enabler		Enabler	

Table 5.3 The relationships between intra-company generic NPD and NBD processes and internal stakeholders

Generic NPD and NBD processes	Internal stakeholders		
	Team process owner	Team member involvement	External involvement
Management and decision making	Chairman	All	Corporate
Prototyping	Shaper	All	
Knowledge generation	Resource investigator	All	
Generation of ideas	Plant	All	
Teambuilding	Team worker	All	
Implementation I and II	Completer	All	Corporate/ sales/ production

Table 5.4 The relationships between intra-company generic NPD and NBD processes and external stakeholders

Generic NPD and NBD processes	External stakeholders
Management and decision making	
Prototyping	Customers, suppliers
Knowledge generation	Knowledge institutes, consultant, customer, supplier, competitor (patents and benchmarking)
Generation of ideas	Customer, supplier, competitor
Teambuilding	
Implementation I and II	Suppliers, distributors, advertisement agencies, media

The resources are inputs, outputs and enablers of the various generic processes. In this way, the processes are linked with each other in a complicated non-linear way. In the next chapter, we will analyze the various non-linear mechanisms present in the NPD and NBD processes in more detail. With all the processes, various stakeholders are shown as process owners, suppliers of the inputs or customers of the outputs. In Table 5.3, we have shown the process owners and described them using the names Belbin (1993) gave the various critical team roles.

We have noted, too, the similar relationships that exist between resources, determining the position of the company, the internal and external stakeholders and the external innovation subprocesses. There are non-linearities here as well that are characteristic of the innovation process and make it one of the most important ways to grow and prosper. The analysis of these non-linear mechanisms will also be discussed in the next chapter. In Part 3, we will discuss how management can profit from these non-linearities and organize the process in such a way that it is more manageable.

A number of authors have published classifications of industries based on one or more elements of the three Ps that may help in the inventorization of the attributes of the processes and, therefore, support the formulation of NPD and NBD policies.

In Part 1, we discussed the classification schemes of Keith Pavitt (1990) and of William Abernathy and James Utterback (1978). Pavitt's scheme was based mostly on the players and their interactions in the different industries. He derived from the roles and motives of the various actors in an industry the characteristics of the innovation process. Although, in general, his scheme helps in understanding differences between industries, within industries large differences may exist that are sometimes even larger than those between industries. In the pharmaceutical sector, for example, we can distinguish strategic groups that are really science-dominated, but also supplier-dominated strategic groups, information-intensive and scale-intensive areas.

We do not want to give general advice; instead we have focused on a more detailed level of analysis so it is possible to develop company-specific strategies.

The scheme devised by Abernathy and Utterback is based on the synchronization between technology, product and industry lifecycles. The innovation process possesses certain characteristics during each of the phases of its lifecycle that affect management practice.

David Teece (1986) also uses the technology, product and industry lifecycles as a starting point. However, he combines these with specific characteristics of technology and derives from this certain best practice for management.

These authors discuss only part of the business system and then draw general conclusions. When you want to give broad advice on how to manage a process, you have to generalize and abstract from the many elements that make every situation unique. Here, in this book, we have done the opposite. We do not want to give general advice; instead we have focused on a more detailed level of analysis so it is possible to develop company-specific strategies.

The idea behind this approach is that general advice for management will never work, because the moment a certain successful strategy is used by other companies, it loses its attractiveness and ceases to work. Management strategies have this in common with technology in general – the moment everybody uses it, it is no longer special. This is the fate of all management methods, which ultimately makes them fad-like.

Management must formulate new strategies that surprise the competition. Richard D'Aveni (1994) has argued that changing the rules is the new rule. This means that every scheme prescribing certain forms of innovation management is old-fashioned the moment it is formulated, recorded and published. Luckily, employees, companies, industries, and even industry clusters, are all different from one another, with their own characteristics. Thus, each situation has to be analyzed separately and when we understand the basis of the dynamics of the processes – that is, the deep structure of the system – we can try to formulate our own, innovative policy, taking into account the possible reactions of the competition.

6 | Determining non-linear mechanisms

Introduction

NPD and NBD are driven by self-reinforcing loops. Especially in the Internet age, the speed with which these loops operate and propel companies towards better positions has been increased dramatically. In Figure 6.1, a number of reinforcing loops are presented that, according to John Hagel and Arthur Armstrong (1998), are central in developing successful Internet businesses.

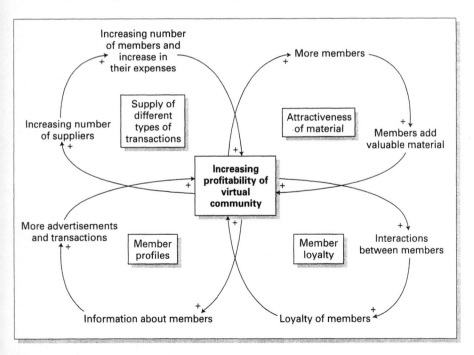

Figure 6.1 The reinforcing loops that stimulate growth of Internet companies

Source: Hagel and Armstrong, 1998

Carl Shapiro, and Hal Varian describe in their book, *Information Rules: A strategic guide to the network economy* (1999), a number of non-linear mechanisms, such as network economies (a reinforcing loop for these will be described later in this chapter), that are fundamental to an understanding of economics today.

Non-linear mechanisms are responsible for the unpredictable dynamics of the innovation process.

In this chapter, we will concentrate on the inventorization and analysis of non-linear mechanisms (see Figure 6.2) in the business system. This analysis will help us to focus the modelling of the system on those parts that contribute to its non-linear behaviour. Non-linear mechanisms are responsible for the unpredictable dynamics of the innovation process.

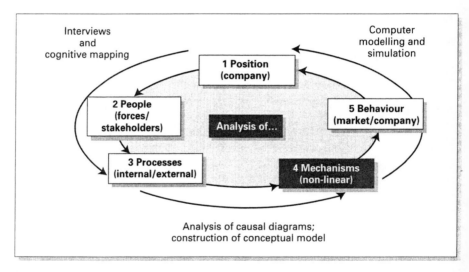

Figure 6.2 The steps involved in the DBM process – the fourth step is analysis of non-linear mechanisms

Microsoft

case study

Fast-growing companies often find that there are several factors responsible for their growth – virtuous reinforcing loops that form customer, shareholder and employee value multipliers. Let us take Microsoft. There is the Wintel reinforcing loop, itself based on the loop consisting of more powerful microprocessors and more user-friendly operating systems that demand more powerful processors. The Windows operating system forms a reinforcing loop via the applications software, acquisition of skills with this software by the users and the number of users. The growth of the company produces attractive returns for the shareholders. This means money for further expansion is relatively cheap and abundant. This increases the strong position of the company, making it increasingly attractive to investors. For employees, working for Microsoft is good for their careers. Therefore, Microsoft can attract among the best of the computing staff. To work with the best is, in itself, a strong argument to work with an organization.

As long as opportunities exist for further growth, it is important to keep such loops running. You have to link with your customers, care for your employees and focus on creating value for your shareholders. However, there have been many occasions in the company's history when the machine that created money for so many stakeholders seemed to stop. The rise of the Internet was such a threat to Microsoft that it was turned into the next territory for Microsoft to conquer.

Sometimes limits to growth must be lifted. New markets, such as the company market, were opened by developing Windows NT, which competed with Unix.

The market position becomes more sustainable when customers are locked into the technology, products and system of the company. Customers are used to Windows and have a large number of applications software and files that make it expensive for them to switch. Supporting applications software developers by providing sophisticated developing environments makes them more dependent on these environments and so makes it more difficult for them to switch.

Whereas locking in customers, suppliers and competitors helps to build a sustainable competitive position, it is important for the company itself to promote the opposite of such a situation, namely discover extra options that can be executed when necessary. This creates flexibility and therefore value for the stakeholders. The availability of knowledge leads to such options. These options to introduce new products can be multiplied by creating marketing options via, for example, the acquisition of companies that operate in new markets.

This case study summarizes a number of non-linear mechanisms that influence improvement in the position of a company.

In the last chapter, we discussed various processes that play a role in NPD and NBD processes. We demonstrated how the various processes inside and outside the company are linked together. This is what is responsible for its behaving in ways that cannot be extrapolated from insight into the behaviour of the constituent parts of the system. Simulation of the system with the aid of computers is the only way we can obtain a deeper understanding of its behaviour and possible outcomes of the planned actions.

This understanding is derived from the fact that computer simulation makes it possible to assess and validate our knowledge because it facilitates the testing of the consequences of our ideas about the business system by comparing simulations with real life.

However, before we are able to simulate a system, we have to model it in an adequate way. We have to try to get a better understanding of its structure, how it changes over time – that is, the various processes that are involved in this change and how these processes interact.

After defining the borderlines of the innovation arena and determining the present and desirable future positions of the company, we have to determine the important parameters that describe this position, together with their past trends. These trends show the changes isolated parts of the business system have undergone and can be considered as timelines of events that are the ultimate result of the behaviour of the system. Next, we need to study the people (stakeholders) involved – the forces acting on the system. Subsequently, we need to analyze the processes that are the result of actions taken by the stakeholders.

These are the steps we have taken so far. Now we will go one step further and discuss the typical non-linear mechanisms that are the result of special configurations of the processes and elements of the system and may influence its behaviour. This analysis helps us to focus on those aspects of the model that affect the NPD and NBD processes the most and aggregate or omit parts that seem to play more or less essential roles.

In principle, there are two ways in which we can model the system. These are by defining the:

- decision rules of the various actors (or agents) and modelling these;
- processes and taking them as a starting point for modelling the dynamic system.

In Chapter 4, we discussed briefly the possibilities for modelling the system as an aggregate of the separate behaviours of the players. In this chapter and Chapter 7, we will discuss ways in which we can model the system as a network of linked processes by means of system dynamics and how this approach helps us to study the behaviour of the system.

The following are all non-linear mechanisms:

- reinforcing loops:
  - virtuous loops;
  - vicious loops;
- limiting loops:
  - control mechanisms;
  - capacity and performance limits;
  - constraints;
- lock-in mechanisms:
  - of the company itself;
  - of other stakeholders, such as customers and competition;
- time delays:

- in negative feedback loops;
- large time variations of processes;
- selection mechanisms:
  - market;
  - intra-company;
  - governmental;
- variation and creation mechanisms:
  - sources of innovation;
  - options and flexibility.

Each of these non-linear mechanisms is now discussed in more detail.

Reinforcing loops

Reinforcing loops emerge when two elements of a system influence each other in a positive way. This means that an increase or decrease in one or more attributes of one item will result in the increase or decrease of one or more attributes of the second item and vice versa. In Figure 6.3, a simple example of such a situation is given.

Figure 6.3 A straightforward reinforcing loop

Virtuous loops

Virtuous loops are reinforcing loops that are beneficial to the company involved. Examples of such loops are abundant. Below, we will describe some examples.

Radical product innovations are defined as products that create new markets. Examples abound because every novel product market combination has started with a radical product innovation. Well-known examples are the introduction of the personal computer in the 1970s, the Walkman by Sony, also in the 1970s, the video cassette recorder for the consumer market, Web browsers, such as Netscape, in the 1990s, 'plastic money' and Internet bookshops, such as amazon.com.

All of these radical product innovations can be characterized by the fact that no recognizable market existed before they were launched. The markets for these products had to be developed. Therefore, at the start, it is not known what determines the quality of such a product. The quality depends on the way the product is used and, often, the product is used in other contexts in different ways than were originally anticipated by the developers. The first users, therefore, are really innovators who experiment and find various ways in which the product can be used. The example of the video recorders made that clear, but the Walkman was also used in a way that was not anticipated.

Without a real product or prototype, it is impossible for even the smartest designer or marketer to imagine how such a product will be used. As discussed before, products have physical quality aspects and these depend on how, in what process and in combination with which other products they will be used. Also, then, the perceived quality depends on the objectives and the expectations of the user. However, all products also have an emotional side as they are used by people who are part of a group. They may help to determine the place of a user in a particular group by affecting their relationships with others. Both aspects determine product quality and only after use for a period of time will the various attributes of quality emerge. A clear example of this is the mobile phone. It has a physical quality component that is dependent on its physical attributes – smallness, quality of the battery, quality of audio characteristics and so on. However, the quality is also dependent on the distribution and penetration of the Internet service provider and the protocols that are used.

The development of products influences the articulation of the market, and the articulation of the market influences further developments of the product.

It is also evident that social attributes result from the fact that, in certain groups, your reputation and authority increase. In other groups, they are better not used when others are present. This determines whether or not the design must be expensive or almost invisible or as sober as possible.

The product, therefore, helps to articulate the various dimensions of quality. What determines high or low quality is always related to defined markets or market segments. When the market becomes well-articulated, further product improvements can be defined and realized. In this way, the development of products influences the articulation of the market, and the articulation of the market influences further developments of the product. In the beginning, this results in a big diversity of products. Certain authors call this the 'pre-paradigmatic stage' of a product and market combination. At a certain moment, a dominant design emerges that affects all subsequent designs. After this happens, we may enter the 'paradigmatic stage' when product development is characterized by only small, incremental changes. We can say that then both products and markets co-evolve.

In a similar way, the development of products and their core technology co-evolve. When new technology is used in an old or new product, its various attributes may not make an optimal contribution to the functionality of the product. The technology may then be used in a different environment. By improving the technology, its attributes will contribute to a better-functioning product. In this way, the product changes, influencing the development of the technology further and so on. The co-evolution of the product and its technology will become a fact and, at a certain moment, the technology may become so differentiated from its original form that it is recognized as a new form of technology. There are many examples of this. Lasers were first used in the so-called laser videodiscs, because it was recognized that large amounts of data could be stored in a small space. However, the very first lasers were large, expensive and used a great deal of energy. The new application of lasers led to the development of much smaller, cheaper and more reliable lasers that also used less energy. With these new lasers, CD players could be miniaturized and a wide variety of new applications was developed as a result.

Technology and science co-evolve in a similar way. Technology often provides the tools for the development of science, and science provides the knowledge that can be the basis of further technological developments. Sir James Black is a famous pharmacologist who has been awarded the Noble prize – one of the few pharmacologists to have been nominated. He is also the developer of two blockbuster drugs – one blood pressure-lowering drug and another used in the treatment of stomach ulcers. This combination is not accidental as he realized early on in his career that he could prove his hypotheses about the existence and role of certain neuro-transmitter receptors only by developing drugs that relied on them in order to be effective.

The process of co-evolution often means that the two or more items co-evolving become more tightly linked to one another. For example, the co-evolution of science and technology has resulted in the fact that, today, the boundaries between technology and science have often disappeared completely, as can be seen in the case of biotechnology.

Co-evolution also occurs when products are used together and, thus, the markets may introduce reinforcing loops for each other. One of the most famous examples is the co-evolution of computer hardware and software, as exemplified by the co-evolution of Intel microprocessors and Microsoft's MS-DOS and Windows operating systems. The development of faster microprocessors provided the opportunity for the development of more user-friendly operating systems. However, these operating systems could only work when faster microprocessors were created. As the quality of operating systems and their applications software also depends on the number of people exchanging documents, as some of us have changed from MS-DOS to Windows and subsequently higher versions of Windows, others have been obliged to do the same. This shift also obliged them to buy new computers with improved microprocessors. In this way, markets become linked and the development of both can only be in one direction.

This example also makes clear that, in this case, a number of software markets are bound together. These are the operating system and applications software markets and the markets of the various software applications that are often used with each other, such as all the software that makes up Microsoft Office.

Product designs, architecture and organizations may also co-evolve. This often results in close links that hinder innovation and the development of new products. This is why new product architectures may require a restructuring of the organization. For example, when IBM decided to develop its own personal computer at the beginning of the 1980s, it realized that the project required a totally new philosophy and architecture and so could be successful only if it took place in a separate organization.

Vicious loops

There are many reinforcing loops that are hazardous to companies – the vicious loops. For example, sometimes the reputation of a company or product may be damaged because a certain event becomes a news item and is repeated a large number of times in the news media.

Another example is the quality trap. In the race to speed up development times, companies have introduced products that still contain large numbers of defects. Whereas in certain applications, such as software, we are used to this (hence, the beta versions), in other situations this may have detrimental effects for the company concerned. There is the example of a company that introduced a new product in the automation market. It was an immediate success and the number of orders increased tremendously in a short period of time. However, after some time had passed, the customers became aware of certain types of bugs. That called for the service engineers. As the number of customers asking for help increased, development engineers were requested to go to the customers to fix the products. At one point, almost all developers were firefighting in the field and so the development of the all-important next versions stopped. Competitors entered the market with improved versions and the company that first brought out the innovation almost went bankrupt. Figure 6.4 shows this sequence of events.

Other examples of vicious loops are the consequence of stress and work overload. When the workload increases, certain co-workers may become ill as a result of the stress. This leads to even greater workloads for the rest of the staff, leading to some of these co-workers collapsing, thus increasing the workload for the rest. Ultimately, the whole department may collapse.

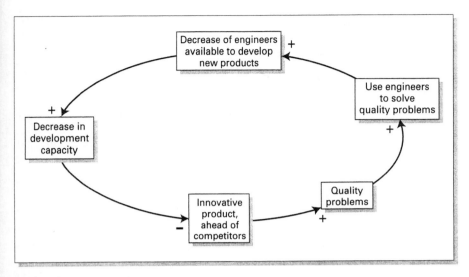

Figure 6.4 The quality trap

What initially may be a virtuous cycle can change into a vicious cycle, as almost happened to Apple when its market share dropped, leading to a fall in the number of software companies developing their new applications for Apple computers. This resulted in a decrease in development of Apple software, making Apple computers less attractive to potential buyers.

Limiting loops

An old proverb says 'the trees don't grow up to heaven'. In other words, all growth comes to an end. There are always limits or constraints that determine how far something may change. These may be physical, economic, social, legal or deliberately chosen limits imposed by the allocation of a particular budget. Innovation is often a matter of taking away these constraints or the shifting of physical and economic limits, as shown in Figure 6.5.

All growth comes to an end. There are always limits or constraints that determine how far something may change.

Whereas the always popular lifecycle – describing the change of a certain attribute of a technology, product or market over time – starts with a reinforcing loop, the ever-increasing rate of change, at a particular moment, will be tempered when it reaches a certain limit. Authors such as Richard Foster (1986) and Rias van Wyk (1996) have concentrated on methods that can be

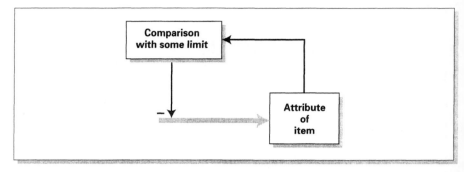

Figure 6.5 A limiting loop

used to determine the limits of technology and products. Once they have been located, management can decide whether to allocate resources to remove the limits or jump to another technology (see Figure 6.6).

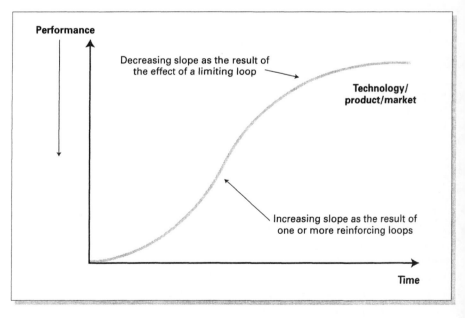

Figure 6.6 The effects of reinforcing and limiting loops on a lifecycle

By adding to a product in terms of functionality, features or styling or decreasing its price, the potential market size is shifted to a higher level, depending on the market's elasticity in terms of volume and quality. This example demonstrates that shifting a limit starts a cascade of events, ultimately resulting in shifting market size, market share and the value of the company. In van Wyk's analysis, it is important to determine what limits the market size, what the causal relationships are between these things and what the company can do to shift the most elementary barriers. Often limits relate to the attributes of the specific material used, such as its strength, weight, melt temperature, conductivity, magnetic density. The toxicity of a compound may restrict the dose of a drug that can be given and, thus, its efficacy. Other constraints relate to the limitations of a certain product.

Besides concentrating on lifting limits or jumping to another technology, it is also important to realize that technology and products are characterized by a bundle of attributes. Whereas for one or more of the attributes the technology may have reached its limits, this does not need to be the case for its other attributes, as shown in Figure 6.7.

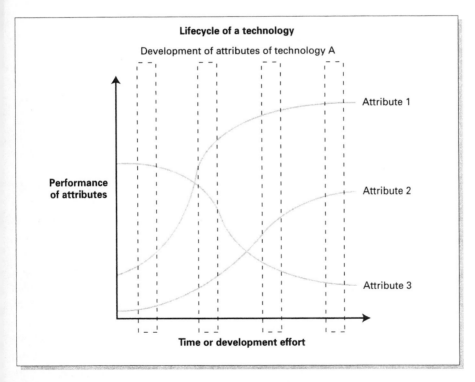

Figure 6.7 Lifecycles of the various attributes of a technology

The relative performance of a technology may change, making it more interesting in terms of its application in other products. Whereas aluminium was, initially, used mainly in aeroplanes, later on it was substituted by other materials but the applications in other areas still rose. At this moment cars may become an increasingly more important area of application for this metal. However, for application in cars the processing of aluminium had to be improved and, for example, sophisticated welding techniques had to be developed.

This example makes it clear that technology interacts with other factors and the development of a certain attribute is dependent on one or more other improvements in technology. Knowing how one technology interacts with another is important if we are to judge the robustness of a limit properly.

The various sets of attributes may subsequently open up a number of markets. Often, in such cases, not all sets of attributes can be fulfilled – choices have to be made between sets. This may mean that different variants of the material must be produced for the different markets – technology will follow specific trajectories for different applications and markets. This may lead to the splitting of a technology. On the other hand, by fusing two or more products, processes or whatever, a new technology may be developed with its own specific sets of attributes, opening up new applications and markets. Examples are composite materials, opto-electronics, electromechanics and genomics.

Other quasi-limits may be caused by increasing interdependencies between one technology and another that emerge during the lifecycle of a product. As explained in Chapter 4, increasing dependencies slow down the speed of evolution (see Kauffman, 1995). At a certain moment, changes may become so difficult and so expensive that it is no longer economically viable to invest in further development. We will discuss this type of mechanism in more detail below, under Lock-in mechanisms.

Aside from these technical and economical limits, legal constraints, assumptions and beliefs pose limits for various developments. Legislation relating to the environment, safety and health impose limits that cannot be lifted by the development activities of the company. This means that companies may shift their activities and, as a result, whole new innovation trajectories may be started. An illustrative example is the development of water-based paint to reduce the pollutants released into the atmosphere. Other examples are the development of substitutes for lead compounds to use in petrol and of new types of propellants to use in all kinds of aerosols.

Besides these more or less 'hard physical' limits, all kinds of soft social and psychological limits may prevent innovation. Sets of values and norms are one of them. Often, mental models impose limits. A certain mental model may blinker companies from seeing certain opportunities or potential threats. A very well-known example is the world view the management of the railways had at the start of this century, which was that railways, as one of the main means of transportation, would last for ever. They did not see the automobile as a growth limiter for their market. Such self-imposed limits are often more difficult to remove than physical or economical limits.

An example of a combination of hard technical and soft socio-economic limits forcing a company to innovate has been the so-called moose test for cars. When the new Mercedes-Benz A series car turned out not to pass the test (it fell over when driven round extremely steep curves), to keep its reputation for superb-quality cars Mercedes had to include new technology to overcome the problem, which it did successfully. Later, it turned out that other cars did not pass the test either. It was because of Mercedes' reputation for high-quality cars that journalists made a point of mentioning this story.

Another type of limit is that of an objective we set deliberately for a certain activity. Such a limit may originate from values or norms, legislation or the organization itself. In the last case, this could be managing via control measurements and corrective actions, activities, such as costs, in such a way that these limits are not surpassed.

Lock-in mechanisms

Lock-in mechanisms result in situations where switching costs prevent actors from moving to a new situation. A lock-in can relate to technologies, investments in plant, organizations, past training efforts and so on.

Often, lock-in is the consequence of co-evolution of technology, products, markets, organizations and so on. Because of this, interdependencies can become so tight that a change in one of the factors required to be successful has to be made at the same time that the other factors are being adapted. To change all of the factors increases the switching costs to such an extent that the costs are perceived as being too high in comparison with the benefits (which are often short-term ones).

The following example illustrates how particular pieces of technology can become more and more intertwined during the lifecycle of the product in which they are embedded.

At the beginning of the 1980s, everyone became aware of the waste caused by internal combustion engines. The engine, as it had evolved in the course of 50 years or so, seemed at the end of its lifecycle – it was considered a mature product. A way to decrease its production of pollutants such as nitrogen and carbon dioxide was to increase the temperature at which the petrol burned. To achieve this, however, other more heat-resistant materials were required. Luckily, ceramics technology and engineering materials were so far developed that these types of materials had properties that made them suitable for use in the construction of engines. A number of companies therefore started new projects with the intention of ultimately developing a ceramic engine. However, during the process, it became clear that the whole engine had to be redesigned. Also, production technology had to be changed to manufacture such engines in large enough quantities for reasonable prices. Altogether, the costs of designing and testing the new engine became prohibitive. At the same time, it became clear that using modern CAD technology, better cylinders could be constructed with improved burning efficiencies.

An example of how hard and soft components of technology can become so much intertwined, resulting in a lock-in situation, is the QWERTY keyboard.

The QWERTY keyboard and the combustion engine are examples of lock-in, characterized by the fact that there are switching costs.

It was developed at the beginning of the lifecycle of the typewriter to actually slow down the typing speed, as the mechanics of those first typewriters did not allow for fast typing. However, the technology of typewriters improved. These improved typewriters allowed for faster typing. Many attempts have been made to introduce keyboards with better arrangements of letters, but none has survived because typists are skilled in using QWERTY keyboards and make too many mistakes using other keyboards.

In this case, the switching costs were too high. The mutual dependency between the typists' skills and the hardware bound the market so tightly that it proved to be a real limiter for change. Thus, the QWERTY keyboard and the combustion engine are examples of lock-in, characterized by the fact that there are switching costs.

Other examples relate to reputation where trust is the important factor and the acquisition of additional information to buy a certain product from another firm determines the switching costs. The importance of customer loyalty for the market position of a company is well known. Corporate and brand images are important ingredients for creating customer loyalty. However, other mechanisms may also be used to increase the switching costs for customers, such as the saving action (saving of air miles) or the possession of videos, CDs and computer applications programs that are very closely linked to a certain hardware platform. The building up of switching costs creates irreversibilities in a certain development path. It results in the fact that history does matter, as we discussed in Chapter 2, and is one of the mechanisms that causes 'path dependencies'.

Strong lock-in effects are connected with investments in capital goods, the acquisition of certain skills or the development of certain models – also called mental models – of how the world around us operates. The last type of lock-in does not normally involve switching costs.

Models help us to interpret what happens around us. At the same time, they determine how we look at our environment and help us to select according to certain signals and patterns. Other signals and patterns are denied. This makes substituting a new model for an established one so difficult, especially when the people in our immediate environment hold the same mental models. We miss the challenge of deviating views, having 'group think' instead, and the organization is locked into certain solutions.

The ways we work determine the structure and systems of the organization. This may determine dependencies between people and the power relationships within an organization. Change will be resisted in these instances by the people who have something to lose and who also have the power to resist change effectively. These organizational lock-ins can be strengthened by the type of technology used and the product architecture.

An example from the computer industry is Digital Equipment Corporation (DEC). Founded in 1957, this was a highly innovative company in the early years and certainly one of the most successful. However, in the late 1980s and early 1990s DEC got locked into its own success formula, denying the upcoming PC industry with its own standards. The company stuck with its proprietary hardware and software too long and ultimately found itself bought by the PC producer Compaq.

Another well-known example is that of the Ford organization in the late 1970s, when top management was convinced that Americans only liked the big comfortable cars that Ford made them and that the popularity of the smaller Japanese and European cars was just a temporary fad. At that time, the designers at Ford were very powerful and prohibited changes coming from manufacturing that would improve production, making cars cheaper and of a higher quality in terms of reliability. The 'not invented here' syndrome comes from such closed organizational mental models.

Lock-in mechanisms decrease flexibility and innovativeness and are similar to the core rigidity concept proposed by Dorothy Leonard-Barton (1995).

Whereas lock-in of the company itself must be prevented, lock-in of customers increases the switching costs they incur if they buy competitors' products and erects barriers to entry for potential new entrants. Thus, it increases the attractiveness of the market and the company's market position. The same may hold true for the positioning of the companies to their suppliers. Of course, competitors who are locked into a certain position are one of the best things management can encounter.

Lock-in mechanisms can be viewed as the memory system of a business as the past is somehow reflected in these situations. This retention of the past makes operation more efficient, but hinders change and innovation. Leonard-Barton discusses in her book *Wellsprings of Knowledge* (1995) how core competences can result in core rigidities. She distinguishes several dimensions of core capabilities that can be the elements of core competences but also of core rigidities. These are:

- physical systems
- managerial systems
- skills and knowledge
- values.

These elements are the same as those discussed here in relation to lock-in mechanisms.

Reinforcing loops, by increasing lock-in mechanisms as a consequence of their operation, result in path dependencies of developments, as discussed in Chapter 1.

Managing lock-in mechanisms is therefore an important route to creating shareholder value.

DBM and business simulation support this approach. In Part 3, we will discuss the applications for management in more detail.

Time delays

Time delays occurring in feedback loops are often the cause of counter-intuitive results. One of the most well-known examples is called the 'pig cycle'. It is a kind of parable. Because of high prices for pork, all pig breeders decide to increase the number of pigs they raise. After a certain period, the result of this decision is that the supply of pork exceeds demand and prices go down. Because, ultimately, people can eat only a certain amount of meat, the market cannot expand beyond a certain size, so prices go down and everybody loses money. The next year, the opposite occurs. Demand exceeds supply and prices rise. This goes on in a cyclical way for a time.

The pig cycle is familiar in mature industries where economies of scale are large and investment decisions take a while to implement.

Pig cycles are also known in science-based industries, such as the pharmaceutical industry where all the companies seem to pursue the same types of drugs, based on this mechanism. At certain times, everybody is working on calcium antagonists or ACE inhibitors or whatever seems to be a unique and profitable scientific option on which to base new drugs.

Time delays are not only visible in pig cycles. There are other cases when time delays result in cyclical behaviour of the system. One such example is in human resource management, where the decision to hire new personnel and the time delay caused by training may result in such cyclical behaviour of the system.

Time delays can be the result of entering a vicious loop that is hard to stop. A familiar example is work overload. You hire extra personnel. They need coaching and training. This requires the input of experienced personnel, decreasing the available capacity for a while. The work overload increases. This may result in hiring even more personnel, with the same effects, and so on.

Selection mechanisms

Selection mechanisms are central to economic systems. Markets are the archetypal social selection mechanisms, where customers decide to buy certain products or services based on their preferences and perceptions of the qualities of the products. Selection is a digital, yes or no, decision. In NPD and NBD, a whole hurdle race of selection mechanisms exists in the form of test screens and milestone reviews. All these selection mechanisms reflect somehow the selection of what creates most net value to the company. Therefore, it reflects the criteria used by customers, shareholders and internal stakeholders.

Besides such selection mechanisms, legislation has become an increasingly important one. In regulated industries, such as pharmaceuticals, it has long played a dominant role, but also now in the chemicals industry it is, more and more, one of the most important driving factors for innovation.

Variation and creation mechanisms

Sources of innovation

The last type of non-linear mechanisms relates to sources of innovation in the system. Sources of innovation are localized 'noise' in the system that can start a reinforcing loop and thus may lead to a complete shift in all positions. Science, suppliers, markets, competition, these may all be sources of innovation. In certain industries well-defined sources are recognized, such as science in the science-based industries of pharmaceuticals, for example, and suppliers in the so-called supplier-based industries of agriculture and construction. Special groups in the markets, such as the leading users, can also be important as a source of innovation, or special trendsetters in the more design-oriented industries.

> *Sources of innovation are localized 'noise' in the system that can start a reinforcing loop and thus may lead to a complete shift in all positions.*

Options and flexibility

The opposite of lock-in mechanisms is options. Whereas a lock-in mechanism destroys value, options create value as they are sources for further innovation. Options are only present when you can change from one state to another. In other words, options are very much related to flexibility. By increasing flexibility, we can choose from alternatives and, at the right moment, go in a direction that generates greater value.

Options, you may recall from earlier, can be defined as rights to buy or sell a certain underlying value. An option costs money, but the downside risk is limited. In cases of uncertainty and dynamic situations, the value of flexibility is higher than in static conditions. Using the real options theory, we can calculate the value of this flexibility. When the possibilities of exercising the option decrease, this lowers the value of the option.

In the case of research, the acquisition of knowledge can be thought of as an option, the utilization of this knowledge as exercising an option. When a new research project is begun, only a vague idea exists as to what can be done with the new technology that will result. By taking into account all the options and trying to evaluate these situations, multiplying the value by the estimated feasibility of these options, you can get an idea of the real value of this knowledge. The value of research, therefore, depends on the various ways in which it will be used and, therefore, on the capabilities of the company.

Keeping options open as long as possible is a wise and valuable strategy. However, doing this often costs money. Specialization delivers cost advantages, as we all know, but decreases flexibility and, therefore, destroys value. Networks open up opportunities for companies, increase their flexibility and thereby create value. Keeping your options open and even creating new ones by, for example, acquiring knowledge by means of partnerships in situations of high volatility creates net value.

Scenario planning and simulation can be strong support tools when you are analyzing the feasibility, viability and economic value of options. DBM and business simulation may support this approach. In Part 3, we will discuss the applications for management in more detail.

Discussion

In this chapter, we have discussed six non-linear mechanisms, each of which can be divided further into a limited number of subclasses. The various non-linear mechanisms are well recognized and play essential roles in NPD and NBD. There are various ways in which to classify them. In Table 6.1, we have mapped these mechanisms to the three Ps. Note that all of them – position, people and process – are linked to these mechanisms.

These mechanisms are the result of certain configurations of processes and structural elements of the business system. They determine the part of the system's behaviour that is of interest with regard to innovation. It makes innovation interesting because small effects, such as small investments, can have large effects. It shows the mechanisms behind innovation – that is, removing barriers, lifting limits to growth, virtuous reinforcing loops and so on. It also shows the mechanisms that prevent innovation and change, such as lock-in mechanisms, and the risks associated with innovation – unintended reinforcing loops. Fundamental to innovation are the variations that happen in certain places, the sources of such variations or new ideas. These variations incorporate the mechanism that separates innovation from random noise in a system–selection mechanism.

Table 6.1 The relationships between non-linear mechanisms and the three Ps – position, people and process

Non-linear mechanisms	Position	People	Process
Reinforcing loops			●
Limiting loops	●		●
Lock-in mechanisms	●	●	●
Time delays			●
Selection mechanisms		●	●
Variation and creation mechanisms			●

In Figure 6.8, you can see how different process configurations can result in the various non-linear mechanisms. In Part 1, we discussed two important aspects of dynamic systems – evolution and self-organization. Evolution is the result of the three fundamental mechanisms of variation and creation, selection and lock-in. All three have been discussed in this chapter. In self-organization, too, a number of non-linear mechanisms play a role, such as reinforcing loops, limiting loops, lock-in mechanisms and time delays.

These non-linear mechanisms dominate the overall behaviour of the innovation arena. It is especially interesting to note their presence in NPD and NBD. Reinforcing loops result in the amplification of small events into large results. Lock-in mechanisms may create customer loyalty or prevent competition from attacking your customer base. Selection mechanisms may result in customers preferring your products to those of the competition. Non-linear mechanisms may benefit the competition instead of your own company, however.

By knowing the mutual interactions that occur in the NPD and NBD processes, we are better able to create reinforcing loops that increase quality and speed and decrease costs at the same time.

Having insight into these non-linear mechanisms can be very profitable for your company. Knowing them better than other companies and being better able to use them to your company's advantage may make the difference between success and failure. As discussed before, Intel and Microsoft profit from these non-linear mechanisms, as do a number of other firms such as Netscape, Yahoo!, IBM, Merck and all the other companies that grow, prosper and create customer, shareholder and internal stakeholder value.

By knowing, for example, the mutual interactions that occur in the NPD and NBD processes, we are better able to create reinforcing loops that increase

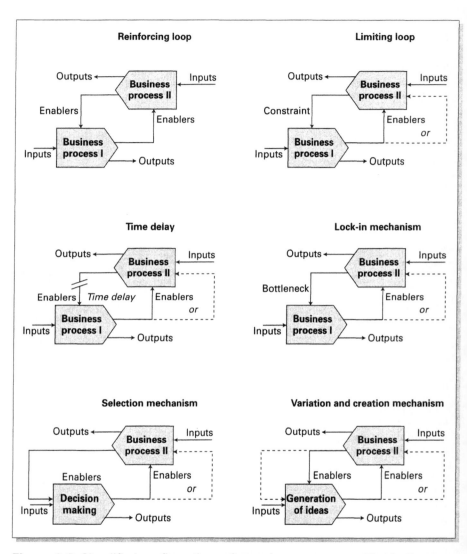

Figure 6.8 Simplified configurations of generic processes resulting in the non-linear mechanisms

quality and speed and decrease costs at the same time. When, hundreds of years ago, German chemical industries started to hire scientists, they made the conditions for the emergence of a reinforcing loop between science and technology development that propelled these companies to the forefront of their industries. The same happened at Bell with Bell Labs and Philips with its Research Labs. Later on, the situation changed and companies that had closer links with their markets created advantage for themselves. Ericsson and

Nokia, for example, benefited from the special situation in their home countries, where low population density means that using mobile phones is cheaper than using conventional telephone lines. The Internet bookshop amazon.com has been able to become one of the fastest-growing because it could remove several of the constraints that other physical bookshops have to deal with. Microsoft has been so successful not only because of the reinforcing loop it created between hardware and software development, but also because it has made use of other reinforcing loops – those of the extended network of users and the lock-in effect brought about by the developed skills of the users of MS-DOS and Windows, which were caused by their accumulation of certain software programs and documents written in these programs.

All companies that profit from economies of scale – be they in production, marketing or R&D – profit from a reinforcing loop that exists between the scale of operations, costs, price and market size. Such economies of scale, in their turn, rest on reinforcing loops of spillovers from numbers of products and projects, costs, prices and market share.

Companies can even profit from their knowledge of time delays if they are better than their competitors at shortening such delays in feedback time and time of implementation. Often the solution is to design another feedback loop with a much shorter cycle.

7 | Modelling the innovation and NPD and NBD processes – dynamic business modelling

Introduction

In this chapter, we will briefly discuss how to translate the model of the NBD processes and the diagnosed non-linear mechanisms into a computer model using system dynamics. We will discuss how to validate this computer model and will also discuss the role of sensitivity analysis. We will then move on to an analysis of parts of the model that can be simplified or must be refined further. It is also possible to discover areas where further study is needed to refine the relationships and 'calibrate' the parameters. Figure 7.1 shows the steps we have looked at so far, highlighting the fifth step, which is the subject of this chapter.

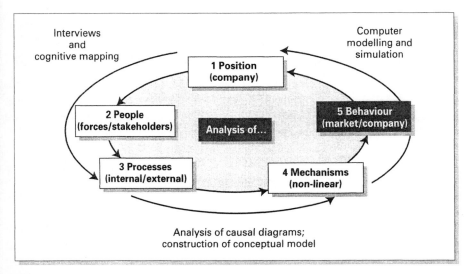

Figure 7.1 The steps involved in the DBM process – the fifth step is analysis of behaviour using computer modelling

Computer modelling

There are two main approaches to modelling business processes with their variants:

- static modelling of flows and transformations:
  - graphical flow diagramming methods;
- dynamic modelling of the processes:
  - discrete event modelling;
  - continuous system modelling or modelling system dynamics.

In the previous chapter, we described the static modelling of business processes. A large number of tools have been developed supporting this type of modelling based on flow diagramming protocols or on soft system methodologies. There are several books on the market that discuss the various approaches, such as Michael Pidd's *Tools for Thinking: Modelling in management science* (1996), and more specialist books, such as *Group Model Building* by J. Vennix (1996) and *Modelling for Learning Organizations* by John Morecroft and John Sterman (1994). This last book deals with modelling system dynamics in particular. It describes both graphic methods and computer modelling using specialized software. In this chapter, we will concentrate on this modelling approach.

Three software packages are available that can be used to model system dynamics:

- Ithink from High Performance Systems Inc, Hanover, USA;
- Vensim from Ventana Systems Inc, Belmont, Massachusetts, USA;
- Powersim by the Powersim Corporation, Virginia, USA, Raston, and Isdalsto, Norway.

All three software packages are derived from system dynamics software programs developed in the 1970s and 1980s at the MIT by Jay Forrester and his colleagues. Demonstrations of these types of software can be downloaded from the Internet by visiting the following websites:

- Ithink at http://www.hps-inc.com
- Powersim at http://www.powersim.com
- Vensim at http://www.vensim.com

All three software packages are operated by using simple icons for certain functions, such as stock, flows, converters and arrows. The stock icon can represent stocks of products or materials or cash, but also market size or soft variables, such as motivation, or else the performance of a certain product or technology.

While the stock icon represents the outputs and/or inputs of a certain process, the flows icon represents the transformation process involved in making the inputs into outputs. Every period a certain amount of the input is transformed into an output according to certain rules and this process is represented by a circle attached to a line. Sometimes the input is, in principle, unlimited, in which case a cloud icon is placed at the start of the flow. When the output forms an unlimited reservoir, the flow ends in a cloud icon.

The transformation of inputs into outputs is dependent on a number of factors which are represented by the converter icons. Connections between the various elements are delineated by arrow icons. Figure 7.2 shows these various elements.

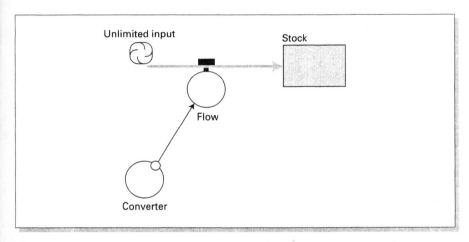

Figure 7.2 Example of the icons used in system dynamics software packages, courtesy of Ithink

Figure 7.2 shows what Ithink looks like, but Vensim and Powersim have similar icons and programming environments.

In the first phase of computer modelling activities, you enter your flow diagrams using the icons of your chosen software package. This is demonstrated in Figure 7.3.

In this model, we have added a number of elements that may influence product development, such as skills, activities involved, limitations and performance of technology. We have filled in certain values in the various converters. While doing this, it is important to be aware of the various units you use.

Now we can simulate what will happen in this simple model. The results are shown in Figure 7.4.

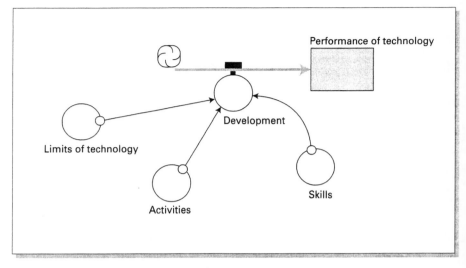

Figure 7.3 A simple model of product development

We can see the familiar sigmoid curve. In the beginning, progress is slow, but gradually the pace increases. When knowledge of the product grows, developing it becomes easier. We introduced here a simple reinforcing loop.

The familiar sigmoid curve. In the beginning, progress is slow, but gradually the pace increases.

After some time, the opportunities to improve the performance of the product decrease because the limits of the technology used are approached. Here, therefore, a limiting loop is becoming apparent. The presence of reinforcing and limiting loops causes this sigmoid curve.

The next stage is to improve our simple model in various ways. For example, we can add other product attributes. The speed of development of the various attributes may be different.

We can also add all kinds of other dependencies. For example, skills may improve during the process. The performance of the technology may depend on research. Furthermore, the dependence on skills, methods and capacity may be non-linear. We can imagine that, below a certain critical level, no progress at all is made and that, above a certain level, there is no additional advantage to be had by adding more capacity or acquiring better skills. We can also imagine that after introducing the product into the market, the growth and feedback from the market improve the testing approaches for the prototypes, which speeds up development. In other words, after starting with a simple, basic model of a central process, we can start to refine this model and add other components. We can introduce other processes and connect the processes with each other.

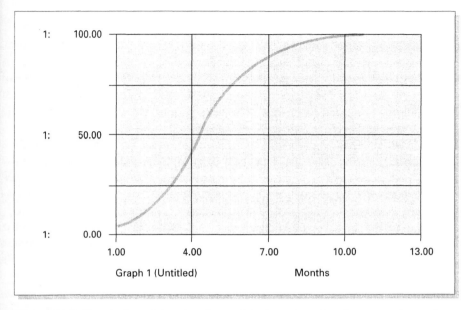

Figure 7.4 Simulation of the simple model of product development shown in Figure 7.3

In this model, we defined four product attributes: efficacy, efficiency, ease of use and design. We also defined different skills and efficiency of methodologies in the development of these various attributes. The result is different rates of progress of the various product attributes.

In the next step, we can add details regarding research, market introduction, milestone reviews, teambuilding processes and so on to this model. We can extend it as far as we want. In building models there is the tendency to overcomplicate things. We need to decide what extra complexity adds to our understanding and at what point the model becomes a kind of black box because of its numerous interactions. All of this depends, of course, on the knowledge and skills of the model's builders and users, how much complexity they think is appropriate. Generally, it can be said that using these types of dynamic models increases the knowledge and skills of both parties and, over time, more complicated models can be built. However, there is an additional factor that may limit the complexity of the model – the need to validate the model and calibrate parts of it.

Validation and calibration of the model

Validation of the model can be divided into internal and external validation. Internal validation means checking that the model does not contain functions and parameter values that are not allowed. The software contains a number of controls that guard the internal validity of a model. Furthermore, a certain amount of mathematical proficiency helps to prevent mistakes being made that lower the internal validity of the model.

External validity can be subdivided into structural and dynamic validity. Structural validity has to do with the quality of the model with respect to how well it resembles the structure of the situation you want to model. This relies on the use of the right parameters and right relationships between the parameters. Structural validity is one of the key factors in the earlier phases of modelling, when the diagrams are constructed. However, it is also important because in translating a diagram into a computer model, certain elements may be presented in different ways. Structural validation can be achieved by consulting experts and comparing the model with those of published studies, where the structure of models of certain processes found there may be based on surveys and statistical research. Although these last types of models are important to use when available, they often lack the connections between additional processes that are included in the models of system dynamics. Also, quite often, they miss out all kinds of feedback loops and mutual interactions. Therefore, models to be found in the literature are of only a limited value and must be used with discretion, making the advice of an expert consultant especially important at the beginning of the modelling process.

Dynamic validation focuses on how accurately the behaviour of the model resembles that of the real system.

In Figure 7.5, you can see a sensitivity analysis, varying the upper limit of the graph. Figure 7.6 shows a sensitivity analysis of the skills identified in the model.

Dynamic validation focuses on how accurately the behaviour of the model resembles that of the real system. If the real system behaves in a rather linear way, a good model of it must reflect this closely. This can be achieved by calibrating the behaviour of the model appropriately. Production and logistical systems are often approximate linear systems.

In the case of models of NBD processes that are characterized by their nonlinear behaviour, and it is this behaviour that is the central point of the modelling effort, dynamic validation and calibration must be approached differently.

Real calibration is impossible, because small, unexpected events may have large consequences. In these cases, it is important to understand the relative importance of the various processes and mechanisms of the qualitative behaviour,

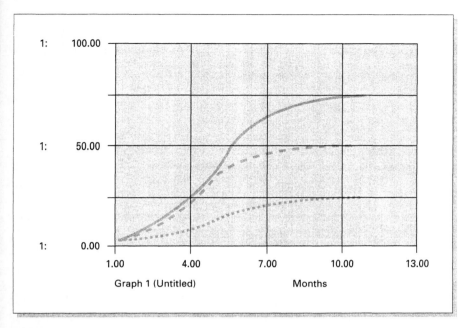

Figure 7.5 A sensitivity analysis

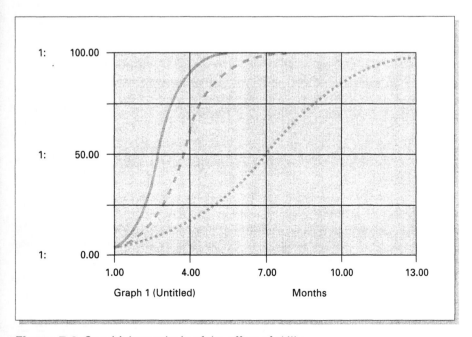

Figure 7.6 Sensitivity analysis of the effect of skills

the trends in the real world. It is especially important to model the consequences of the various interventions we or other stakeholders can perform. We want to learn more about the relative importance of time, quality, market position. We want to know more about the effects of allocating limited resources to, for example, marketing versus research or development.

This type of validation is best done by using well-known cases and trying to validate the qualitative behaviour – the trends in the model – to what happened in the case.

It is necessary as you are doing this to ask questions that are important to getting a better understanding of the case and the real world. In other words, the modelling process becomes a learning experience in itself, where all involved members will learn from each other. While 'jogging' their own memories, they can become aware of things they had either long forgotten or never put into words, such as intuitions.

Sensitivity analysis

The objective of sensitivity analysis is to learn more about the effect of changes in parameter values on the outcomes of the simulation. This is an important area where computer modelling proves its superiority over the other modelling methods. We can learn more about the importance of the various parameters in relation to certain structural characteristics of the model. For example, by means of sensitivity analysis of model variants of the NBD process it has become clear that often time to market is more important when:

- there are reinforcing loops present relating to market share;
- there are lock-in mechanisms present relating to customer behaviour.

In cases of connected markets, time to market is one of the most crucial elements. For example, hardware and software markets are connected and when customers do not shift easily to other hardware or when they are used to certain software, the time it takes for new products to be available is very important to them.

In other cases where switching costs are not present, the quality to price ratio may be more important.

When, however, quality is related to network externalities, time to market will be essential. For example, the number of users of word processing programs is such a factor.

In this way, computer simulation helps to find what the important elements in NPD and NBD are so that these may be incorporated into the development strategy.

The validation process – looking for the important parameters and gathering new data and information about field cases – is iterative and so is a learning process.

What DBM does is to codify and increase the speed of this learning process. A company using these methods can gain competitive advantage because it is faster in sensing new trends and recognizing successful behavioural procedures, and has a laboratory at its disposal to help it formulate new rules to compete in the marketplace.

> *The validation process is iterative and so is a learning process. What DBM does is to codify and increase the speed of this learning process.*

This last point has been stressed by the various pioneers in this field of applying system dynamics methodology to the creation of business strategies, such as Peter Senge (1994), John D. Morecroft and John Sterman (1994), and many others.

The most important attribute of the computer modelling approach to solving complicated problems in business is not that it delivers ready answers, but that it helps managers to ask much more sophisticated questions and this speeds up the learning process. In addition, it helps to formulate shared/joint models that we can use to interpret the world around us. This can support teambuilding and, in this way, may also lead to more successful strategies being designed. We will come back to this in Chapters 8 and 9.

Part 3

Dynamic innovation in chaotic markets – profiting from the non-linearities of the innovation process

8 | DBM – speeding up organizational learning

Introduction

In Chapter 1, we referred to John L. Casti (1997), who has studied complex adaptive systems and the behaviour of non-linear systems. He has summarized the characteristics of the behaviour of complex adaptive systems as being the following:

- inconsistent phenomena – that is, the existence of paradoxes;
- large effects from small changes – that is, instability
- behaviour transcends rules – that is, incompatibility;
- behaviour cannot be broken down into parts – that is, connectivity;
- self-organizing parts – that is, emergence.

These principles apply to a large number of non-linear systems. The emergence of the Internet can be considered as one of the most recent and well-known examples to which these principles can be applied.

The important issue, however, is how can insight into the characteristics of the innovation process be translated into more successful innovation management?

Let us look at Casti's principles a little more closely.

- **Large effects from small changes**
  We have demonstrated a number of times that, because of the fact that small effects can have large effects, instability is what makes innovation so interesting as a way to improve your position.
- **Behaviour transcends rules**
  Richard D'Aveni (1994) in his book about hypercompetition has argued that constantly inventing new rules of competition and developing new business models – that is, reinventing the industry – is the only way to keep ahead of the competition. However, you never know beforehand whether or not a new business model will be successful.

⦿ Behaviour cannot be broken down into parts

We have stressed over and over again that behaviour cannot be broken down into parts – that is, connectivity drives the non-linear behaviour of the system.

⦿ Self-organizing parts

Self-organizing parts – that is, the emergence of new businesses and internal structures of companies – can often be observed. For example, e-mail has had a larger effect on how organizations operate than many deliberate management interventions.

⦿ Inconsistent phenomena

This principle recognizes the existence and importance of paradoxes. This, the first of Casti's principles, we have kept until the end to explore further.

Innovation has often been characterized by paradoxes such as:

- ⦿ 'innovation is creative destruction';
- ⦿ 'successful innovation needs both chaos and control';
- ⦿ 'innovation management is directed at reducing uncertainty, but, at the same time, makes use of uncertainty';
- ⦿ 'innovation is focused on removing barriers or bottlenecks, but also creates new barriers and bottlenecks, both anticipated and unanticipated';
- ⦿ 'innovation can be considered to be an event as well as a process'.

Managing these paradoxes seems to be one of the most conspicuous differences between this and other management fields, such as production and logistics.

Managing paradoxes seems to be one of the most conspicuous differences between this and other management fields, such as production and logistics.

It is these paradoxes that were the starting point for Shona Brown and Kathleen Eisenhardt (1998) when they defined their management principles in their book *Competing on the Edge: Strategy as structured chaos*. Christensen (1997) has shown in his book *The Innovator's Dilemma* how the success of innovators may prevent them from making further innovations. In Parts 1 and 2, we have discussed a number of times how virtuous loops, which help companies to grow, may result in lock-in effects.

How to handle these inconsistencies and paradoxes and how to profit from the non-linearities of the innovation process are the subject of Part 3.

In the next three chapters, we will discuss how dynamic business modelling (DBM) can support innovation management. We will describe various ways in which companies can profit from their insight into the peculiarities of, and linkages between, the generic processes and the non-linearities of the innovation process, both inside and outside the company.

In this chapter, we will discuss how DBM can help in gaining insight into those dynamic parts of the business system that have the strongest influence on the outcome of the innovation and new product development and new business development (NPD and NBD) processes and in locating the white spaces – those parts that are important and about which knowledge is incomplete or even absent. The combination of the knowledge about the important parts and the white spaces of the DBM can help us to focus our business intelligence activities and market research effectively. It helps us to formulate better research questions and, in combination with the performance measurements, using, for example, balanced scorecards, can provide a tool that helps to integrate the management of the NPD and NBD processes with strategic management.

The learning organization

Innovation, by definition, changes the structure of markets, industries, the organization of companies, and, by definition, all this, in turn, affects the innovation process itself. Therefore any insight we have into the process will age quickly and so we need to be learning constantly. We must continually revise our mental models of the innovation process. It is therefore best to think of DBM as a continuous activity that can be divided into a number of phases.

The first phase of DBM provides us with a prototype model based on the readily available knowledge within the organization. It supports the inventorization, codification, integration and validation of the existing knowledge about the business development processes inside and outside the company. This initial model of the business system is the starting point for a process of continuous improvement and adaptation of the business model.

DBM supports the knowledge spiral as proposed by Ikujiro Nonaka and Hirotaka Takeuchi (1995) (see Figure 8.1). They distinguish four phases in this knowledge-creation spiral; from tacit to explicit, externalization; from explicit to explicit, combination; from explicit to tacit, internalization; and from tacit to tacit, socialization.

DBM includes externalization and the combining of knowledge about the dynamics of business systems. Such combination of distributed parts of knowledge increases the knowledge base of all participants. It helps them to acquire knowledge, or generate even more. It starts as tacit knowledge that can only be transferred to other partners by working together.

DBM helps the validation of knowledge by comparing the results of computer simulations of real-life situations with actual outcomes and studying the reasons for any differences.

This situation can best be demonstrated by the learning loop devised by David Kolb (1981) (see Figure 8.2).

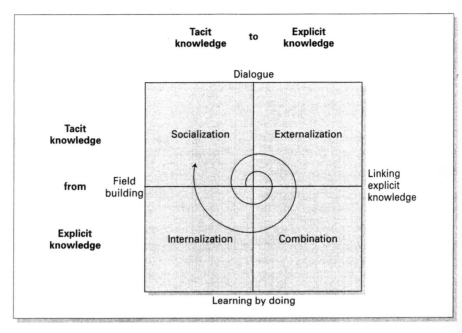

Figure 8.1 Nonaka and Takeuchi's knowledge spiral

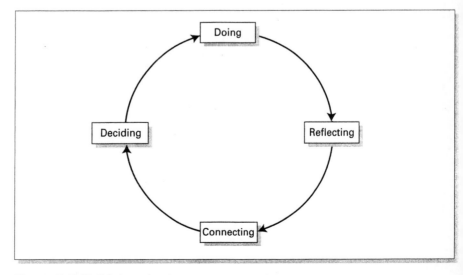

Figure 8.2 Kolb's learning loop

The learning activities in this model consist of 'doing', 'reflecting', 'connecting' and 'deciding'. By reflecting is meant analysis of the results of our acts. Often this will be on the gap between expected and actual outcomes.

Connecting is the incorporation of the results of our analysis into our previous experience. This includes our modelling activity. It supports organizational learning because it helps develop system thinking, which, according to Peter Senge (1994), is one of the five disciplines essential to learning organizations. It helps us to develop shared mental models.

Irrespective of whether our model is implicit, tacit or explicit, codified and communicable, we will use it to act and compare the expected outcomes of our actions with what happens in reality. Subsequently, we will reflect on any discrepancies between the expectations and actual events and try to learn from this. As a result, we will improve our implicit or explicit model.

Being aware of what we do not know and realizing how important this lack of knowledge is, is essential for the quality of data that must be acquired by subsequent studies.

DBM provides us with a model of NPD and NBD processes that is based on the integrated mental models the various managers have of the innovation arena. It is a necessary starting point, but, often, especially in the beginning, it is far from ideal. By performing sensitivity analysis and relating it to the robustness of the knowledge about those sensitive parts, we can reveal the white spaces of the model. This is already a very valuable outcome because, being aware of what we do not know and realizing how important this lack of knowledge is and, subsequently, asking the right questions in order to explore further, is essential for the quality of data that must be acquired by subsequent studies. Before the model is valid enough to be used as a support tool in decision making, it has to be adapted, improved and validated up to a certain level. This is also required in order to build enough trust and confidence in it within the team.

It is important to note that no model will ever be complete because:

- it must help in decreasing the complexity of real life to a point that makes it useful in decision making;
- businesses are changing rapidly, so our insight will always lag behind reality.

As in science, we constantly have to challenge our models. This continuous process of increasing our knowledge thanks to the models we use and our knowledge aging results in a situation where we never reach a state of complete knowledge. This makes it clear that learning is as important as delearning.

However, it is not absolute knowledge that is important, but what we know relative to what our competitors know. Having a knowledge advantage may result in designing better and smarter strategies than the competition and lead to more effective R&D management. This, in turn, may lead to more effective and efficient NPD and NBD and, thus, extra value creation for all the stakeholders. This, ultimately, may lead to a faster-growing and more prosperous company than would otherwise be the case.

It is important to run faster along the learning curve than our competitors and DBM may help to do this.

Because DBM helps to inventorize the relevant white spaces, formulate better questions and interpret new data better, it can be best to apply it first to business intelligence activities. These include all activities that have as their objective to increase our business understanding, such as external studies of the markets, competition, government activities, as well as the supply chain and internal business processes.

These studies are more productive when they are used together with a consistent model of the business involved. They may be even more productive when the model, at an early stage, integrates the important performance indicators and their drivers, as are used in shareholder and customer value calculations, activity-based costing methods and balanced scorecards.

In this chapter, we will discuss the integration of the various control and performance measurements into the DBM and will demonstrate how this may improve the business intelligence activities, increase the learning and innovative capabilities of the company and serve as a knowledge management instrument.

DBM and business intelligence – improving the extra-company process model

Sensitivity analysis provides us with insight into the relative importance of the various parameters and subprocesses (see Figure 8.3). Comparing this information with estimates about the exactness of the knowledge about these parts of the model helps us to localize the white spaces and formulate the right research questions about them.

One of the things that is often overlooked in marketing research of consumer goods is the way the product is used in the consumer process. The quality of the product may be dependent on the functionality of complementary products and the social setting in which the product is used. Changes in the features of the complementary product(s) may therefore affect the definition of product quality. This may affect the dynamics of market development and become apparent only after some time.

DBM may help us to gain insight into the importance of these various product markets to each other. For example, whereas the 386 computers were high-quality machines, and, even today, may provide enough computing power for most users if they were to have present-day operating systems and software programs installed, they would be too slow for almost all tasks. Equally, the fact that almost all households now have a refrigerator has led to the need to develop margarine and butter that can be spread on bread even at low temperatures.

DBM may also help to indicate that companies are not only competing against their direct competitors, but also against indirect ones. For example, in one model of the steel market, it became evident that, at a higher level, the steel sector was competing with the non-steel sector when it came to certain applications. In the long run, the model showed that this higher-level competition could well be more important than the direct competition. This situation suggested that cooperation with competitors in the steel industry to develop certain new types of steel or designs that made better use of the specific attributes of steel could be more profitable in the future than competing solely on price.

Figure 8.3 shows how the process of sensitivity analysis fits into a DBM.

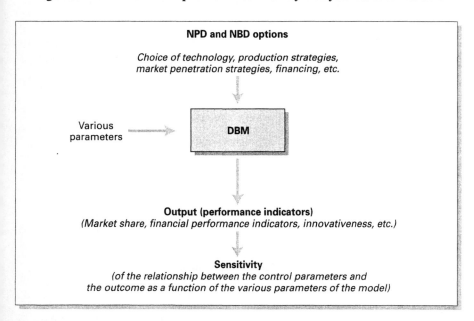

Figure 8.3 The process of sensitivity analysis

Business intelligence may provide us with information that may be used to improve the model. At the same time, it may help us to focus future business intelligence activities and make better use of scarce resources. Moreover, as a result of being able to interpret data better, we can make more use of it and plan future data collection better, too (see Figure 8.4).

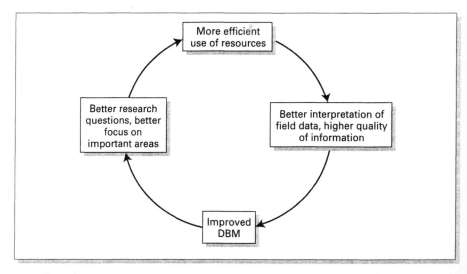

Figure 8.4 Causal relationships between business intelligence and DBM

In reality, in the situation shown in Figure 8.4, two learning loops can be distinguished – one relating to the interpretation of data, the other relating to improvement of the model on the basis of gaps observed between expected and real outcomes. This is presented in Figure 8.5.

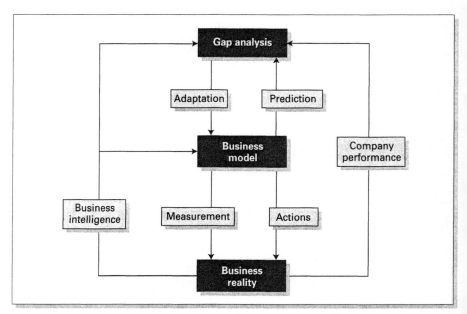

Figure 8.5 DBM and business intelligence and the two ways of learning

These two loops can be compared with, respectively, C. Argyris and D. Schon's (1978) single-loop and double-loop learning concepts. Single-loop learning is simple feedback learning based on data interpretation, with no change of rules and/or models.

Double-loop learning is higher-order learning in which rules and/or models are adapted. By using DBM in double-loop learning, this type of learning will be facilitated and accelerated.

Being the fastest and smartest-learning company in the industry may be one of the most important assets a company has when it tries to outrun the competition.

Being the fastest and smartest-learning company in the industry may be one of the most important assets a company has when it tries to outrun the competition.

Scenario planning as a means of accelerating organizational learning

Scenario planning is often recommended as a way of accelerating the learning process because it helps us to think 'out of the box' – that is, consider possibilities that are not normally given much thought when planning future activities. Especially when the time horizon is long and the dynamics of the environment are great, scenario planning can greatly help the learning process.

The use of scenarios was pioneered at Shell and developed further by a number of people who were involved in these early developments, such as Arie de Geus (1997), Kees van der Heijden (1996) and Paul Schoemaker (1995).

The most important role of scenario planning in the strategic management process is that of helping managers to step out of their established mental models and create possible futures that are not simply extrapolated in a limited way from the present. In this process of creation, it also helps managers to listen more closely to each other and not to focus on discussions relating to futile differences of opinion.

Kees van der Heijden distinguishes a number of steps in this strategy development and learning process:

- acknowledgement of aims, either as a result of an externally imposed mandate or the internal organization's dual purpose of survival and self-development;
- assessment of the organizational factors for success, including its ability to change;
- assessment of the environment, current and future, in all its uncertainty and ambiguity;
- assessment of the fit between the two;
- development of policies to improve the fit.

He explains the link between strategy and organizational learning as follows:

- the aim of strategy has to do with the driving force of the learning loop;
- the organizational success formula depends on the mental model and theories of the world;
- environmental scenarios are based on perceptions, differentiation, reflection on experience and seeing new patterns;
- the assessment of strategic fit happens when there is an integration of reflection into mental models;
- the development of policies to increase strategic fit is achieved by planning future steps.

The building of scenarios calls for creativity – artistic skills that go beyond the systematic analysis of DBM described in Part 2. DBM requires good analytical skills and provides a methodology that supports the systematic analysis of a business.

Combining the two approaches delivers a very strong approach that makes it possible to mobilize all knowledge about and insight into the business and, by using the creative potential of the company, stretch the models based on existing knowledge to become models of possible futures.

In Figure 8.6, you can see the relationships between the classical approach to strategic management, DBM and scenario planning.

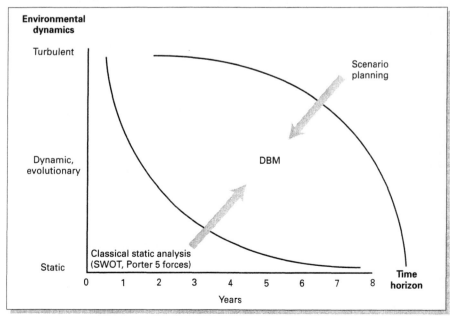

Figure 8.6 The relationships between classical, DBM and scenario methods of strategic management

The classical approach to strategic management was developed in the 1960s and continued into the 1980s. It was based on static analyses of the structure of the market and positions of the various stakeholders in the business. This approach is valuable in situations where extrapolations from present positions and trends is sufficient. This is the case in static environments or for short periods of time.

However, scenarios are the only possible approach to finding out about the future in very dynamic or turbulent environments or when we want to take into account long time periods of, say, more than ten years. Accurate extrapolations can be achieved only for the very stable and basic elements in a business, and we have to take into account all possible events that may happen in between.

DBM is an intermediary between these two extremes. The investment in time required to do this is too much when we are confronted with stable environments and we do not expect changes or when we only want to develop a policy for the coming six months to one year. However, for instances of situations, environmental dynamics and time periods in between these extremes, DBM is ideal.

It is also methodologically linked to both approaches in strategic management. On the one hand, it starts with the classical analysis of the business and extends this analysis by adding a dynamical analysis of forces, processes and mechanisms that affect the changes in accumulation and control over resources by the company and, consequently, its market and competitive position. On the other hand, it can be adapted to look at certain scenarios by including descriptions of processes that are not in place yet, but may become prominent in the future. Sometimes the model can be adapted quite easily to include these processes by changing the parameters. However, sometimes when changing a scenario, a more dramatic adaptation is called for. For example, it is possible to develop certain scenarios for the energy market in which a new type of stakeholder will appear and act as energy broker between energy producer and energy user – a role that is not present in regulated energy markets. In other words, the development of scenarios may help to develop DBM variants that have a certain flexibility. This may increase the value of DBM for strategic management because more options can be simulated and the value of these options, their critical factors and constraints can be studied better before taking any risks in the real world. In Figure 8.7, we have depicted this use of DBM in the development and valuation of strategic options.

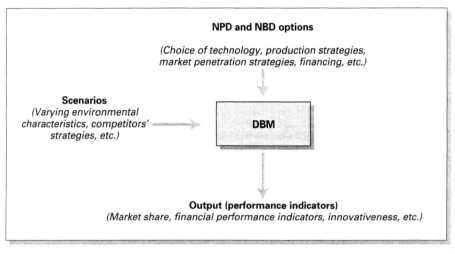

Figure 8.7 Using DBM in scenario planning

Growth strategies must be based on the creation of value for the various stake-holders, customers, shareholders and employees, and value creation is linked to the valuation of options.

DBM and benchmarking – improving the internal processes

Benchmarking is a longstanding way in which you can compare yourself to competitors in order to increase the company's competitiveness. It has been developed to a high level at Xerox. By benchmarking its internal processes with its Japanese competitors, staff at Xerox learned where they were lagging behind and what had to improve. In this way, the company was able to improve its processes and restore its competitive edge.

Growth strategies must be based on the creation of value for the various stakeholders, customers, shareholders and value creation is linked to the valuation of options.

Traditional benchmarking was restricted to comparing products, trying to obtain knowledge about the technology used and then imitating the best features. During the last decade, it has been developed further and is now an important instrument for learning from the 'best in class' in a certain function, process or activity, independent of industry, interpreting the lessons learned and improving internal processes.

This type of benchmarking is critically dependent on the insight into the generic processes that are encountered everywhere before translating the lessons learned to one's own situation.

DBM may play a critical role and be used as a tool that helps to look for the related processes, abstract from the idiosyncrasies, and then apply it to the special situation. In Figure 8.8, a template for benchmarking, as developed by G. Watson (1993), has been presented.

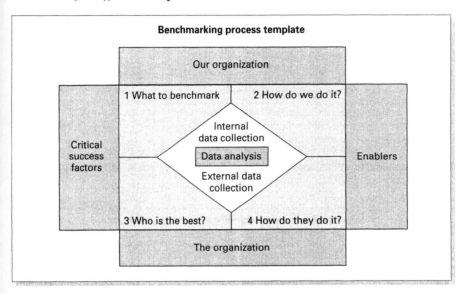

Figure 8.8 Watson's benchmarking template

Source: Watson, G., *Strategic Benchmarking*, © 1993. Reprinted by permission of John Wiley & Sons, Inc.

This template makes clear that insight into the basics of the business processes is essential for benchmarking, as, without real understanding, it is not known what to search for, how to interpret the critical success factors and enablers, and how to relate this information to an organization.

In Chapter 5, we discussed the generic internal NPD and NBD processes, and these make a good starting point for benchmarking.

In the benchmarking process, we want to learn more about the relationships between the enabling factors and performance of the business processes by learning from the best in class. In Figure 8.9, this is depicted using the general model of a business process.

For example, in this chapter, we said that the NPD and NBD processes could be classified into seven generic processes. It is essential that they are always in place, but, because the conditions for optimal working of these processes may be contradictory, usually one of the processes is optimized at a time, keeping the others in subordinate, supportive roles. One observation that can be made is that besides phasing the generic processes, particular ones are prominent in certain industries or certain types of companies, whereas others may not be recognized

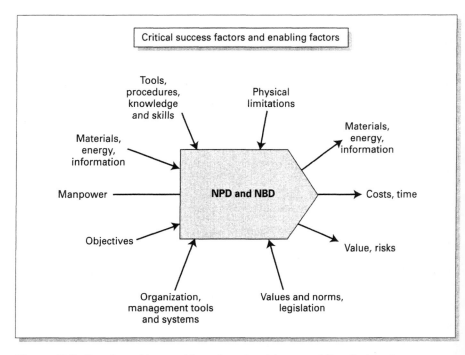

Figure 8.9 Benchmarking and learning about how enabling factors improve business processes

as being critical. For example, teambuilding is now known to be critical and so an emphasis, especially at the start of a new project, is put on building a high-performance project team. Such a team is one in which no one single person dominates all the time, but, rather, the team members leave room for each other in such a way that, when appropriate, others may take over the lead. This will not only prevent the situation where some disciplines dominate and others are underused, decreasing the number of options to choose from for a certain problem, but will also avoid certain generic processes dominating in all phases of the NPD and NBD processes, leading to stagnation in certain phases.

A few years ago, teambuilding was not recognized as being at all critical. Benchmarking has revealed, however, that certain innovative companies, such as 3M, put special emphasis on teambuilding. Similarly, it became apparent, by comparing practices in western and Japanese companies, that Japanese companies make better use of the knowledge distributed in them. By means of knowledge management, companies everywhere try to imitate this through a systematic inventorization of the various sources of knowledge inside and outside the company, a systematic analysis of its importance and codification of this knowledge. In this way, relevant knowledge is made accessible to a wider circle of employees.

Similarly, in certain professional organizations, such as management consultancies, where knowledge is their main asset, a good infrastructure for assembling, classifying and making accessible best practices to a wide internal audience has existed from a very early stage.

Benchmarking has shown that so-called 'skunk projects' – the making of very rough prototypes in the generation of ideas phase – help to formulate ideas and communicate these to each other. In other words, in this phase, linking ideas with prototyping is very helpful. However, the prototyping has to play a subordinate role to the ideas.

'Skunk projects' – the making of very rough prototypes in the generation of ideas phase – help to formulate ideas and communicate these to each other.

Benchmarking has also revealed that Japanese companies put more emphasis on the pre-project phase to inventorize the uncertain or risky aspects of the project and gather extra information about these aspects. Again, building prototypes to study these aspects in more depth and investigate the feasibility of the proposed solutions has paid off later on in terms of shorter development times, less repetition and improved quality.

DBM can also be used as a tool for benchmarking the best way to profit from the characteristics of processes outside the company. Studying how markets interact is most useful in highly connected markets, such as those in the information and telecommunications industry. Communication with investors is especially important in the biotechnology sector and, as it is so specialized an area, this may be one where the ability to communicate with relatively 'ignorant' investors, who do not know about the specifics of the technology, needs to be and so is highly developed. Most of these lessons have been well elaborated on in the literature on benchmarking. However, DBM provides a tool that facilitates and improves this aspect of benchmarking further.

The findings of research by Shell into companies that have lasted a long time, described by Arie de Geus (1997), were that such companies are tolerant of and sensitive to their environments. Both aspects play essential roles in the processes of generation of ideas and teambuilding. As both processes are essential for innovation, it is understandable that they played such a dominant role in survival.

Another aspect of DBM that relates to benchmarking is the inventorization of non-linear mechanisms inside and outside the company. For example, how other companies handle lock-in effects, caused by activities of separate departments being too closely linked together. Also, how other companies have established virtuous reinforcing loops between the various stakeholders by creating mechanisms that, in the process of growth, create value not only for customers and stakeholders but also for other stakeholders – internal and external partners, suppliers and retailers. Last but not least, how other companies integrate the sources of innovation into their overall NPD and NBD processes.

Discussion

In this chapter, we have discussed the use of DBM in a number of business intelligence activities that not only help to validate the business model but also aid the process of interpreting and relating the data to the particular business context being studied.

DBM is a continuous activity once it has started. At the beginning, a DBM prototype is constructed based on the existing knowledge distributed among the various managers and experts. This initial model is often far from optimal. However, when the core of the model is correct, it provides a sound basis that can be improved and elaborated on. The evolutionary metaphor discussed in Chapter 1 is very relevant here. Stuart Kauffman (1995) explains how systems that are based on a number of interacting elements can be projected on to a fitness landscape that consists of many hills and valleys. In Figure 8.10, such a fitness landscape with hills and valleys is represented. The higher the top of the hill, the fitter the system – fitness being represented by that hilltop. At the beginning, it is important that we start at the foot of a high hill. Then, as we improve, we change the model, we continue to measure its fitness. During this process, the fit of the model will become better and better – that is, more useful. Using the existing knowledge as well as possible gives us a greater chance of landing on a good, high hill. By optimizing the various steps in the improvement process, the rate of the evolution of the model will be as fast as possible, adding to the learning and innovative ability of the company.

As in nature, the business environment may change drastically and, thus, the fitness landscape may also change shape radically (see Figure 8.11). Hills that were once very high may become less so. How do we prevent ourselves from being stuck with a model that is outdated and may even be detrimental to us in the new situation? How do we avoid the problem of once successful models preventing us from changing to better ones?

DBM may also help to look out for parts of the environment that function as early warning signals, revealing new developments.

In this situation, a total revision of the model is necessary. Combining DBM with scenario planning can achieve this. Constantly challenging our models requires the kind of critical attitude essential in science. One way to stimulate this is to be always validating the model; another is to stimulate lateral thinking in the team.

Besides the aforementioned applications for DBM, it may also help to look out for parts of the environment that function as early warning signals, revealing new developments, and use these to assist in choosing which are the most important sources of data that become available via information and communications technology. In other words, a virtuous loop may be created of data warehousing improving DBM improving data warehousing.

During these activities, the DBM improves and needs to change constantly to reflect the situation within and outside the company. In this way, the company can better accommodate itself to the hypercompetitive environment discussed in Chapter 1.

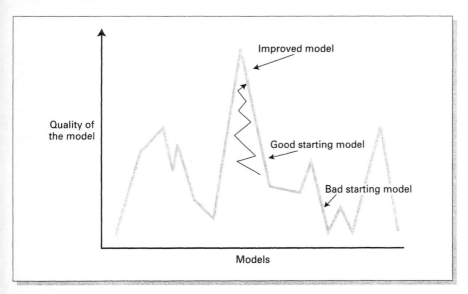

Figure 8.10 The way in which DBM improves the construction of optimal models of the environment

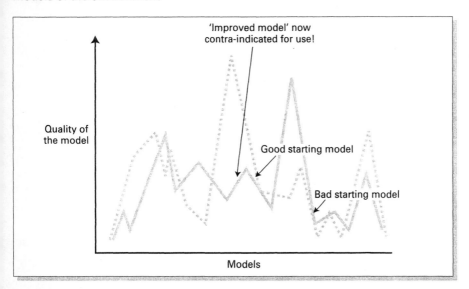

Figure 8.11 Changing situations can result in a model no longer being a good starting point

9 | Designing and redesigning business models and strategic management

Introduction

Strategic management has as its objective to develop, direct and mobilize the innovative capabilities of a company towards those targets that deliver most value to the stakeholders in the company.

Ideally, strategic management starts with a vision of the mission and position of the company in its environment. Based on this mission, a trajectory for the company is decided on and a plan drawn up to make this happen. Taking as the starting point our generic model of business processes at a high aggregate level – that is, the level of a business unit or at corporate level – strategic management has to set the goals of the company in such a way that the optimum net value is created by using its resources and abilities in the most effective and efficient way possible (see Figure 9.1).

Ideally, strategic management starts with a vision of the mission and position of the company in its environment. A trajectory for the company is decided on and a plan drawn up to make this happen.

The abilities of a company are determined by the enabling factors of the business process – namely, the tools (including the physical systems), knowledge and skills, organization, management systems and values. These are identical to the four dimensions defined by Dorothy Leonard-Barton (1995).

The trajectory is ideally based on a more or less shared model of the future business. This must not only be shared by most of the organization, but also be as close as possible to reality.

Strategic management consists of a number of activities, such as:

- monitoring and analysis of the trends in the environment and (re)definition of the mission of the company;
- (re)design of a business model that best fits the mission, abilities, characteristics and strategic goals of the company;

- selection of technology-product-market (TPM) combinations and allocation of resources to develop them – that is, portfolio management and (re)formulation of the business models and business objectives for these TPMs;
- planning the trajectory from present portfolio to future desirable portfolio – roadmapping;
- controlling the developments – strategic control.

In turbulent environments, strategic planning is difficult because of the unpredictability of markets. Such environments are characterized by the fact that, as we have seen, small events may have large consequences. Thus, operational decisions about, for example, product design and architecture may have significant consequences for the future.

Under these circumstances, it is important to look extra carefully for those vital weak signals and interpret them as early as possible. They are often observed first at the operational level by co-workers in close contact with the

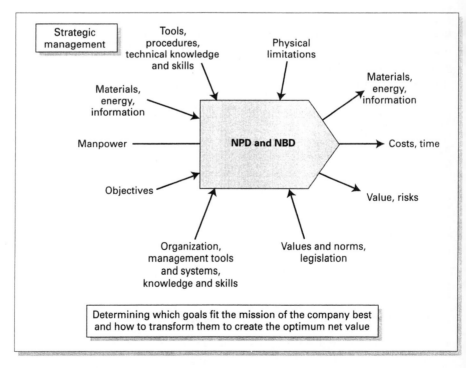

Figure 9.1 Strategic innovation management in relation to the various inputs and outputs of the business processes

key aspects of the environment, such as sales representatives and marketers, engineers and designers, plant managers, personnel staff and so on. The use of DBM may help to interpret these weak signals faster than would otherwise be possible because sensitivity analysis may indicate which parameters affect the outcome of the model most, and discrepancies between outcomes of the model and reality may stimulate analysis of the reasons for this deviation at an early stage. Working with the same DBM at all levels in the company – strategic and operational – helps to communicate these signals faster and less ambiguously. In this way, monitoring and analysis of the environment will become a continuous endeavour for the whole company.

In this chapter, we will focus on the second to fifth points in the list of strategic management activities above. First, we will describe the selection and planning of TPM combinations. Second, we will discuss the topic of strategic control with the help of a combination of DBM and balanced scorecards techniques.

Designing and redesigning business models – non-linear mechanisms and innovation strategies

In Chapter 6, we discussed in detail the various types of non-linear mechanisms that are so characteristic of the NPD and NBD processes.

In Table 9.1, the effects of non-linear mechanisms on a number of factors that affect strategic planning are summarized. The factors we have taken into account are:

- innovativeness
- growth
- flexibility
- quality
- speed
- cost
- risk.

The first three determine the overall shape of any strategic plan. The last four can also be applied to operations.

Table 9.1 Non-linear mechanisms and their effects on factors affecting strategic planning

Non-linear mechanisms	Innovativeness	Growth	Flexibility	Quality	Speed	Cost	Risk
Limiting loops	–	–	–				
Lock-in mechanisms		–		–			
Time delays		–	–	–			–
Selection mechanisms				+		+	+
Variation and creation mechanisms	+		+				
Reinforcing loops		+		+	+	+	–

Key
+ = positive effect
– = negative effect

One of the first objectives of strategic management is to determine the limits of the various parts of the business system. The technology, markets, legislation and the economy determine business limits, while the limits of these elements determine what opportunities exist for innovation and the areas where new breakthroughs in technology or its applications are needed. Lifecycle analyses of technology, products and markets are therefore the basis of strategic planning.

> *Technology, markets, legislation and the economy determine business limits, while the limits of these elements determine what opportunities exist for innovation.*

Because of the connectivity between various types of technology, using impact analysis, the most basic of these may be found on which to concentrate development activities. When technological limits cannot be lifted, it is better to leave that technology aside, outsource or consolidate.

Another way to look for sources of innovation is to analyze areas of high variation. Traditionally, these can be found in science and technology research centres, but there are others, such as market sectors where innovation holds a central position, such as the military sector, or there are new technical infrastructural systems, such as the Internet. Looking for special, innovative customers who can become lead users also falls into this area of analysis.

Strategic management must focus on localizing such sources of innovation and linking them to the business development process. This can be done by either incorporating them in one or another form or by partnering.

One point must be made in this context. In the past, a number of small, innovative companies have been acquired by larger companies, the objective of this being to increase the innovativeness of the acquiring company. In a number of cases, the early promise was not fulfilled because the huge number of rules the larger companies imposed on the acquired company killed all initiatives and the creative people left. The lesson to learn from this is that, for creativity to occur, there needs to be room for original ideas, lateral thinking and freedom to experiment. This may mean that, sometimes, certain common knowledge about technology, markets or customers must be ignored.

Kauffman (1995) has called this the 'logic of the patches' (see Chapter 3). He demonstrated in his simulation studies that the evolution of a system that is composed of a number of subsystems is faster when the subsystems are loosely linked to each other and can find their own optimum way of working than when, by means of co-evolutional forces, the various subsystems influence each other's evolution. The lesson that Kauffman draws from this is that departmentalization of organizations and modularization of products may have a positive effect on flexibility and development speed. We may add that compartmentalization of time – by defining phases separated by milestone reviews – may have a similar effect on the speed of developments. A certain isolation between the sources of innovation and the mainstream activities of the company is needed so that the opportunities are there to vary and experiment. We will discuss this topic in more detail in Chapter 10.

An important issue for strategic management is how to turn innovation into growth. Growth strategies must be based on the creation of virtuous loops, in which the creation of value for the various stakeholders takes centre stage.

The development of new technology, applications, markets and organizations will succeed only when they are linked to the creation of net value for the customer. Growth means that, in one or more of the reinforcing loops of the NPD or NBD processes, net value creation for customers, shareholders, suppliers and employees is linked. For example, the loop 'increase of market share, economies of scale, lower costs, lower prices' increases net value, as does the loop 'increase of market share, increase in economies of scale, progress along the experience curve, lower costs and/or higher quality, higher net value, higher market share' (see Figure 9.2).

Another reinforcing loop is that linking value creation and other stakeholders – the shareholders. This loop consists of innovations, higher levels of sales, higher income for shareholders, decreases in the cost of money, more investment in innovative projects and on to higher levels of sales. Another important reinforcing loop is that innovative companies are interesting places to work for innovative people. These companies may hire more innovative people by offering higher salaries. This makes the company more innovative and so on.

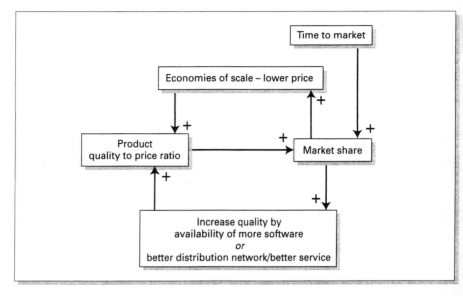

Figure 9.2 Time to market and the effect of reinforcing loops linked to market share

From this we can see that the global reinforcing loop (shown in Figure 9.3) is composed of a number of these smaller reinforcing loops.

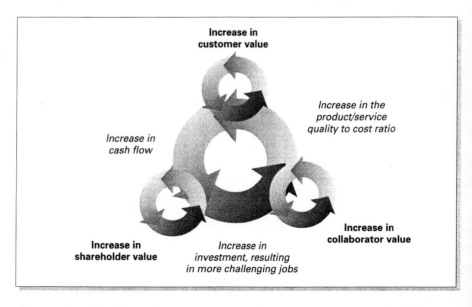

Figure 9.3 The circle of growth as a reinforcing loop composed of a number of smaller reinforcing loops

However, as we know from earlier, 'the trees' don't grow up to heaven. There are 'natural limits' to growth. If we know about them, we can see if we can shift or partially remove some of them. In this way, growth may continue. Limits to growth may be linked to the potential of markets. These may be shifted by developing other markets in other regions, other applications, other distribution channels, defining other market segments and so on.

The options for further growth may depend on the flexibility of the company. To what extent can the company switch to exporting, develop other markets, use other distribution channels?

The options for further growth may depend on the flexibility of the company.

Flexibility is highly dependent on lock-in mechanisms with respect to technology, organization, and investments in plant. The presence of such a mechanism means that there is a switching cost. Such costs are mostly financial, but sometimes the origin is psychological. Trust and perceived risks can constrain switching just as much as not having a big enough budget. Mental models may limit the scope of our visions and so determine our decision to switch or not. The 'not invented here' syndrome may be one of the outcomes.

Switching costs for other stakeholders, however, may be profitable for the company. It may prolong their being in favour of any move that maintains or increases the share value of the company. The lock-in effect other stakeholders can have when they oppose management's decisions has the opposite effect, of course. Such a lock-in mechanism also decreases flexibility in other ways because switching takes a lot of time – it cannot be done overnight.

Flexibility is related to variation and creation mechanisms. These mechanisms may feed flexibility. The creation of new products and alternatives increases the flexibility of the company.

Time delays also affect flexibility. Insight into time delays is therefore essential. For example, the hiring and training of new employees takes time. It also may decrease the existing capacity, because the new people need to be coached by the existing staff. This may mean that strategies planned previously may not succeed.

Quality is, as discussed before, not only determined by the attributes of the products or services *per se*, but also, at least partially, by their interactions with other complementary products, services and network effects. Economists call these effects 'network externalities'. Examples are the effects of the availability of complementary products (hardware, software and attendant services) or the penetration of other products (telephones and mobile phones). These network externalities can also lead to lock-in situations. For example, having invested heavily in certain software makes switching to other software standards costly.

These are the dynamic aspects of quality. In a similar way, costs have static and dynamic aspects. To know what these are is important for strategic management. The dynamic aspects largely determine speed and risks.

Achieving the right balance between quality and speed is also important in strategic management. In Chapter 7, you will recall, we discussed the dynamic elements that may affect this balance. An example of a mechanism that makes speed more important is the existence of reinforcing loops linked to market share.

Knowledge about the existence of vicious loops is also important, because these are the areas we want to stay far away from. Vicious loops are so detrimental that they can ruin the company. If we have to deal with a vicious cycle (related to quality aspects, reputation, organizational meltdown because of stress), it is like a physician dealing with a patient. A patient becomes ill because his body cannot rectify the situation. When the patient suffers shock, his blood pressure is too low for it to be rectified by increasing his heart rate. The low blood pressure results in less blood flow through his vital organs. Cells die and toxic components are freed that suppress the healthy functioning of the heart. His blood pressure reduces further, restricting blood flow to more essential organs. More detrimental toxic compounds are freed, and so on.

The physician tries to interrupt this cycle by taking away one of the elements in the loop. For example, he may give extra fluid, to boost the circulation, or vaso-constricting substances, to raise the blood pressure sufficiently so that the vital organs receive enough blood and oxygen.

In management, too, we can try to treat the company when it is taking a detrimental course by giving it strong medicines, such as cutting costs drastically. In the case of a vicious loop affecting its reputation, it may be wise to admit mistakes and correct them openly. In the case of organizational meltdown, because of stress and illness, we have to temper the number of projects we take on, refocus our efforts and restrict the rate of growth.

It is clear that such interventions cannot be part of normal management practice, being used solely to redirect a downward vicious loop. It is also clear that cost-cutting measures do not bring about NPD or NBD.

A number of authors have recommended generic strategies for NPD and NBD. Michael Porter's (1985) strategies are well known. He distinguishes four strategies along two dimensions, one of these being focus and diversification and the other distinguishing between cost and quality. Other authors have also set out simple rules that, when followed properly, may lead to the development of successful strategies. In this book, we will not follow this trend because we believe that permanently innovating technology, applications, markets and the organization is the only successful strategy for gaining sustainable competitive advantage. As soon as successful strategies are codified in rules and heuristics, they are no longer innovative, but can be imitated easily and so are no longer successful.

We think it is more important to understand your business better than the competition and, based on this better insight, new, innovative strategies can be developed and pre-tested with the help of DBM.

Maximizing stakeholder value

The wheel of growth is turned by the continuous creation of value for the stakeholders, especially that for customers, shareholders and internal stakeholders. These three drivers of growth are particularly critical and dissatisfaction among any of these groups may stop the wheel in its tracks. Networks are vehicles for growth only when all the partners have their part in the profits generated by them.

Various instruments have been developed to evaluate value creation for the stakeholders. Although they have become quite sophisticated, they are better suited to static situations than dynamic ones. Let us explain.

The various tools used to estimate customer value are based on the products' attributes, whereas the rest of the world is kept constant. In combined analysis, the value of various attributes is determined by investigating a limited number of products that differ in certain ways from these attributes. By statistical means, information is produced on the perceived value of each of the attributes. Subsequently, with this information, we can investigate products that have different combinations of the various attributes. This method of analysis presupposes that the way customers use these products is constant. However, when we use products in a different way, our appreciation of the attributes changes, and then the results of the combined analysis no longer apply.

A simple example of this problem is that of CD-ROMs. When they were first introduced, most CD-ROMs contained games. For customers who did not like games the value of CD-ROMs was next to zero. Nowadays, most computer software requires so much memory that putting new software on our computers using floppy disks would be very time-consuming. Often you would need 10 or more disks, sometimes more than 50. CD-ROMs have therefore become necessary components of every PC and so acquired value for *all* users, not just those who play computer games. This has happened because the world in which PCs are used has changed. Today product lifecycles are becoming shorter and shorter and totally new functionalities are being commercialized almost daily, so determining value using such a static method is no longer justified. One way to deal with this situation is to build options into product platforms that may be exercised when the situation demands change.

We must think in terms of options and a dynamic way of analyzing these is required. The value of various options can be studied by means of simulations in which markets are linked to each other. For example, the hardware market may be linked to the software market. Therefore when the software market changes this may affect the potential and preferences of the hardware market.

As well as other markets, the value of a certain product may be dependent on the infrastructure, as with telephones, or on the availability of certain services. All these situations can be simulated and studied in terms of what this means for the company's strategy.

Options to enhance the product platform by enabling it to encompass new developments are not only valuable for the company but also for customers.

Investing in knowledge and skills enhances the flexibility of the company. It creates options.

When customers can swap a CD-ROM for a DVD-ROM in a laptop or they can enhance the capacity of a computer by adding extra RAM memory or extra hard disk memory storage, the system becomes more valuable to them and they are even willing to pay more to have such flexibility built in. In short, such flexibility within products has a value, which we can call the dynamic value component of a product.

A similar argument can be used for shareholder value. Building options into the operation of a company so that future opportunities can be used better to create value for its stakeholders has a value. Investing in knowledge and skills enhances the flexibility of the company. It creates options that can be valued by the real option theory. The value that can be put on such options can best be studied by simulating situations in which there are opportunities to use them and multiply the cash they generate by the estimates of the probability of these events happening.

Let us turn now to value creation for internal stakeholders. The value of working for a company is measured in terms of numerous factors, of which pay is one, but a limited one. Workload, motivation and stress may determine, to a large extent, how an employee values their job. In situations where the workload is excessive, stress may increase to such a level that certain co-workers suffer burnout. Then, the workload for those who remain increases, leading to more stress, leading to further burnout. In other words, the value of working for a company may collapse, leading to the departure of its most valuable co-workers. Companies have collapsed because of just such a situation.

case study

Exit of good people because of excessive workload

During the late 1980s and early 1990s the Aluminium Company of America (Alcoa) established a construction industry group of companies in The Netherlands. One of the subsidiaries, a producer of standard-sized aluminium windows and doors, was reorganized so that it could also supply the non-standard building project market with curtain walls, even though there was no system available to deal with such orders. On an *ad hoc* basis, a dedicated project facility was set up, with design and engineering capacity, in just a few weeks. The aluminium curtain wall system was developed, literally, overnight, on the basis of competing systems and architectural drawings. The project was prefabricated and installed on site.

As a result of this policy, the first projects were neither engineered nor executed optimally, resulting in a host of small and large complaints from customers. Engineers and production people spent a large amount of time on 'firefighting' instead of improving the initial system design. Meanwhile, new orders came in. The amount of rework and repair required had a negative effect on profitability. After about a year, the situation had worsened to the extent that the management team and director as well as the people within the departments were blaming each other for the increasing stream of customer complaints and costs incurred. People left for competitors or took long periods of sick leave because of poor workplace atmosphere. In the end, the holding company had to replace the director in order to give the whole project a new impetus.

This situation may have started as a result of a small difficulty, but it caused the collapse of the company.

Value for the stakeholders is dependent on the context in which the value is created and consumed. As the world – the context – is dynamic, the values change and so they have a dynamic component. The importance of this dynamism can be studied best by using DBM and simulations. These techniques support the analysis of this dynamic component and the effects on the growth of the company.

A similar argument can be used to support analysis of the dynamics of the reputation of a company with its various stakeholders and the effects various changes have on stakeholders' preferences regarding the company. An example of this is provided by the emergence of so-called green funds on the various stock exchanges. These are investment funds that invest only in companies that have a sound environmental policy. Thereby, such funds enable potential investors, who place a high value on ecologically viable growth, to combine their personal beliefs with – formerly contradictory – capitalistic aims.

Strategic management, flexibility and the management of options

The term 'strategic management' is commonly restricted to understanding and influencing the position and stakeholders of a company. Kees van der Heijden (1996), however, distinguishes three paradigms:

- rationalistic
- evolutionary
- process.

He underscores that the rationalistic paradigm is appealing to managers because of its claim that planning can be done and is a valuable activity. This paradigm is based on understanding the positions and objectives of the stakeholders.

The evolutionary paradigm makes clear that prediction is not possible. Therefore, planning is a hazardous activity and does not add much value. The process paradigm focuses on learning and, therefore, by discerning certain patterns and reacting to them faster and more adequately, companies can outperform their competitors. Our approach is based on this paradigm, but also integrates certain parts of the rationalistic and evolutionary paradigms.

Kees van der Heijden stresses the fact that scenario planners try to find structure in a range of events. He uses an iceberg model, with events as the top of the iceberg. Under the events lie the trends and patterns. Under the trends and patterns lies the structure. This is composed of a large number of elements – encompassing resources, culture, legislation, technology and so on – in causal relationships with each other. DBM helps to reveal this causal structure. Thus, whereas extrapolation gives an unjustifiable feeling of certainty, by means of intelligent analysis of the business, we can estimate a restricted number of scenarios and design a strategy based on these. By being flexible on those points where we expect changes but cannot predict which direction they will take and by making choices regarding those aspects where the environmental changes can be foreseen with less risk, we keep a balance between efficiency and flexibility. When no flexibility is needed, focusing on efficiency helps to save costs, but when flexibility is needed, being able to respond in this way increases value because we keep options open as long as possible, executing them only when we need to. Comparable with stock options – the price of which is higher when the volatility of the underlying value is higher and when the time period available in which to exercise them is longer – the 'price', or value, of these real options is positively influenced by increasing the number of alternatives we have to choose from and the length of time we can keep these alternatives open. In this way, we create the most value for *all* stakeholders – customers, shareholders, employees and partners.

The evolutionary paradigm makes clear that prediction is not possible. Therefore, planning is a hazardous activity and does not add much value. The process paradigm focuses on learning.

A simple example will make this clear. In the process of development of a new radio we would start with a global design and, during the process, the details would be filled in. At a certain stage we would have to choose the design of the box. Only after we have done this can the mould that will be used to make it be developed. This takes a certain time. When we keep the choice of colour open for as long as possible, we create flexibility and can, at a later stage, choose a colour that will be most highly appreciated by the customers. We create more value for the customer and at the same time for the shareholder, without increasing the development or production costs. Other well-known examples relate to reference architectures and standard designs that can be used in a number of subsequent generations of the products.

When we build in flexibility by using not the leanest design, which can only be used for one product, but by increasing the costs a little bit, enabling the development of a standard design for several of its components, we may earn these back by reducing the costs of subsequent product design by shortening the development time. Then, this may enable us to use more mature technologies, decreasing the technical risk. We may also, therefore, be able to incorporate more recent wishes from the customers and/or new technology, increasing the quality of the product, in a wider sense, decreasing costs further by profiting from quantum effects. One last example of creating options and, thus, flexibility is when we decide to acquire a company to enter a new market. We will profit from the creation of this option when we bring new products to this market. All acquisition of knowledge can be seen as the creation of options, but they are only exercised when we apply this knowledge in new products. In the book *Competing on the Edge: Strategy as structured chaos* (1998), Shona Brown and Kathleen Eisenhardt discuss a number of areas where flexibility can be created by making use of the insight provided by complexity and chaos theory. Here we will stress how these insights, those of financial theories of options, from strategic management literature and flexibility and scenario thinking can be brought to DBM.

Innovation in networks and supply chains

The various non-linear mechanisms of the innovation system and the resulting non-linear behaviour of the NPD and NBD processes are not evenly spread. This means that innovation management does not stay the same in the different parts of the innovation system and the phases of the NPD and NBD processes. The management style may – depending on the number and types of non-linearities present in the system – vary from a supportive style to an entrepreneurial style and then change again to a more hierarchical and bureaucratic style.

In order to match the management style and organization to the requirements of the segments of the innovation system or phases of the innovation process, we have to decide where to end each phase and start another. Insight into the attributes of the various processes and the presence of the various non-linear mechanisms and their relevance for the NPD and NBD processes helps in this.

In parts of the system or phases of the process where the extrapolation from historical trends and into the future is feasible, we can rely on the traditional ordinary forms of management. In other parts, we must rely more on what Ralph Stacey (1993) has named 'extraordinary' forms of management.

The success of a company depends, to a large extent, on its partners in the network in which it operates. Networks are groups of companies that work together. This cooperation encompasses multiple sequential transactions. Networks decrease the uncertainty that companies encounter in a dynamic environment. However, the stability of a network depends on trust and the mutual reputations of the companies involved, as well as the value that is generated and distributed among them. Networks may increase

Innovation in networks may increase the development and marketing power to the level that is needed to transform the business.

the flexibility of a company to grasp new opportunities. At the same time, networks may also decrease the freedom to be opportunistic. Networks may increase flexibility when there is a balance between stability and freedom, when the partners are loosely linked to each other. Shona Brown and Kathleen Eisenhardt explained in their book *Competing on the Edge: Strategy as structured chaos* (1998) how this loose–tight linking of organizations keeps networks on the edge of chaos. Operating at the edge of chaos provides the greatest flexibility to react to disturbances. In complicated systems such as business systems, evolutionary processes will move organizations to this edge because extremes, real chaos and stiff structures such as bureaucracies will not survive the environmental challenges.

Innovation in networks is also important because it may increase the development and marketing power to the level that is needed to transform the business. For example, Duphar is a Dutch pharmaceutical company that registered the first of a new class of antidepressants, Fevarin, in 1983. This new class of drugs was more effective and safer than the tricyclic type of antidepressants that had been used up to this point. Duphar, however, was, and is, a small company that lacks the muscle to transform the market. Eli Lilly introduced the antidepressant Prozac, which belongs to this same class of drugs, three years later and, by making use of the favourable messages in the media, did transform the market and made a billion-dollar drug of Prozac. Fevarin had managed to attract only a minor market share. Duphar realized that it needed a stronger partner and chose Upjohn to reverse this situation, but it was too late – Prozac is the drug everyone knows.

Warner Lambert, another pharmaceutical company, developed Lipitor – a drug that lowers cholesterol levels in the blood. At the time it was introduced onto the market, there were a few other cholesterol-lowering drugs available. Although Lipitor had some advantages, it was not able to gain a large market share. After going into partnership with Pfizer – a company well known for its marketing muscle – Lipitor became a market success.

Even at the beginning of the 1990s, most biotechnology companies wanted to become large, integrated pharmaceutical companies. Centocor, a biotechnology company that developed antibodies for diagnostic and therapeutical purposes, had this as its aim. In 1993, Centocor introduced Centoxin, an antibody medicine for treating blood poisoning. It was allowed to release it onto the market faster than usual because of the military campaign against Iraq. After a while, papers were published that doubted its efficacy. Centocor, at that time, had invested heavily in its production and sales capacity for Centoxin. The authorities demanded more research and the drug had to be removed from the market. Centocor's share price dropped and it almost went bankrupt.

The company's management realized that Centocor's core competence was transforming research findings into new technology and products but that it needed the larger pharmaceutical companies to transform these products into registered market successes. So, since that time, Centocor, and other biotechnology companies, have been involved in extensive partnering projects with other pharmaceutical companies, to the benefit of both. Centocor, has introduced a new antibody medicine called Rheoprin and is now one of the big five independent biotechnology companies in the world.

Examples of innovative companies are the small, high-tech companies in software development and biotechnology. Often these companies are spinoffs from universities or large companies. Xerox has learned from its experience with inventions created at Parc Labs in the early 1980s. It was not Xerox that profited from its inventions but Apple, which applied the mouse, icons and many more inventions in its Lisa and Macintosh computers. The result of this is that nowadays when employees develop something that does not fit the strategy of Xerox, but is still generally promising, these employees are supported to found their own companies.

In pharmaceuticals, large companies are focusing more and more on development and marketing, relying on partnerships with small, dedicated biotechnology companies as sources of new technology and products. It is their experience that small companies can take more risks because they are more innovative.

On the other hand, there are companies, such as Solectron, that specialize in manufacturing new products. These employ a new breed of subcontractors, ones who are superflexible and so can dramatically reduce the time between coming up with an invention and it reaching a new customer (*Business Week*, 24 August 1998, pp 61–2).

One of the most prominent companies exploiting innovations successfully is Microsoft. Even when it was late in recognizing the impact of the Internet, it was able to take it up and turn it into a success.

An example of a reproduction company is Matsushita. It is much less innovative than companies such as Sony and Philips, but is very able at turning innovations into mass market products by making them high-quality and low-cost items.

These types of companies operate successfully in different phases of the product lifecycle. The NPD and NBD processes differ in focus and different ones are prominent in the different phases. How can management profit from knowing these sorts of things about the complicated nature of the business system?

Knowledge of how markets interact provides a first clue about how complementary products, services and networks together deliver quality to the customer. What happens when the customer uses them gives these products their positions in the environment. A change in one product may affect the value of the others. It is interesting that a lot of energy nowadays goes into developing partnerships and establishing standards – DVD being a case in point.

Moreover, supply chains operate more and more as networks, where suppliers co-develop their products with the producer of the end product. Similarly, suppliers of knowledge (universities), services (accountants and management consultants) and finance develop closer bonds with certain companies in a sector. However, bonds that are too tight reduce the manoeuvring space and so companies may lose power over their suppliers.

Therefore three aspects of the relationship between partners in a network are important:

- power and control;
- trust and mutual reputation;
- the value generated for the various stakeholders.

The power one participant has over another depends on the alternatives or options a company has, on the switching costs or lock-in mechanisms and time delays involved in exerting these options.

Trust or mutual reputation is built up after multiple transactions. Trust creates a kind of lock-in because switching costs money in terms of gathering extra information and the extra risk it imposes.

Value consists of the present operations, expected future operations, the extra flexibility the network provides to its participants and the decrease in perceived risk.

Portfolio management and roadmapping

In portfolio management, we try to allocate our resources to developing those TPM combinations that will maximize the shareholder value of the company. Portfolios must be balanced in terms of the phase of the lifecycle, time to market and length of development, risk and uncertainty, development of breakthroughs, new platforms and line extensions. Constraints that have to be taken into account are the total resources available and, especially, the length of time that critical resources in development and market launches will be needed.

Market launches, in particular, require a lot of financial resources and management time, so they must form a steady flow rather than ending up with a concentration of products to be launched.

Last but not least, synergies between projects in the portfolio must be maximized in such a way that skills developed in one project can be used in other projects and economies of scale can be obtained with respect to investments in new instrumentation, design and testing facilities and specialized expertise. For this reason, process models must be complemented by cash flow

> *Roadmapping is a method used to relate the development of technology, products and markets in time.*

models, in which the values of NPD and NBD options can be calculated, and by human resource models, in which the presence and evolution of the available human resources in the company are mapped out. Because of the non-linear relationship between the allocation of resources and any returns on this investment, being the first on the market may make a lot of difference to the return, or working on too many projects may dramatically decrease the productivity of scarce talent. Thus, designing the optimal portfolio is hampered by the large number of parameters that have to be taken into account. We humans can only deal with a very limited number of factors at any one time. Using computer models, however, we can greatly increase the number of relationships between more parameters.

Roadmapping is a method used to relate the development of technology, products and markets in time. In Chapter 1, we discussed that, often, these developments require organizations to adapt. Organizational development takes time and so it too can be approached as you would a project. Including such projects in the roadmaps is recommended.

The roadmaps describe the trajectory of the company in the innovation arena as discussed in Chapter 1. As the innovation arena can be considered a starting point for translating structure into process, the innovation arena or its derivative, the roadmap, can be used to translate the outcome of DBM into structural parameters that indicate the progress of the development of technology, products, markets and the organization. Using DBM in roadmapping may help to reveal bottlenecks or critical factors with respect to cash flow, human resources or investment in new facilities in the whole development plan at an early stage.

DBM and the balanced scorecard – setting up improvement measures

Balanced scorecards – as described by Robert Kaplan and David Norton in their book *The Balanced Scorecard: Translating strategy into action* (1996) – are increasingly used as a tool to provide managers with the instrumentation to navigate their way to future competitive success. The balanced scorecard translates the mission and strategy of an organization into a number of performance measures (see Figure 9.4). It emphasizes the importance of balancing the four main performance drivers:

● financial
● customers
● internal business processes
● learning and growth.

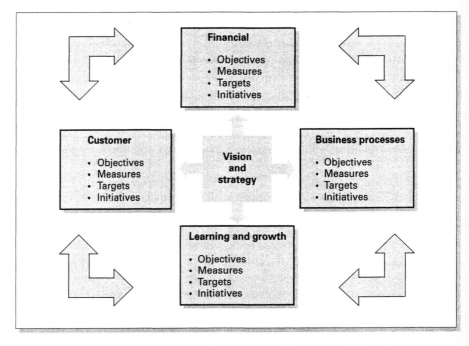

Figure 9.4 The balanced scorecard as a strategic framework for action

Source: Adapted from Kaplan and Norton, 1996

In Figure 9.5, we have taken the business process as a starting point and depicted how the various performance indicators relate to our general scheme of business processes. The success of the approach depends on the following factors:

● recognition of the best indicators for performance and the operationalization of these parameters;

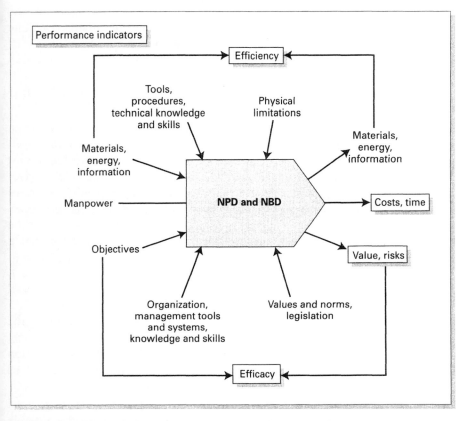

Figure 9.5 The balanced scorecard, performance indicators and their role in business processes

- insight into the connections, the cause and effect relationships, between the various performance indicators and, especially, between the performance drivers of the financial objectives and the financial objectives themselves.

A number of constraints that influence the application of the approach must be recognized:

- the choice of the time window – the relative weight of the drivers is dependent on the time window used;
- no important changes in the situation may occur – the cause and effect relationships between the drivers and the financial performance may change over time and depend on other conditions that are not monitored.

This second point is important because cause and effect relationships are often non-linear. For example, this may mean that, in certain conditions, small deviations may have large effects on the financial results, but in other situations the financial results may be rather insensitive to changes of these parameters. Time to market is also just such a parameter and everybody now knows that it is critical, but others may be less obvious. For example, team performance is a vital parameter that cannot easily be overestimated. Also, measuring the relative positions of the various generic processes during the subsequent phases of the NPD or NBD processes is often not taken into account.

DBM can be applied to study exactly all the relationships shown in Figure 9.4. Growth depends not only on learning and applying this knowledge to the development of better products, services or businesses, but also the creation of new options and the potential effort that must be put into exercising them. DBM gives insight into what options may be available to the company by studying various scenarios. It results in a model that encompasses both the external processes, including the customer and market processes, and the

DBM gives insight into what options may be available to the company by studying various scenarios.

internal business processes. It makes clear which processes contribute to learning and growth of the company and indicates its financial performance in the various scenarios. For this reason extending the balanced scorecard approach with DBM is advantageous.

Two objectives can thus be combined. First, the objective of the balanced scorecard to enhance strategic feedback and learning. Second, the objective of DBM as a tool to support the codification and integration of managers' knowledge about the cause and effect relationships of the various elements of the NPD and NBD processes and to facilitate the learning process.

DBM may accelerate the learning process started by applying the balanced scorecard approach, because it helps to define hypotheses about the possible relationships between performance drivers and financial results. By using real-time measuring, it is possible to create a disciplined system for validating and improving the model. Moreover, it may suggest, even at an early stage, what other parameters may be important drivers, though these had not been recognized at the start, and which ones may be signals that cannot be controlled but give information about the importance of the drivers.

Using the balanced scorecard may also show the developers of the model what target parameters they should concentrate on.

In summary, integrating of the balanced scorecard and DBM approaches may create various synergies that increase the value of both tools.

One of the important aspects of using the balanced scorecard is that strategic management and operational management become better linked to each other. In this way, not only is the manner in which strategies are translated into operational plans facilitated, but also how events at the operational level and in the markets are translated into adapted strategies. Simulating strategies in various situations facilitates the adaptation of strategies to the emergence of new or only recently recognized opportunities at the operational level.

10 | DBM and the management of NPD and NBD

Introduction

In NPD and NBD, operational and strategic management are closely linked to each other because not only are strategic plans executed during the process of R&D and market development, but, also during this process, new information is obtained and new opportunities become apparent that may result in the strategic plans being adapted. A large part of innovation strategies are in reality emerging strategies.

In Figure 10.1, we have depicted the objectives of operational NPD and NBD management using our general scheme of business processes.

In this chapter, we will discuss how operational management can profit from a better insight into the NPD and NBD processes, which consist of the various interacting generic processes. We will focus especially on the relationships between the various performance indicators of the NPD processes, the generic process model and its consequences for the organization and management of NPD and NBD.

Managing NPD and NBD performance

Projects undertaken in NPD and NBD are evaluated according to five performance criteria:

- quality
- speed
- costs
- risks
- the creation of spinoffs or new options and the building of skills and new core abilities.

In Figure 10.2, these criteria are depicted in relation to the outputs of the NPD and NBD processes.

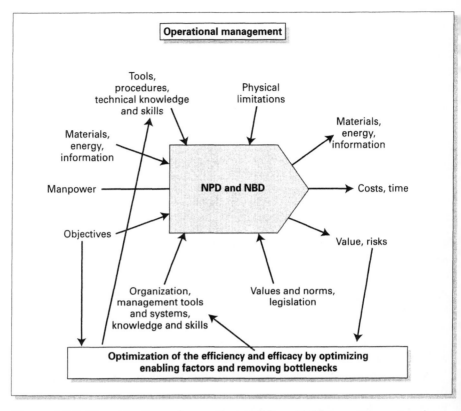

Figure 10.1 The objectives of operational NPD and NBD management and their role in business processes

The first four performance indicators are generally acknowledged. The last is often overlooked in assessing the performance of the NPD and NBD processes, but sometimes it is one of the most critical. Especially in young, high-tech companies, it is the one that has proven to be very valuable in the case of takeovers by established companies. For example, the dedicated biotechnology company Plant Genetics System was bought for more than $1 billion even though it did not have any products on the market – it was the staff's skills and competences that proved to have that value.

The building up of competences must therefore be viewed separately to the activities of NPD and NBD *per se* because it adds to shareholder value. It is largely, but not exclusively, concentrated in the R&D department.

The management of NPD and NBD must be directed at optimizing all five criteria at the same time. This can be done by:

● improving the performance of the various generic NPD and NBD processes (see Figure 10.2);

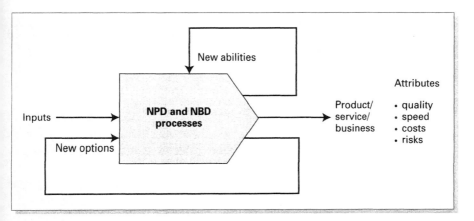

Figure 10.2 The five performance indicators of the NPD and NBD processes

● promoting their integration.

However, there is a certain state-of-the-art frontier or barrier where decisions have to be made about the trade-offs between the criteria (see Figure 10.3).

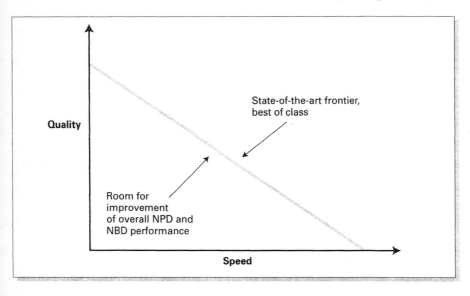

Figure 10.3 The state-of-the-art frontier with respect to NPD and NBD performance

In Figure 10.3, only two dimensions are represented. In reality, we can think of the figure containing five dimensions and the frontier represented as a plane in this five-dimensional space. Below this plane, the NPD and NBD processes can be improved by better structuring, use of more advanced tools and systems, better staffing, a more innovative climate and so on. The plane itself will only move when we discover an innovation concerning one of these factors.

At a certain level, companies have to decide whether or not to substitute quality for speed or costs for quality. Where to strike the balance is determined by the effects on stakeholder value. What has the most influence on market share – speed or quality – depends on the strategies of the competition and the behaviour of the customer. At that stage, we have to decide how to allocate our scarce resources to the various generic processes.

The project attributes of quality, speed, costs, risks and future options are complicated aggregated results of the attributes of the underlying parts of the projects.

The project attributes of quality, speed, costs, risks and future options are complicated aggregated results of the attributes of the underlying parts of the projects. Speed can be increased in a multitude of ways, such as by executing activities in parallel, outsourcing, using more standard designs, allocating the resources to fewer projects and so on. All these ways, when executed at a best practice level, have consequences for quality, innovativeness, costs and risks. The overall contribution of the four aspects in terms of subprocesses has the same consequences for the total project.

Below, we will elaborate first on the individual and combined aspects, respectively, and demonstrate how DBM may help the management of the various aspects in isolation to reach the state-of-the-art frontier. Subsequently, we will discuss how DBM may support decisions concentrating on what is the best trade-off. In Table 10.1, an overview of the main generic processes in NPD and NBD that contribute to each of the five performance criteria is given.

Table 10.1 Overview of the main generic processes in NPD and NBD that contribute to each of the five performance criteria

Generic NPD and NBD business processes	Quality	Speed	Costs	Risks	Options
Management and decision making	+	+	+	+	
Prototyping		++	+	+	
Knowledge generation	+	+		++	++
Generation of ideas	++			+	++
Teambuilding	+	+	+	+	
Implementation I and II		+	++		

Next, we will discuss the relationships between the various generic processes, their contributions to the performance criteria and R&D management in more detail.

The relationships between the five NPD and NBD performance criteria and the generic processes

The quality of prototypes and new product, service, production or business processes

We define quality as more than just reliability. Quality is closely linked to customer value. It also encompasses functionality, ease of use and styling.

Three generic processes seem to contribute especially to quality:

- decision making;
- knowledge generation, acquisition and exploitation;
- generation of ideas.

The last two processes dominate at the start of the NPD and NBD processes, when flexibility is highest. The availability of ideas and knowledge about the combination of customers and technology contribute most to the quality of products. The outputs of both processes are intimately related to the quality of the team and decision-making processes.

> *We define quality as more than just reliability.*

The leverage of a dollar invested in quality at the front of the NPD and NBD processes is much higher than it is later in the lifecycle. The return on investment reduces towards the end of the lifecycle and is lowest when the quality must be lifted by after-sales service or by reworking in production (see Figure 10.4).

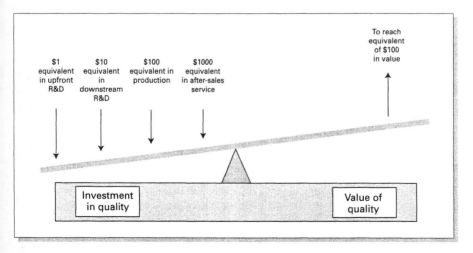

Figure 10.4 The quality lever, depicting the value of investments in quality during phases of the product or business lifecycle

Since the 1970s, quality improvement has been an important issue in management. Whereas in the 1970s this was focused on the production process, nowadays everyone realizes that quality must be built into the product or business from the start, and the best and cheapest way to do this is to invest in the NPD and NBD processes. Especially early in the process, when the specifications are formulated, most of the quality is determined. Using knowledge from multiple sites, marketing, customers, technology, production and logistics, and integrating these into the product or business specification, defines most of the quality. Tools such as quality function deployment, failure mode effect analysis, design for manufacturing and so on support this process of the integration of distributed knowledge. The use of databases where best practices are documented and made available to everyone in the company may promote the use of widely distributed knowledge in the company to improve quality. The generation of ideas may provide options for alternative ways to fulfil certain quality needs. Aside from using knowledge to improve quality, making better use of available knowledge may also lead to better tests being devised in the prototyping process.

When quality issues have to be tackled by combining the distributed knowledge available in the various functions and disciplines, the quality of the team becomes important. This determines the efficacy with which knowledge will be exchanged and integrated to solve quality and other problems. Starting a project with a phase in which the focus is on teambuilding seems to be a good investment of time and money. Almost all research shows that high-performance teams build high-performance products (Deschamps and Nayak, 1995; Thomas, 1995). High-performance teams are those in which members trust, support and depend on each other. They easily switch roles without much loss of energy and time. They guarantee high-quality decision making. In the process models used in DBM these causal relations become clear immediately.

Between teambuilding, decision making and prototyping performance there is a reinforcing loop. It is possible to stimulate this loop in the right direction by giving small, clear-cut assignments to the team in the first phases of the teambuilding process. Peter Senge (1994) has named one of his archetypes after such a situation – 'success to the successful'. Positive outcomes stimulate the teambuilding process and start a virtuous reinforcing loop. Early failures, on the other hand, may hamper or even ruin the teambuilding process, resulting in teams in which everybody accuses each other and cooperation will stop, resulting in a group of individuals that will never become a real team.

Speed

Preston Smith and Donald Reinertsen (1998) have summarized the reasons for the importance of speed as being that it:

- increases sales;

- beats the competition to market;
- is responsive to changing markets, styles and technology;
- maintains a market leadership position.

Several possibilities exist for speeding up the development process. Two of the ideas mentioned most often are the simultaneous execution of activities (concurrent engineering) and outsourcing. Both are related to the prototyping and implementation process. However, using knowledge more effectively and, especially, making sure that the developers can easily monitor and use knowledge that helps to solve design problems contributes to shortening time to market.

Modularization of the product and standardization of the interfaces makes concurrent engineering easier, because it reduces the need to communicate and discuss all changes to the modules with the separate development groups.

Still, a lot of consultation between the groups is necessary. Creating a multidisciplinary team in which the core members are the leaders of the separate development groups facilitates this consultation process. However, the quality of the core team is an essential prerequisite for effective communication and decision making among its members.

In order to avoid time delays due to revisions later on of a design because of forgotten issues relating to manufacturing and applications downstream in the primary process, addressing such matters at the start of the product or business definition phase is important.

Smith and Reinertsen suggest a number of ways in which the development process can be speeded up, including by:

- improving front-end processes – generation of ideas, planning and knowledge generation, acquisition and exploitation;
- deciding carefully about incremental versus radical innovations;
- capturing customer needs in an efficient way;
- deciding on the best key architectural designs – planning and prototyping;
- forming and energizing teams – teambuilding process;
- good communication – teambuilding and knowledge generation, acquisition and exploitation;
- designing fast development processes – prototyping;
- controlling the process – milestone reviews, decision making;
- bridging the R&D manufacturing gap – implementation I and II.

In short, the authors emphasize, in effect, that speed is increased by performing all the generic NPD and NBD processes more efficiently and integrating them more effectively.

We think that one of the most critical issues in NPD and NBD is the phasing of the development process. Earlier, we discussed the paradox of the NPD and NBD processes. They consist of a number of generic processes that are linked to each other, creating multiple reinforcing loops. By integrating them, we speed up the process. However, the various processes often require conflicting optimizing conditions. This paradox is solved by the compartmentalization of the processes into phases in which one generic process is dominant and the others play only subordinate roles. The phases are separated from each other by milestone reviews. It is necessary to ensure that all the processes can play a role in all the phases and, when they play only a subordinate role, the owners of the different generic R&D processes must be present in the team. The essential team roles, as classified by, for example, Belbin, can be interpreted as roles that are linked to the generic NPD and NBD processes. A balanced team, therefore, is essential for efficient and rapid NPD and NBD processes.

The stagegate process as proposed by Robert G. Cooper (1993) can be at least partially understood and explained using this model. (The other effect of having milestone reviews is an increase in the flexibility to stop or continue. This may increase the option value of the project.) It helps to follow the trajectory from idea to product, which lessens the risk of a project getting stuck halfway and never reaching the finish.

However, one of the most difficult things is preventing the generation of ideas, or knowledge generation, playing dominant roles later on in the NPD and NBD processes, while another is prototyping starting too early. The dominance of certain roles in the team or absence of some others may cause this problem. The project leader must be able to promote the desired shift in focus on the various generic processes in each of the phases. High-performance teams, we have seen, are defined by the fact that no one team member dominates during all phases. Rather, the members accept the contributions each person makes. Therefore, high-performance teams make the transformations easily.

The project leader must be able to promote the desired shift in focus on the various generic processes in each of the phases.

Being aware that reinforcing loops may exist between various activities – for example, between defining the product or business specification, testing, realization of certain holes in the available technical and customer knowledge and the acquisition of additional knowledge – may stimulate linking these processes more closely to each other. Concurrent engineering may provide the conditions for such tighter links. However, only when team members are cooperating with each other can such reinforcing loops be established.

Lock-in mechanisms of certain routines can prevent the early recognition of deadlocks in design that cost time and money. Stimulating the inventorization of multiple options early in the process may mean that time-consuming redesigns are avoided later on.

Finally, it can be remarked that all phases take time, and a month won at the start in the first phase or in the last phase contributes to shortening the duration of the process in exactly the same way. Although it is bad practice to skip the solution of certain problems, leaving this to later stages, where often solving them is much more complicated, time-consuming and costly than would have been the case in the early stages, prolonging these early stages and letting them consume precious time because the market launch still seems far away is equally bad practice.

Costs

Most of the costs of NPD and NBD are incurred during the ramp-up and early commercialization of the implementation phases. It is clear that a 1 per cent decrease in costs in these stages means a lot more than 1 per cent decrease in costs in the generation of ideas phase. Working efficiently, therefore, in the ramp-up and commercialization stages is more important than it is in the early phases.

Whereas the requirements become better defined and more exact as the project progresses, the overall planning can be more precise. Freedom in the early phases of the NPD and NBD processes will therefore slowly be substituted by control and a move from a democratic to a more autocratic leadership style may take place. However, the flexibility also decreases and it becomes more difficult to change specifications to less costly solutions.

This is the paradox of NPD and NBD projects. At the stages when flexibility is greatest, the uncertainty is also greatest and a lot of decisions are made using rough estimates and intuition. The postponement of these decisions costs money, but decreases the risk of making the wrong decisions. For these reasons, even during the generation of ideas the other generic processes, such as knowledge generation, acquisition and exploitation, prototyping and implementation, must be performed. Prototyping often means skunk work at this early stage. Also, looking at the consequences of a realization of the ideas may help to prevent the wrong direction being chosen. Knowing how to build options into designs and when to execute these options so that the optimal balance of quality, risks, speed and costs is achieved defines the difference between artist designers and the knowledgeable designers. Again, NPD and NBD involve teamwork, and this also applies to the team's quality. High-performance teams enhance the abilities of the individuals within them and create synergies that make a difference.

Risks

At the start of a project, uncertainties are at their greatest. These uncertainties can be transformed into calculated risks when knowledge about the technology, products, organization and markets is gathered. However, uncertainties that are not recognized as such and so not addressed appropriately may result in the wrong decisions being made and so may add to the level of risk. Because the highest chances of mistakes being made and money wasted occur at the beginning of projects, the cheapest, but most selective, activities and tests are planned for the front end of a project and the more expensive processes downstream. This simple calculus also determines how far the other generic processes can be brought into the earlier phases. By using the right tests during prototyping, general knowledge becomes increasingly more specific. In areas of development where the effects of failure are great – such as in the development of drugs or aeroplanes – the testing phase makes a large contribution to the duration and total cost of development. The quality of the tests is important and knowledge generation, acquisition and exploitation (research) are in large part related to the development of new and/or improved tests.

Options and core competences

The main process that affects the building of competences is the knowledge-generation, acquisition and exploitation process. This can result from research in the company, during prototyping, production preparation and, last but not least, from outside the company. By means of the generation of ideas, options can be thought of to exploit this knowledge. The R&D department is traditionally where this takes place. Also, advanced development projects may have as their main objective the acquisition of new competences that expand the options of the company (Clark and Wheelwright, 1993). Today it is recognized that all parts of the company may contribute and, by using information and communications technology, we can attempt to organize this activity in a more effective and efficient way. In all planning and performance evaluation sessions of NPD and NBD, the acquisition of new and the extension of existing competences must be added to the agenda as an extra objective and valued separately.

Finding the right balance

It is obvious that success in NPD and NBD is achieved only when we know how to maximize the acquisition of new competences and skills at the same time as improving quality, speeding up the process, and decreasing costs and risks as soon as possible during the course of the project.

Improving all these performance indicators at the same time constitutes the golden route to success. Improving the performance of all the generic processes helps to improve the overall NPD and NBD processes. This can be done by removing bottlenecks and optimizing the enabling factors, which are:

- structuring – linking processes;
- introducing the best tools and systems;
- training staff and increasing their management skills;
- introducing certain management styles and building an innovative climate;
- adjusting the strategy and competences in line with the company's mission.

Teambuilding especially has proven to be critical to the other generic processes.

Teambuilding especially has proven to be critical to the other generic processes. It is the most basic of the processes linked to the style of decision making and the quality of planning the NPD or NBD processes upfront.

Furthermore, all these processes can be improved by introducing better tools that function as the enabling factors of these processes. This applies to knowledge management tools and infrastructure, quality management tools, rapid prototyping techniques, simulation tools and so on.

Next, we will discuss in more detail the organization of the NPD and NBD processes. We will focus on the phasing of NPD and NBD processes.

The compartmentalization and phasing of NPD and NBD processes

A variety of authors have classified organizations according to a number of dimensions, such as centralization versus decentralization or control versus freedom. A dimension often mentioned is closed, inward-looking versus open, outward-oriented (Hardjono, 1996; Ramondt, 1996). Both these dimensions can be linked to the characteristics of the inputs, outputs, enablers and/or constraints of the generic processes. The generation of ideas and options can only prosper in an environment where freedom to experiment with new ideas exists. Inputs for the generation of ideas process are often weak signals from outside or discrepancies between expectations and reality. Open organizations, therefore, seem to offer better environments for the generation of ideas than do closed ones. Options are often formulated down the organization in the functional departments close to the operations.

The processes of prototyping and implementation are linked to the outside world via the processes of generation of ideas and knowledge generation, acquisition and exploitation. In both processes, fulfilling specific requirements is becoming increasingly important, changing the balance between freedom versus control to the control side of the axis.

Therefore, we can classify the various generic processes and matching phases using the two dimensions of a control to freedom axis and a closed to open axis (see Figure 10.5).

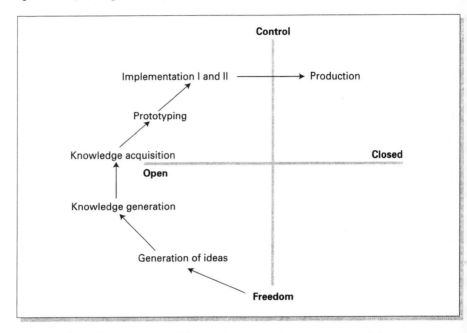

Figure 10.5 Classification of the various generic processes and the subsequent phases in which they dominate along the two dimensions of control to freedom, open to closed

The conclusions from our discussion above seem to also fit the observations of several authors who have stressed the fact that management practices and the attributes of organizations differ depending where in the lifecycle of products and industries they are (Abernathy and Utterback, 1978).

- One of the important questions for management is up to what level can the NPD or NBD processes be integrated because the organization is flexible enough to accommodate the various requirements or to what extent must the processes and transfer of technology between organizations be split? In other words, what is the optimal balance between transfer of technology and transformation of organizations?

- Closely linked to this question is another – what is the optimal proportion of emergent to planned strategy (Mintzberg, 1994)? Opportunities arise, especially early on in the process of NPD or NBD, that are often outside the planned strategies. How much strategic flexibility can be allowed to accommodate these opportunities?

● A third question is what coordination mechanisms are best within and between the organizational units?

Now that we have discussed organizational segmentation and product lifecycle phasing, we can relate this to analogue segmentations of the market and products or product systems.

This whole issue is related to the much-debated make, buy or cooperate issue. It is also related to the issue of innovation in networks.

Improving the NPD and NBD processes – arranging the interfaces between organizational boundaries and phase transitions

Here, we will discuss how the performance of the NPD and NBD processes can be optimized by adapting the organization, implementing management subsystems and adjusting the culture, including management style.

Certain patterns in the application of heuristics and tools in management practice summarized above can be observed.

● In the various phases of the process just one generic process will dominate, while the others are present but remain subordinate to the dominant process.

● In the team, roles are related to the various owners of the generic processes.

● To ensure that the type of work done in the team changes during the progress of the project, other team members must become more dominant. The more mature the team, the better this switch. Teambuilding activities must be focused on creating high performance.

● The more innovative the project – that is, the more different it is from the other products of the company – the more independent the project team must be from the rest of the organization, the more responsible the team members are for the results, the more authority the project leader must have, moving from a project coordinator to a lightweight project leader to a heavyweight project leader as required.

● Application of information and communications technology makes it possible to create more virtual teams. However, the virtual teams must become actual teams, which means that they must occasionally meet each other face to face and have an opportunity to do things together.

Various classifications of organizations, or parts of them, have been proposed. In this book, earlier we took as a starting point the classification of organizations using the two dimensions of control to freedom and closed to open.

Hardjono (1996) has used these two dimensions and distinguishes from these four classes of organizations:

- innovative
- expansive
- efficient
- flexible.

These organizations are located in, respectively, the freedom to open, control to open, control to closed and freedom to closed quadrants. Hardjono argues that organizations change over time and go through each of these four phases in turn. According to his theory, organizations can only transform along one dimension over time and will do this only in one direction. This means that organizations change from innovative to expansive, efficient to flexible and then start the cycle over again. However, although organizations are located dominantly in one phase, isolated parts of them can be located in another phase. These reservations are then considered to be alien and play only marginal roles in the policy-making processes of the organization. Over time, however, these aliens may influence the rest of the organization and prepare the way for the rest of the company to follow.

Often, R&D is such an alien. During the lifecycle of a product or business, from idea to implementation and beyond, parts of the organization are the main location where the activities related to the product or business are concentrated. Taking this standpoint, we may rearrange the organizational phases so that they relate to the phases of the lifecycle.

Taking as our starting point the fact that a product or business lifecycle can be divided into a number of subsequent phases, from idea to prototype, introduction, articulation, growth, consolidation, we can map these phases to the various characteristics of the organization. We have named these:

- innovation
- transformation
- exploitation
- reproduction.

We have renamed these phases to stress their relationship to the lifecycle phases, but their resemblance to the phases as defined by Hardjono (1996) should be obvious. We have renamed the flexible organization the transformation phase, the expansive phase, the exploitation phase, the efficient phase and the reproduction phase. Innovation is located in the freedom to open quadrant, transformation in the freedom to closed quadrant, exploitation in the control to open quadrant and reproduction in the control to closed quadrant. Change along each dimension is accompanied by a change in various organizational attributes, such as structure, use of management systems, management style, type of staff, skills and so on, each differing from the other (see Figure 10.6).

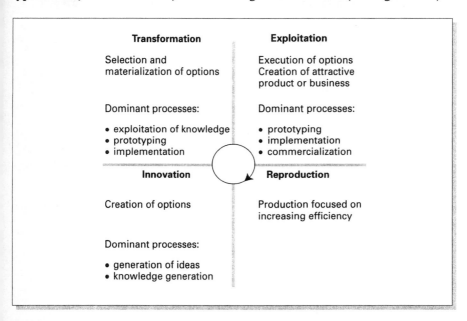

Figure 10.6 The dominant behaviours of the different types of organizations and their main attributes

The dominance of different generic NPD and NBD processes is linked to variations in non-linear mechanisms. Table 10.2 lists the types of organizations and the particular non-linear mechanisms associated with them. The changes in the non-linear mechanisms during these phases are linked to changes in the dominance of the generic processes and organizational dimensions. The differences between the phases characterize the transitions and determine the best way to organize them.

Table 10.2 Summary of the types of organizations and their dominant non-linear mechanisms

Non-linear mechanisms	Innovation	Transformation	Exploitation	Reproduction
Reinforcing loops	Science, technology, product, market	Organizational learning Product to product interactions	Product, market	Economies of scale Learning curve
Limiting loops	Finance		Product technology	Market
Lock-in mechanisms	Competitors Customers			Product technology in dominant design Products in relation to other products in technical system
Time delays				
Selection mechanisms	Accepted by customers			
Variation and mechanisms	Science, technology		Market	Production

The relationship between DBM and quality systems

In the 1980s, it became clear that quality had to become an important issue for western companies. Quality is one of those fuzzy management concepts for which everybody has their own definition. Some define quality as conformance to standards.

J. M. Juran (1992) distinguishes between quality with a big Q and with a little q. Conformance is quality with a little q. Quality with a big Q concerns all products, all processes, all industries, and is viewed as a business problem based on the universal trilogy (quality planning, quality control and quality improvement), which is to be included in the business plan. Improvement is to be directed at company performance, based on responsiveness to customer needs, and is a company-wide responsibility, coordinated by a quality council of top management. Quality planning is, according to Juran, the activity of establishing quality goals and developing the products and processes required to meet those goals.

Bounds *et al.* (1994) define quality as 'a principle that encourages excellence in everything: products, strategies, systems, processes and people'.

Three of the important outcomes of the emphasis on quality are, first, the recognition that the quality of products and services depends on the quality of all the processes that play a role in their creation; second, the recognition that many customers can be distinguished besides the final customer; and last but not least, that to improve quality we have to measure the performance of the various processes.

Since it first came to prominence, a multitude of tools have been developed that help in ensuring quality and net value for the stakeholders, measuring performance of the various processes that deliver the products and that help to conceal the link between the net value of a product or service for the various customers or stakeholders and the performance of the processes that deliver those products or services. Important instruments are, for example, process flow charting, Pareto analysis, and cause and effect analysis.

The quality of products and services depends on the quality of all the processes that play a role in their creation.

Although the quality movement started in manufacturing, it became evident that the best way to improve quality was to start in the design phase. However, the relationship between quality and process performance is more complicated than it is in manufacturing, because it is not only the quality or net added value of the end products that count, but also speed, costs and risks of development, and added shareholder value and added value for the internal stakeholders. How to generate most value for the various stakeholders in the product development process is still one of the most relevant issues.

DBM provides a tool that supports the quality management process, because it increases the insight of the managers into the relationship between the organization of the various processes and the generation of net value for the stakeholders, between resources, strategies and skills and competences, process management and the co-workers and customers' satisfaction. Moreover, tools developed for quality management, such as SPC, cause and effect analysis, and QFD, may also be used in conjunction with DBM. Quality function deployment relates attributes to components and process technologies. As such, it links marketing with engineering, product realization and knowledge generation, acquisition and exploitation. By entering certain values for the product and technology parameters in the model, DBM can be applied to real-life cases.

Epilogue

In this epilogue the main topics of this book are summarized point by point.

The starting principles of this book are that:

- in the present world, one of the most important strategies for survival is constant innovation;
- for successful innovation, you need to have insight into the innovation process.

The three main questions addressed in this book are the following.

- What are the main attributes of the innovation process that it is important for management to know?
- How can management profit from the peculiarities of the innovation process?
- How can management get insight into the peculiarities of the innovation process?

In the book the following topics were discussed in relation to the questions posed above.

- Companies operate by, consciously or subconsciously, using a certain business model. The success of a company depends on the fit between its model, the characteristics of the industries in which it operates and its own abilities. This model rests on certain assumptions about the company's abilities and the main market, supply chain and competitive processes. The success of the company also depends on the extent to which the various functions within the company use the same business model. Inconsistencies between business models can result in inefficient and ineffective use of scarce resources.
- As the environment changes, the dominant business model used by the company has to change.
- Globalization of markets, international competition, fast technological advancements, the development of the information infrastructure and

deregulation are just some of the trends that have affected almost all industries, and increased the connectivity of the economy and the unpredictability of environmental change.

● Innovation has become the main way in which to improve the market position of a company and create value for its stakeholders.

● In order to innovate successfully, we have to be more effective, more efficient innovators than our competitors. A prerequisite for this is having better insight into the innovation process than the competition.

● In innovation, the structure of the innovation arena influences the innovation process and the innovation process, by definition, changes the structure of the arena. These are very closely linked and this is the basis of the non-linear dynamics of the innovation process.

● Non-linearity is the main characteristic of the innovation process, making it different from other processes such as production and logistics. This results, among other things, in the fact that small causes may have large consequences. Thus, small investments may result in large profits. On the other hand, this adds to the unpredictability and risks involved in innovation.

● To understand the innovation process, we have to use the distributed knowledge about the process that is present in the company. In addition, we need to have tools to model this knowledge, validate it, recognize the white spaces in it and ask ourselves the right questions so we can gather additional information to improve our knowledge of the innovation process.

● Modelling starts with a definition of the scope of the model – that is, the boundaries of the arena and dimensions of our present and future position that we want to take into consideration.

● Next, we have to inventorize the internal (disciplinary, departmental, functional and personal interdependencies) and external (market, suppliers and competitive) forces. This involves an inventorization of the internal and external stakeholders together with their motives, goals, expectations, value perceptions and interdependencies.

● Next, the processes have to be explored – that is, the internal business processes, market, supply chain and competitive processes. In this analysis, the individual processes have to be defined by their inputs and outputs in technical as well as in economic and social value terms and by their enabling factors and bottlenecks, again, in both technological and organizational terms. The ways in which these individual processes may interact must also be inventorized.

- The interactions between the individual processes may give rise to non-linear dynamics of the system. Study of these interactions may suggest a number of ways in which they affect the dynamics. Six large classes of interactions with their specific effects on the dynamics of the system can be recognized.

- Comparing the dynamics of the model with reality gives a means of evaluating the validity of the model. This helps us to explore any white spaces and the possible consequences of management decisions.

- Having a model of the innovation process helps in setting up and interpreting balanced scorecards. It supports the benchmarking process and the setting up of other business and marketing research studies.

- Innovating companies must all have the generic NPD and NBD processes in place and 'high-performance' teams to integrate and balance the processes.

- Innovative companies use a variety of tools that support the various generic NPD processes and can adjust organizational settings and leadership style to meet the demands of the various phases with their respective dominant generic processes.

- The success of innovation management can be improved if we know when and how to profit from the non-linearities of the NPD and NBD processes and when and how to circumvent or neutralize these non-linearities.

- Management of NPD and NBD is improved when the non-linearities are concentrated in the less costly front end of the process and then, in the more expensive parts, the non-linearities are brought more or less under control by focusing and phasing of the process.

In this book, we have introduced a new approach to innovation management and NPD and NBD that builds on methods described earlier based on the application of system dynamics to strategic management, and encompasses a large number of additional methods and approaches introduced before, and we have discussed how these can be applied. As such, it can be considered as an architectural innovation of a management tool.

As with all new approaches, there are several issues that have to be developed further in future. These are that:

- the models of the generic NPD and NBD processes must be elaborated further – especially important are better ways to measure the performance of the individual processes, and the relationship between the organizational setting, application of management tools and performance must be studied in more depth;

- the integration between DBM and financial, planning and resource allocation tools must be elaborated further;
- a broad inventorization of industries, peculiarities of the innovation process, non-linear mechanisms, prevailing business models and performance must be executed – this could help in choosing industries and companies for benchmarking studies.

DBM as described in this book can be considered as a starting point for further development. Advancements in computer hardware, software and methodologies for analyzing, modelling and validating all parts of the innovation process may make it an indispensable tool for management to design more competitive strategies and innovate more effectively and efficiently.

Glossary

Business process This can be defined as a set of activities (organization), by which specific inputs are transformed into outputs (application) according to certain predetermined specifications in order to create value for a customer. This process is enabled by the application of certain tools and techniques (technology).

Business system The system that fulfils a certain class of need, defined as product market combinations. It encompasses all actors involved in the functioning of the system.

Deep structure That part of a business system is that shapes the NPD and NBD processes.

Dominant design Such a design in a product class is, by definition, the one that wins the allegiance of the marketplace, the one that competitors and innovators must adhere to if they hope to command a significant market following.

Innovation Introduction of something new to the business.

Innovation arena A space that is described by the four dimensions of innovations – namely, technology, applications, markets of customer groups and (internal and external) organization (TAMO). In the innovation arena, innovation trajectories can be localized and described.

Innovation system All the actors and factors involved in the generation, diffusion and implementation of innovations.

Non-linear mechanisms Mechanisms that affect the non-linear behaviour of business systems. We distinguish six main classes of non-linear mechanisms – reinforcing loops, limiting loops, lock-in mechanisms, time delays, selection mechanisms and variation.

Power This can be defined as control over resources in the system. Jeffrey Pfeffer (1992) defines power as being the potential ability to influence behaviour, change the course of events, overcome resistance and get people to do things that they would not otherwise do.

System memory The part of the business system that is shaped by history and plays an important role in shaping NPD and NBD processes.

Technical system The system that fulfils a certain class of needs, defined as technology and product combinations. It encompasses all artefacts, skills and knowledge that play a role in the functioning of the system.

Bibliography

Abernathy, William and **Utterback, James** (1978) 'Patterns of industrial innovation', 80 (7) 40–7

Akao, Yoji (1990) *Quality Function Deployment: Integrating customer requirements into product design*, Productivity Press (English translation)

Argyris C. and **Schon, D.** (1978) *Organizational Learning*, Addison-Wesley

Arthur, W. Brian (1994) *Increasing Returns and Path Dependency in the Economy*, The University of Michigan Press

Ayas, Karen (1996) 'Design for learning for innovation', Thesis, Erasmus University, Rotterdam, Netherlands

Bak, Per (1996) *How Nature Works: The science of self-organized criticality*, Springer Verlag

Belbin, R. Meredith (1993) *Team Roles at Work*, Butterworth-Heinemann

Bell, C. Gordon (1991) *High-tech Ventures: The guide to entrepreneurial success*, Addison-Wesley

Bijker, Wiebe (1991) *The Social Construction of Technology*, Printer Alfa, Enschede

Bolwijn, Piet T. and **Kumpe, Ted** (1990) 'Manufacturing in the 1990s: productivity, flexibility and innovation', *Long Range Planning*, 23 (4), 44–57

Bounds, Greg, Yorks, Lyle, Adams, Mel and **Ranney, Gipsie** (1994) *Beyond Total Quality Management: Toward the emerging paradigm*, McGraw-Hill

Brandenburger, Adam and **Nalebuff, Barry** (1996) *Co-opetition*, Currency Doubleday

Brown, Shona and **Eisenhardt, Kathleen** (1998) *Competing on the Edge: Strategy as structured chaos*, Harvard Business School Press

Callon, M., Laredo, P. and **Radeharison, V.** (1992) 'The management and evaluation of technological programs and the dynamics of techno-economic networks: the case of the AFME', *Research Policy*, 21, 215–36

Casti, John L. (1997) *Would-be Worlds: How simulation is changing the frontiers of science*, John Wiley & Sons

Christensen, Clayton M. (1997) *The Innovator's Dilemma: When new technologies cause great firms to fail*, Harvard Business School Press

Clark, Kim B. and **Wheelwright, Steven C.** (1993) *Managing New Product and Process Development: Text and cases*, The Free Press

Collins, James and **Porras, Jerry** (1996) *Built to Last: Successful habits of visionary companies*, Century

Compton, W. Dale (1997) *Engineering Management: Creating and managing world class operations*, Prentice Hall International

Cooper, Robert G. (1993) *Winning with New Products: Accelerating the process from idea to launch*, Addison-Wesley

Copeland, Tom, Koller, Tim and **Murrin, Jack** (1990) *Valuation: Measuring and managing the value of companies*, John Wiley & Sons

D'Aveni, Richard (1994) *Hypercompetition: Managing the dynamics of strategic manoeuvring*, The Free Press

de Geus, Arie (1997) *The Living Company: Growth, learning and longevity in business*, Nicholas Brealey

De Wit, Bob and **Meyer, Ron** (1994) *Strategy, Process, Content, Context: An international perspective*, West Publishing Company

Deschamps, Jean-Philippe and **Nayak, P. Ranganath** (1995) *Product Juggernauts: How companies mobilize to generate a stream of market winners*, Harvard Business School Press

Dyson, Robert G. (1990) *Strategic Planning Models and Analytical Techniques*, John Wiley & Sons

Eden, C. L. (1989) 'Using cognitive mapping for strategic options development and analysis (SODA)', in Rosenhead, J. (ed.) *Rational Analysis for a Problematic World*, John Wiley & Sons

Epstein, Joshua M. and **Axtell, Robert** (1996) *Growing Artificial Societies: Social science from the bottom up*, The MIT Press

Farrell, Winslow (1998) *How Hits Happen: Forecasting predictability in a chaotic marketplace*, HarperBusiness

Foster, Richard (1986) *Innovation: The attacker's advantage*, Summit Books

Freeman, G. (1988) *The Pursuit of Innovation: Managing the people and processes that turn new ideas into profits*, Amacom

Gale, Bradley (1994) *Managing Customer Value: Creating quality and services that customers see*, The Free Press

Ghoshal, Sumantra and **Bartlett, Christopher** (1997) *The Individualized Corporation: Great companies are defined by purpose, process and people*, HarperBusiness

Goodman, Malcolm (1995) *Creative Management*, Prentice Hall

Hagel, John III and **Armstrong, Arthur G.** (1998) *Net Gain*, Harvard Business School Press

Hakansson, H. (1987) *Corporate Technological Behaviour: Cooperation and networks*, Routledge

Hamel, Gary, and **Prahalad, C. K.** (1994) *Competing for the Future: Breakthrough strategies for seizing control of your industry and creating the markets of tomorrow*, Harvard Business School Press

Hardjono, Teun W. (1996) *Ritmiek en organisatiedynamiek – Vierfasenmodel (Rhythmic and dynamics of organizations – four phases model)*, Kluwer

Henderson, Rebecca and **Clark, Kim B.** (1990) 'Architectural innovation: the reconfiguration of existing product technologies and the failure of existing firms', *Administrative Science Quarterly*, 35, 9–30

Hinssen, Peter (1998) 'What difference does it make? The use of GroupWare in small groups', Thesis, Delft, Netherlands

Holland, John H. (1995) *Hidden Order: How adaptation builds complexity*, Addison-Wesley

Imai, Masaaki (1986) *Kaizen: The key to Japanese competitive success*, McGraw-Hill

Juran, J. M. (1992) *Juran on Quality by Design: The new steps for planning quality into goods and service*, The Free Press

Kaplan, Robert and **Norton, David** (1996) *The Balanced Scorecard: Translating strategy into action*, Harvard Business School Press

Katzenbach, Jon, and **Smith, Douglas** (1994) *The Wisdom of Teams: Creating the high-performance organization*, HarperBusiness

Kauffman, Stuart (1995) *At Home in the Universe: The search for the laws of self-organization and complexity*, Oxford University Press

Keeney, Ralph (1992) *Value-focused Thinking: A path to creative decision making*, Harvard University Press

Kline, S. J. and **Rosenberg, Nathan** (1986) 'An overview of innovation', in Landau, R. (ed.) *The Positive Sum Strategy: Harnessing technology for economic growth*, National Academy of Education

Kolb, David (1981) *Learning Style Inventory*, McBer and Co

Leonard-Barton, Dorothy (1995) *Wellsprings of Knowledge: Building and sustaining the sources of innovation*, Harvard Business School Press

Luehrman, Timothy (1998) 'Strategy as a portfolio of real options', *Harvard Business Review*, September–October

Mintzberg, Henry (1994) *The Rise and Fall of Strategic Planning*, Prentice Hall Inc

Moore, Geoffrey (1995) *Inside the Tornado: Marketing strategies from Silicon Valley's cutting edge*, HarperBusiness

Moore, Geoffrey (1999) *Crossing the Chasm: Marketing and selling high-tech products to mainstream customers* (revised edition), HarperBusiness

Moore, James (1996) *The Death of Competition: Leadership and strategy in the age of business ecosystems*, John Wiley & Sons

Morecroft, John D. and **Sterman, John** (1994) *Modelling for Learning Organizations*, Productivity Press

Nonaka, Ikujiro and **Takeuchi, Hirotaka** (1995) *The Knowledge-creating Company: How Japanese companies create the dynamics of innovation*, Oxford University Press

Oakland, John (1984) *Total Quality Management: The route to improve performance*, Butterworth

Pasternak, Bruce A. and **Viscio, Albert J.** (1998) *The Centerless Corporation: A new model for transforming your organization for growth and prosperity*, Simon & Schuster

Pavitt, Keith (1990) 'What we know about the strategic management of technology', *California Management Review*, 32, 17–26

Peters, Tom (1997) *The Circle of Innovation: You can't shrink your way to greatness*, Alfred A. Knopf

Pfeffer, Jeffrey (1992) *Managing with Power: Politics and influence in organizations*, Harvard Business School Press

Pidd, Michael (1996) *Tools for Thinking: Modelling in management science*, John Wiley & Sons

Porter, Alan L., Roper, Thomas A., Mason, Thomas W., Rossini, Frederick A. and **Banks, Jerry** (1991) *Forecasting and Management of Technology*, John Wiley & Sons

Porter, Michael (1985) *Competitive Advantage: Creating and sustaining superior advantage*, The Free Press

Prietula, Michael, Carley, Kathleen and **Gasser, Less** (eds) (1998) *Simulating Organizations: Computational models of institutions and groups*, The MIT Press

Quinn, James Brian (1992) *Intelligent Enterprise: A new paradigm for a new era*, The Free Press

Ramondt, Joop (1996) *Organisatie diagnostiek (Diagnostics of organizations: A method for questions directed research)*, Academic Service, Schoonhoven

Ries, All and **Trout, Jack** (1997) *Marketing Warfare: How to use military principles to develop market strategies*, McGraw-Hill

Rothwell, Roy (1992) 'Successful industrial innovation: critical success factors for the 1990s', *R&D Management*, 22 (3), 221–39

Roussel, Philip, Saad, Kamal and **Erickson, Tamara** (1991) *Third-generation R&D Management: Managing the link to corporate strategy*, Harvard Business School Press

Sanchez, Ron (1996) 'Strategic product creation: managing new interactions of technology, markets and organizations', *European Management Journal*, 14, 121–38

Schoemaker, Paul (1995) 'Scenario planning: a tool for strategic thinking', *Sloan Management Review*, 36, 25–45

Scott-Morgan, Peter (1994) *The Unwritten Rules of the Game*, McGraw-Hill

Senge, Peter (1990) *The Fifth Discipline: The art and practice of the learning organization*, Doubleday

Senge, Peter (1994) *The Fifth Discipline Fieldbook: Strategies and tools for building a learning organization*, Nicholas Brealey

Shapiro, Carl and **Varian, Hal R.** (1999) *Information Rules: A strategic guide to the network economy*, Harvard Business School Press

Smith, Preston and **Reinertsen, Donald** (1998) *Developing Products in Half the Time*, John Wiley & Sons

Stacey, Ralph (1993) *Strategic Management and Organizational Dynamics*, Pitman

Teece, David (1986) 'Profiting from technological innovation', *Research Policy*, 15 (6) 78–98

Thomas, Robert J. (1995) *New Product Success Stories: Lessons from leading innovators*, John Wiley & Sons

Twiss, Brian (1992) *Managing Technological Innovation*, Pitman

Urban, Glenn and **Hauser, John** (1993) *Design and Marketing of New Products*, Prentice Hall

Utterback, James (1994) *Mastering the Dynamics of Innovation: How companies can seize opportunities in the face of technological change*, Harvard Business School Press

van Breukelen, Rinus *et al.* (1996) *Facts on Factories: In search of manufacturing excellence*, Thesis

van der Heijden, Kees (1996) *Scenarios: The art of strategic conversation*, John Wiley & Sons

van Wyk, Rias (1996) 'Technology analysis: a foundation for technological expertise', in **Gaynor, Gerard**, *Handbook of Technology Management*, McGraw-Hill

Vennix, J. (1996) *Group Model Building*, John Wiley & Sons

von Braun, Christoph-Friedrich (1996) *The Innovation War: Industrial R&D ... the arms race of the nineties*, Prentice Hall

von Hippel, Erich (1988) *The Sources of Innovation*, Oxford University Press

Watson, G. (1993) *Strategic Benchmarking: How to rate your company's performance against the world's best*, John Wiley & Sons

Wee Chow-Hou, Lee Khai-Sheang and **Bambong Walujo Hidajat** (1997) *Sun Tzu: War and management*, Addison Wesley Longman

Weick, Karl (1995) *Sensemaking in Organizations*, Sage Publications

Index